A Commentary on Heidegger's *Being and Time*

A Commentary on

Heidegger's

Being and Time

Revised Edition

Michael Gelven

NORTHERN ILLINOIS UNIVERSITY PRESS

DeKalb, Illinois 1989

© 1989 by Northern Illinois University Press
Published by the Northern Illinois University Press,
DeKalb, Illinois 60115

Design by Julia Fauci

Library of Congress Cataloging-in-Publication Data
Gelven, Michael
    A commentary on Heidegger's Being and time / Michael
Gelven. — Rev. ed.
        p.   cm.
    Includes bibliographical references.
    ISBN 0-87580-145-5. — ISBN 0-87580-544-2 (pbk.)
    1. Heidegger, Martin, 1889–1976. Sein und Zeit. 2. On-
tology. 3. Space and time. I. Heidegger, Martin,
1889–1976. Sein und Zeit. II. Title.
    B3279.H48S465   1989   89–8585
    111—dc20   CIP

10 9 8 7 6 5 4 3

To My Students

Contents

PREFACE

The first edition of this commentary was published in 1970, at which time Heidegger was not overly well known and certainly not properly understood in this country. For the most part he was perceived then as one among many European "existentialists" or "phenomenologists," and his works were often buried in anthologies along with other figures whose names have long since faded, but whom the editors found fit to label with the popular tags. Since that time, however, Heidegger's fame and reputation have developed to such an extent that he is now recognized as the single most important thinker in the twentieth century. The labels of twenty years ago have, thankfully, fallen away, and Heidegger is seen as a figure of such stature that there is no adequate label to designate him except his own name. The far-reaching impact of his thought promises to extend well into the future.

Although the 1988 French translation and the Japanese translation of the *Commentary* give evidence of the continuing need for a clear, section-by-section analysis of Heidegger's greatest work, the English edition of the *Commentary* was taken out of print in 1981. As interest in Heidegger, rather than abating, has continued to grow, it is a pleasant and fitting opportunity to be able to present this extensively revised edition. Not only will a new generation of students have the opportunity to use it to help them work through the troubling masterpiece, readers already familiar with the original edition will, hopefully, find the revisions beneficial and worthy of reflection.

I have entirely rewritten the Introduction and added extensively to the sections on the authentic-inauthentic distinction, the discussion of "The Who of Dasein," the chapters on truth and history, as well as many smaller revisions of paragraphs and smaller segments. I have added an important clarification to the end of the section on anticipatory resoluteness. The postscript "Why Existence?" has been replaced with an essay on how Heidegger's later works develop many of the central themes of *Being and Time*.

I resisted the temptation to allow the *Commentary* to become an arena for scholarly disputation. Since 1970 a remarkable amount of literature on Heidegger has appeared, some of it rather good but most of it quite bad. These scholarly battles have no place in a commentary whose chief purpose is to assist the reader in working through a challenging text. My additions and revisions are all designed to clarify and explain; and whenever alterations were made it was solely for the sake of clearing up what may have needed improvement. The success of the original edition was surely due to this concern for clarity of exposition and the avoidance of undue complexity and jargon. The revisions in this present edition have not wandered from the original simplicity; indeed I hope to have made some passages even more readable in an uncluttered and straightforward style.

However, lest this endeavor sound overly simplistic, it should be pointed out that to explain a thorny passage clearly and in simple terms is itself an immensely difficult challenge. Nothing is easier than to seek refuge from a troubling passage by an appeal to vagueness and the maddening reiteration of ponderous terms that are intoned like sacred rituals without explanation. Obfuscation is ultimately a confession of ignorance or deceit. In order to simplify a profound notion, to make it readable and intuitively available, the deepest thinking and greatest mental effort are required. Honest readers will recognize that in seeking to explain Heidegger's complex analyses in clearer terms I have never meant to reduce the profundity of his thinking to mere synopses or slogans. To be simple is not to be simplistic. The point is not to render the ideas so basic as to make them no longer worthy of thought. Quite to the contrary, by clarifying them, and hopefully making them more readily available by interpreting them in simple English, I intend to show how profound and powerful they really are.

Of course, over these twenty years my own thinking has matured, and

I believe that from the vantage of teaching many seminars on Heidegger to many rather wonderful and gifted students, and even wincing at a few telling criticisms, the present revised edition will provide an even better resource for understanding Heidegger's ideas, which, I fully admit, continue to fascinate and astonish me. I hope this *Commentary* will help others to appreciate their true greatness.

A Commentary on Heidegger's *Being and Time*

I.

INTRODUCTION

Martin Heidegger's *Sein und Zeit* first appeared in German in 1927; the English translation, *Being and Time*, appeared in 1962.[1] Since the appearance of this work, the reputation and influence of its author has spread to such international dimensions that it may be said that Heidegger is the most important and widely influential philosopher of the twentieth century. Even now, as the century enters its final decade, no thinker is more significant in terms of intellectual impact and controversy. There are many who deeply resent his works, who detest his personal association with Nazism in 1933, who defy his most fundamental principles. But even among these, his most ardent enemies, he is recognized as the singular dominating force with which to be reckoned. Among his countless admirers he is considered the greatest European philosopher since Immanuel Kant. Interest in this Freiburg philosopher is in no way waning; indeed the future seems to promise ever expanding respect, and in some cases even reverence, for his vast accomplishments. Although Hei-

1. *Being and Time*, trans. John Mcquarrie and Edward Robinson (New York: Harper & Row, 1962).

degger has written voluminously since 1927, there remains little doubt that *Being and Time* will continue to be recognized as his major work, and shall be for many decades to come.

It is somewhat odd, however, that this seminal work, *Being and Time*, so formidable in its language and so immense in its undertaking, should find such eager readership among nonscholarly men and women. It is a truly intimidating book, challenging even to the experts and scholars, and even in its less demanding passages it remains an enormously difficult endeavor. Why then, do so many people consider it worthwhile to work through? Surely one answer, though not the only one, is simply because the book is both fascinating and true. It concerns itself with many of the greatest questions the mind can ask, and it does so with remarkable insight. We forget that many people remain genuinely interested in the truth, no matter how difficult the text may be, or how challenging the depth of thinking. The topics Heidegger analyzes in his book are among those which cannot but provoke our deepest interest, for who is not concerned about authentic existence, guilt, death, truth, and dread? But it is not merely the topics that have attracted so many and such fine readers; it is also the profundity of thought with which these fundamental ideas are penetrated and analyzed.

It is the purpose of this *Commentary* to make the profound analyses more readily available to the interested reader. In the following I endeavor to explain and clarify each section exactly as they occur in the progression of Heidegger's own thought. My task is to render Heidegger's thinking accessible to the English-speaking reader without putting any labels on his thought or criticising his ideas from an external perspective. There are, in our history, a few figures who simply rise above all movements, labels, and epochal identification. Shakespeare obviously is not merely an Elizabethan; Beethoven cannot be understood by labelling his music classical-romantic. In the same way, Heidegger should not be trivialized by reducing his thought to such labels as existentialist or phenomenologist. He is a philosopher who must be understood solely in terms of his own thought and in terms of his own peculiar question. And there can be no doubt that, for Heidegger, the single, all-pervasive question haunting not only *Being and Time* but all his subsequent work is the question of Being.

The reader who wishes to grasp what Heidegger is saying must make the initial effort to confront this single term, "Being." What does it mean, for Heidegger? How does he raise the question? What *is* the question? Unless one takes this first, and perhaps most challenging step, and tries to establish at least a sympathetic willingness to comprehend what Heidegger means by this term, one shall never succeed in understanding anything Heidegger has written. And yet, that is precisely the paradox involved, for an understanding of Being is exactly what the entire work is designed to achieve. If we must first understand what Heidegger means by Being in order to read *Being and Time*, and if the whole purpose of reading the book is to understand what Being means, then it seems we must end before we begin. This paradox is not insurmountable, however; indeed the paradoxical nature of the inquiry is an essential part of its success.

THE TRANSLATION OF SEIN

Preliminary steps can, however, be taken right away to avoid some serious misconceptions. The term Heidegger uses is *das Sein*, which is usually translated into English as "Being." However, the term *sein* is an infinitive: to be. In German it is permissable to take an infinitive, like *rauchen*, for example, to smoke, and use it as a noun: *Das Rauchen ist ungesund*: Smoking is unhealthy. This would seem to be adequate as a translation, although it may be more precise if we were to retain the infinitive form and translate the sentence: It is unhealthy to smoke. But since both sentences seem to say the same thing, it seems picayune to quarrel. However, the seeming similarity in translations is misleading. Suppose I were to say "I enjoy singing." One might interpret this to mean that I like to sing. But it also might mean that I like to hear others sing. "I like to sing" therefore cannot be equated with "I like singing"; so the infinitive form *does* mean something not contained in the participle. For this reason, the term *"Sein"* really should be translated in the infinitival form whenever possible. But this is prohibited in English, for we cannot say "The To Be," which is what *Das Sein* would mean if it were transliterated. It is possible, however, to protect the infinitival meaning in some cases by altering the syntax slightly, so that the phrase in German, *"die Frage nach dem Sinn von Sein"* becomes "to question what it means to be" rather than "the question of the meaning of Being."

These refinements may seem unduly pedantic, but they are extremely important. For Heidegger, *Sein* (Being) never should be thought of as an abstraction, or an entity, since, as an infinitive it is a verb used as a noun. Yet, the term "Being" is often, perhaps even usually, considered an abstract noun or simply an entity. In order to accommodate some semblance of translational respect for Heidegger's term, the procedure that has been more or less accepted by translators is to capitalize the letter *B* when translating *Sein*, so that when we use the term "Being" the reader should mentally bear in mind that what it really means is "to be." This may seem cumbersome, but it avoids the far greater difficulty of miscomprehension.

The difficulty is enhanced by Heidegger's use of a similar term, *das*

Seiende, which can also be translated "being" in the sense of an entity. Translators do not feel comfortable with "entity" because one loses the etymological connection with Being. Thus they often use "being," particularly in the plural since Being has no plurality; though it is perhaps better to use the term "entity" when any possible confusion may arise. Thus we have two terms, "*das Sein*," usually translated "Being" but which should be thought to mean "to be" and "*das Seiende*," usually translated as "being" or "entity." What is important is that the reader bear in mind that Heidegger wants to make the distinction between these two terms the very foundation of his entire philosophy.

How can such a fine, grammatic distinction be the foundation of an entire ontological revolution? And we must make no mistake about it, *Being and Time* is exactly that, a *revolution* in ontology. Even the most casual readers of this work recognize that the approach taken is one that establishes an entirely new way of thinking and totally rejects a tradition that has grown so entrenched it is almost indiscernible. Since much confusion and misinterpretation results from a failure to recognize exactly why this seemingly innocent, purely "grammatical" distinction has such far-reaching effect for philosophy, it may be helpful to include as a part of this Introduction an analysis of this approach.

HEIDEGGER'S REVOLUTION

Whenever one seeks to understand any revolution, whether in art, the political order, or philosophy, it is necessary first to sketch out what precedes the revolution itself. We must, so to speak, briefly examine the *ancien régime* before we can appreciate the violence that overthrows it. Such sketches of the prior institutions always suffer, to some extent, from oversimplification; and, in the case of Heidegger's revolution against traditional metaphysics, a certain degree of oversimplification cannot be avoided. Nevertheless, since the point here is to appreciate the importance of the change, such simplification may be advantageous. Briefly, then, we may characterize pre-Heideggerian ontology as being concerned with what kinds of things exist. That is, the fundamental question asked by metaphysics is this: Given any notion or idea, what we want to know is does such a thing actually exist? Does God exist? Does freedom exist? In making sense of our own existence, we ask: Do we possess an independent entity called mind, and another independent entity called body? What justification do we have for believing in such external entities as rocks and trees? How can we justify the existence of the external world, even? All of these questions are serious and important, and there is no doubt that if we could answer them we would have a better understanding of the world. But all such questions are raised in a rather curious way; for we ask them as if we already knew what "existence" means, and as if the only serious question is one of disjunction between only two possible answers: it either exists or it does not. To be sure, among the greatest of such thinkers, many do indeed consider what existence means. Aristotle tells us that whatever exists is either a fundamental kind of thing, called *prote ousia*, "first being," or a derived characteristic or predicate that depends on a primary existent like a "first being." This allows Aristotle to give as one of his definitions of *prote ousia* the purely formal or grammatical definition that it is a notion that can never be a predicate of anything else but is only predicated by other things. "Socrates is white" therefore means that "white" is a predicate, whereas "Socrates" is a "first being." Such analyses, brilliant as they are, have, over the centuries, cemented themselves as unquestioned absolutes. The quest becomes a search for the kind of things that exist and for the fundamental definitions of such existence. Descartes, for example, not only asks *whether* such a thing as material substance exists, he actually tells us what it means for such a thing to exist: if it takes up space it is a material thing that exists.

Heidegger, however, argues there is an even more fundamental question that can be asked: What does it mean to exist at all? The question is not whether something does exist or how to characterize the existence of particular *kinds* of things, like material things or mental things, but simply to ask about the very meaning of Being. In raising this question, one notes a subtle shift in what is being asked. If I am concerned with entities, such as God, minds, bodies, the earth, this page, I seem to ask two questions: Do such things in fact exist; and, if so, What *kind* of things are they? But what can I possibly ask about Being itself? I surely cannot ask *whether* Being exists, nor can I ask what *kind* of thing it is. Indeed, precisely because these familiar questions cannot be asked, one is inclined to wonder if Heidegger's question is legitimate at all.

There is, however, one question I can ask about Being: What does it mean? Indeed, if we reflect upon it, it appears that this is the *only* question we can ask. But since it is at least a legitimate question, and since it turns out to be the only question we can ask about Being, and since Being does seem to be presupposed in all other questions, Heidegger identifies this question as the fundamental question. To ask what it means to exist or simply to be is to engage in the most fundamental kind of questioning possible. Heidegger calls this *die Frage nach den Sinn von Sein*, "to question what it means to be," or simply, "the Being-question."

Why would such a question be fundamental? And how on earth can one go about even raising such an abstract and elusive question? In point of fact, this question is in no way abstract: it is rather the most concrete and immediate of all questions; for after all, I do exist, and, if I turn my attention to the question of what it *means* to exist, I am not abstracting from anything. As to why the question is fundamental, an example may prove helpful.

Suppose I ask "What is a jail?" You answer, "The jail is that red-brick building down the street with bars on the windows and locks on the cells." In this case, the question is about an entity, and the answer provides one with characteristics that describe or identify the entity. Suppose I ask, "What does it mean to be in jail?" In response, you say, "To be in jail is to be guilty of a crime and to be punished for it by suffering the loss of liberty. To be in jail thus is to be punished, to feel reprimanded, to suffer, possibly to be afraid, to be lonely, to feel outcast, etc." The second question is answered by reference to what it means to exist in various ways, such as being guilty or being unfree. The question What is a jail? is answered by the description of other entities, bars in the windows, locks, unsavory patrons; but the question of the meaning of anything is answered by reference to other meanings. In this we simply recognize there must be a parallel between the kind of question asked and the kind of answers given.

But suppose I press this distinction and ask Which question is prior? A moment's reflection will assure us that what it means to be in jail is the reason or the ground for the jail being built the way it is. In other words, what it means to be in jail is prior to what kind of thing a jail is, for the meaning determines the entity. If I understand what it means to be in jail I will know what is required to make a jail. So, in the formal sense of what explains what, meaning precedes entity. The inquiry into what it means to be in jail is not only different from the question about what kind of thing is a jail, it is also prior to it, for the meaning ultimately explains the entity.

Let us take the principles learned from this simple example and apply them to some traditional metaphysical problems. I ask: What is the mind? This question is the traditional metaphysical one; it asks for classification and identification. I also ask: Do I have a mind that is anything more than the physical brain? Here the question is one of whether something exists. Let us now re-ask this all-important question in terms of Heidegger's revolution. What kind of question could we ask? *What does it mean to think?* Notice what happens when we rephrase the question in this way. By asking What does it mean to think? I avoid completely the metaphysical questions of whether something exists or what kind of thing it is. Yet, at the same time, the question probes just as deeply into what I want to know. It is possible for example, to point out that what it means to think is quite distinct from what it means to sense or feel. A Cartesian would insist that this distinction shows there must be a body separate from a mind. And perhaps there are two kinds of entities, but why even bother with them if I can focus my attention directly to the real question, which is about thinking? It may or may not be valid to infer that if I think I therefore must have a mind, separate from a body, to think *with*, but even if this inference were valid it depends on the more fundamental inquiry into what thinking means. So, I can ask what it means to think without bringing in whether there exists a thing called a mind that does the thinking. This alone is a huge advantage, since the entire tradition of the agonizing mind-body problem can be avoided. Furthermore, it is obvious that the question of meaning is precisely what is appealed to in determining *whether* something exists anyway, which proves the meaning-question is more fundamental.

It is possible of course to go through a list and rephrase all the great questions: Is there a body? becomes What does it mean to take up space and to feel things? Is there a God? becomes What does it mean to worship that which is utterly magnificent yet ineffable? Is there an external world? becomes What does it mean to be in the world? But these translations are not the most important thing at this point. The example of the jail is used solely to focus our attention on just what Heidegger is doing to the question of Being.

In the same way that we can ask of any entity the prior question about its meaning, we now question Being itself in the same way. We do not ask, What is the ultimate kind of thing? Or even, What kinds of things really exist? We ask rather, What does it mean to be at all? This is the fundamental question, but it cannot simply be posed and answered. For it is important to bear in mind that this fundamental question must first be *approached*. That is, even to *ask* such a question requires much preparatory analysis and careful reasoning. We have seen that the question of what it means to be is already lurking even in such ordinary questions as what does it mean *to be* in jail. Indeed, all of these retranslated questions contain the infinitival form of the verb "to be"; so that we find ourselves asking, What does it mean *to be* in space? or What does it mean *to be* a mind?; or, if that formulation seems to entail an entity, we could ask, What does it mean *to think*?, which contains the being-question only implicitly, as in the formulation, What does it mean *to be* as thinking. The point is, that in all of the ways we find ourselves existing or doing or being acted upon, it is possible to reformulate the question so that the infinitive "to be" becomes the unifying and underlying question. And so the technique or method becomes obvious.

If I can ask, What does it mean to be a body? or What does it mean to exist as thinker? then the underlying question, which is, What does it mean to be at all? can obviously be approached by first analysing the specific questions. In other words, it is precisely because I *can* ask What does it mean to be a body? that I am already, to some extent, responding to the question, What does it mean to be at all? For, in carrying out an inquiry into what it means to be a body I am already making sense of what it means to be in a particular way or mode. An investigation into the various fundamental ways in which I can be said to be, such as "what it means to be in the world" or "what it means to have possibilities" reveals the important ways in which I can be said to be, and from a consideration of how these various *ways* of existing share a common meaning, it is possible then to focus on what it means to be at all. In this way, the approach to all the great questions not only is raised in terms of what it means to be, it also provides a thematic unity to the various inquiries. As we shall soon see in the analysis of the actual text, Heidegger begins by actually carrying out an inquiry into the various ways or modes of existing and then discerns the underlying meaning shared by all of these ways. In doing this he avoids the necessity of having to assume some kind of entity or referent that lies behind these modes of being. In short, he has simply, but profoundly, turned the entire metaphysical approach upside down. We do not first ask what a man is and then wonder what it means; rather we begin by asking what it means to be a man, and then can decide what a man is.

Any philosophical inquiry can be understood in terms of the primary danger or fear which the thinker seeks to avoid at all costs. We understand Descartes just because we also understand the threat he is seeking to overcome, namely total epistemic scepticism. It is the fear of scepticism that requires Descartes to find a truth so obvious and clear it cannot be denied. In the same way the reader of Kantian ethics recognizes that what dominates Kant's reasoning is his desire to avoid moral relativism at all costs. The Categorical Imperative makes sense to us simply because the threat of multiple opinions renders the entire edifice of moral reasoning crippled. In understanding Heidegger, one must recognize that the threat to reason and thought which he identifies as the supreme evil to avoid at all costs is nihilism. By nihilism is meant the denial that existence, particularly human existence, is meaningful. Heidegger's approach to fundamental ontology takes its focus from his revolutionary question, what does it mean to be? as a total and unalloyed rejection of the nihilistic threat. For if Heidegger can show that the question of meaning *is* capable of being asked and responded to, then the challenge from the nihilist has been met squarely and decisively. And so, before turning to the analysis of the text, one final introductory discussion may prove beneficial.

HEIDEGGER AND NIHILISM

It is a source of considerable annoyance to any serious thinker that, after a lifetime of succesful inquiry into the questions of what exists and what is right, the entire endeavor may be derailed by the simple, arrogant question, How do you know? or Prove it! This is the threat of scepticism; and by this threat the entire philosophical enterprise is held hostage. Unless it can be shown that there really is a difference between knowledge and opinion, the great labor of mighty thinkers is no more significant than the idle ruminations of a lazy and rebellious youth. Scepticism thus is a formidable threat of misology—a hatred of reasoning—which, if not confronted will destroy the importance and value of philosophy altogether. Luckily there are meaningful responses to scepticism, and the thinker need not abandon his entire endeavor because of this lurking threat. Nevertheless, scepticism is always there, perhaps held at bay by superior thinking, but always threatening to break in on an endeavor and render it sterile.

A slightly more sinister form of misology is moral relativism. This criticism of reasoning admits that one can carry out schemes of explanation designed to show us the proper moral principles, but we then simply shrug our shoulders when the effort is complete and archly assure him that although this may be his opinion, we too can opine about such matters, and our opinion is different. As in the case of the sceptic, there are defences against this threat, but it too remains always lurking in the shadows of our inquiry, ready to pounce on an unsuspecting theorist or thinker who is not armed against it. For both scepticism and relativism are absolutist critiques, that is, they undermine the entire edifice of reasoned inquiry altogether by rendering it impotent.

The third of these great misological attacks on thought is nihilism, and it is the most sinister of all. The nihilist may admit that we do indeed have knowledge rather than opinion. He is willing to admit that $3+2=5$, that sugar dissolves in water, and that we know these things for certain. He may even admit that it is wrong to break a promise and that we are able to show, by reasoning and analysis, that this censure against promise-breaking is not a matter of opinion but is absolute. He may even act according to these principles himself, and admit that he feels an obligation to keep promises and respect the dignity of others. But, he claims, in the last analysis, so what? To have knowledge and to know the moral law do not *mean* anything. In the last analysis, a world that is revealed by cognitive principles and a world governed by discernible moral laws are simply no more or no less meaningful than a world lacking such laws and principles. In short, though we may have knowledge and may even know what we ought to do, it does not matter. Nothing matters. For knowledge and morality of themselves do not make the world *meaning-ful*. And since these principles cannot show us why the world matters or why it is meaningful, there can be no overwhelming reason to carry out the difficult inquiries that discover the principles, since in the last analysis, who cares?

The most dangerous approach one can take to the problem of nihilism is one of attitudinal persuasion, or to treat the threat as a mere incidence of bad psychology. For the argument is genuine and the threat real. Even if you can change my attitude or my psychological outlook, it does not challenge the *truth* of what I say. Why should any of this matter? In what way is the world meaningful? In the absence of good reasons to the contrary, what is to stop me from simply abandoning the entire enterprise of thought because it does not matter? Unless the fundamental discipline not only provides me with a sense of what is true and good, but also what is meaningful, the entire endeavor is threatened.

Heidegger's analysis of Being *begins* with the argument that Being matters, and it does so by analysing the *meaning* of Being rather than the knowability of Being or the advantage of moral conduct. In his approach, Heidegger overcomes the sharp distinctions between fact and value and between subject and object. Rather than isolating the powers of reason and thought by restricting them to the determination of what is the case, Heidegger shows that the fundamental discipline, the study of what it means to be, is already (i.e., *a priori*) a study of the meaningfulness of existence. He shows that I not only exist, but that I exist meaningfully.

A casual glance at the table of contents reveals that many of Heidegger's concerns are focused on questions that seem to belong to the field of values or value-theory. Yet, these analyses are presented not as values at all but as dimensions of Being itself. It may be helpful to the reader to consider this argument in a general way before attacking the individual sections.

Traditionally, philosophers have approached the fundamental questions by distinguishing the knower from the world it knows. "The World is my representation," Schopenhauer says in the opening sentence of his great work; and with this sentence he reflects the beginnings of all modern thinkers, from Descartes through Kant. The world is out there, and the task of the thinker is somehow to accommodate what is in us, or in our minds, with what is outside us; we are subjects, and the world is our object. Thus, if we are to uncover any values, whether they be moral, aesthetic, or simply hedonistic, they cannot be found in the neutral, objective reservoir of all things, the world as it is. Even truth is beguiled by this sharp distinction between subject and object, for what we finally come to mean by truth is the *disvaluing* of our perceptions: what is true is objective. The logic is thus inescapable: if truth is objective and values subjective, then all values are necessarily untrue; i.e., they are merely subjectively provided assessments or measurements *attributed* to the world by our private preferences. But Heidegger entirely repudiates the distinction, and thus reestablishes a unified account of what it means to be.

It is impossible to argue that the world is objective, and the knower merely the subject set over and against the object, for it is palpable upon reflection that I am already in the world. To be a subject *and* to be an object presupposes that we are already in the world. The world cannot be my representation, for I am already a part of the world. Being in the world is thus a characteristic of my existence; the world is not "outside" of me; rather I am in the world. When I talk about Being, therefore, I must talk about what it means to be in the world. But to be in the world is *already* (i.e., *a priori*) to care about certain things, to concern myself with others, to recognize the ways in which I matter, not only to myself but to others. It is not the case that my existence is somehow neutral, that values are somehow made-up, and that facts are merely discovered. Rather, to be at all is to be as meaningful, to matter, to care. It is, of course, possible to focus our attention on aspects of any given object solely in terms of its physical properties, but such a focus is a specialized, rarefied, and indeed abstract consideration only of entities conceived in a highly artificial and specialized way. The establishment of a fundamental discipline, which Heidegger calls "Fundamental Ontology," must precede all distinctions between fact and value, with the realization that an unvalued fact and a pure value are both abstractions.

Once it is seen that the subject-object distinction is valid only within a certain restricted realm of what it means to exist, and that the fact-value distinction is an artificial one, sustained only by purely formal abstraction, the initiation of Heidegger's inquiry into what it means to be, in the manner he develops, makes perfectly good sense. And with this realization, the threat of nihilism is profoundly answered. It is difficult to understand why so many contemporary theorists, especially among the followers of Leo Strauss, and to a lesser extent the movements in contemporary French philosophy following J. P. Sartre and Jacques Derrida, should make the outrageous claim that Heidegger espouses nihilism, or that his thinking "leads" to nihilism. Nothing could be further from the truth. As this commentary unfolds, and the critical accounts of the existential modalities are revealed, the reader can discover for himself the tremendous advantage of Heidegger's wisdom in initiating his inquiry by focusing on the fundamental question, What does it mean to be? The only consideration *not* allowed by such a beginning is that Being has no meaning. If Being has no meaning, how is it possible to carry out an inquiry into what it means to be? It is the very fact that Heidegger can and does carry out such an inquiry that ultimately refutes any possibility of nihilism.

STRUCTURE OF *BEING AND TIME*

The scope, then, of *Being and Time* is immense. According to its original projection the work was to have been almost three times as large as its present published form—which is incomplete. In its original design the work was to contain two major parts; but only two-thirds of the first part were ever published. The missing third section of Part One has been the subject of much debate as to its possible future publication;[2] in place of the second part a series of other works have appeared, which deal with the so-called destruction of the history of philosophy.[3]

But even the incomplete form that we have at our disposal is rich and varied in its scope and content. Excluding the two-part introduction, in which Heidegger explains his method and procedure, Division One of *Being and Time* concerns the "existential analytic." The meaning of this term is to be taken literally; it is an analysis of existence. Heidegger takes the accepted and normal problem areas of philosophy and reinterprets them in terms of transcendental awareness. He takes a concept like "world," for example: instead of treating the world cosmologically as an objective entity, or epistemologically as an object of knowledge, he examines what it means for a human being *to be in a world*. He asks: What does it mean for us to be in a world? He pursues this kind of question regarding several major concepts: e.g., What does it mean to be one's self? to be afraid? to be such that one understands? In this way, "world," "self," "fear," and "understanding" are not objective entities divorced from the type of subjective concern about them, nor are they "definitions" in any abstract or verbal sense. Each is, instead, a *way* in which one exists; one of the many ways in which I exist is to be aware of the world. What the world actually *is*, is replaced by the question of what

2. Too much debate, perhaps. To be sure, the fact that the final synthesis is missing is doubtless something to be regretted; but this does not mean that the entire attempt of the first sections is thereby made useless or invalid.

3. Heidegger himself, in the Foreword to *Kant and the Problem of Metaphysics*, specifically points to his study of Kant as a part of the original project of *Being and Time*. The historical section and the analytic section were to be worked out together as a twofold attack against traditional metaphysics.

it means *for me to be* in a world. Heidegger calls these modes of existence whose analysis reveals what it means to be *existentials*. In many of his arguments in which he describes the nature of these existentials, Heidegger points out that, like the Kantian categories, they are not the result of an abstraction from an experience; rather, they are presupposed in an experience and make that experience *possible*: hence they logically come prior to any experience and are *a priori*. When I ask, How is it possible for me to understand what it means to be in the world? my answer cannot lie in any consideration of the factual world that I indeed do experience. For when I ask how something is *possible*, I am not asking for its factual characteristics, but rather for what might be called its transcendental presuppositions. When Kant points out that the category of cause and effect is presupposed in scientific explanation and thereby makes science possible, he is stating an essential philosophical point. If one tries to find evidence of cause and effect in empirical observation, one is bound to end in a fruitless search, as David Hume so adequately demonstrated. Kant is right in saying that causality is *a priori*; and it is the condition under which science itself is made possible. In a similar way, when one realizes that one is aware of one's own existence, one must ask for the modes of awareness that *make possible* such confrontation of one's meaning. Whatever the explanation for any such awareness, it must be of the character of an *a priori*, otherwise it would not *explain* the fact of awareness. The explanation of a fact cannot ever be the *result* of a fact; it must, indeed, logically *precede* it. For this reason, Heidegger's existential analytic is an analysis of the *a priori* conditions under which one's existence is made meaningful.

The table of contents of *Being and Time* reveals what these existentials are. But the examination of such concepts in the existential analytic is, by itself, insufficient. For the entire investigation of the existential analytic is done, according to Heidegger, from an "everyday" or "inauthentic" perspective. In order to achieve the higher ontological level needed for a truly fundamental ontology, one must reanalyze and reinterpret the entire existential analytic, but from a new perspective. This new perspective follows from the first analysis; it amounts to the fact that the one who is investigating—who, in this case, is also the investigated—is limited by, and takes his dimensions from, time. This second or higher kind of analysis is the task of Division Two of the published *Being and Time*, entitled "Dasein and Temporality." In the second analysis, those characteristics of the human species that are peculiarly reflective of the person's awareness of himself, such as death and guilt, are analyzed under the influence of his temporality—a term that is discussed at great length in the second half of Heidegger's book.

FUNDAMENTAL ONTOLOGY[4]

This twofold analysis of what it means to be, first on the level of the existential analytic and secondly on the level of the temporal dimensions and limitations of who we are, is by no means to be meant merely as one among many possible philosophical considerations. Rather, because the analysis necessarily includes all the ways in which we can exist, and hence all the possible problems of philosophy, the investigation is, for Heidegger, the foundation of all philosophy. Heidegger therefore calls his entire discipline "fundamental ontology"—i.e., a study of the meaning of Being as the foundation of the entire edifice of philosophy.

It is this claim that fundamental ontology is the foundation for all philosophy that most truly reflects what Heidegger is attempting in *Being and Time*. His rejection of the Neo-Kantians is most pronounced here; for they had argued that the whole purpose of philosophy was to examine the possibilities and language of science, whereas Heidegger considers such a view of philosophy an "embarrassment."[5] It is an embarrassment because such a view leaves unconsidered all the rich and demanding questions of human concern, such as the meaning of life, virtue, morality, freedom, and death. After all, such problems were the original impetus

---

4. The terms "ontology" and "metaphysics" have uncertain status in Heidegger's writings. In *Being and Time* and *Kant and the Problem of Metaphysics*, the term "metaphysics" is treated with a certain amount of respect, almost as though the term has something to do with Heidegger's own form of inquiry. In these early works, he prefers the term "ontology" or, more specifically, "fundamental ontology" as descriptive of his own form of inquiry. In this early usage, fundamental ontology was seen as a kind of *metaphysica generalis*—i.e., the ground or general inquiry into Being which lies at the basis of all other forms of metaphysical inquiry. But Heidegger's resistance to traditional metaphysics and ontology grew more and more emphatic, until finally the term "metaphysics" came to represent that form of inquiry against which all of Heidegger's energies were directed. Metaphysics became the source of error—a discipline that concerned itself solely with objects and entities, and as such covered up the true philosophical goal, a study of Being. Consequently, Heidegger later came to abandon the term "ontology" as descriptive of his own form of inquiry, since that term for so long had been identified with traditional metaphysics. In *Being and Time*, however, the term had not as yet lost its function as describing Heidegger's own thought; and even the term "metaphysics" had not as yet become the object of his attack.

5. At a meeting with Ernst Cassirer at Davos, Switzerland, Heidegger accused the Neo-Kantians of embarrassing philosophy by limiting it to the inquiry of scientific method. The discussion with Cassirer at Davos was oral, but a *Referat* was taken by a student who attended the conference. This *Referat* was subsequently published by Guido Schneeberger in *Ergänzungen zur einer Heidegger-bibliographie* (Bern: Suhr, 1960). Neither Heidegger nor Cassirer ever had occasion to repudiate this report, and nothing said in the report is at variance with the general thought of either philosopher. Hence it has achieved a limited though respectable authenticity among scholars.

to philosophy, and to discard these problems as either secondary in importance or even "meaningless" is to do violence to the whole reasoning behind why people philosophize at all.

The search for a fundamental discipline that serves as a basis for all philosophy is by no means new in the history of thought. Aristotle, for example, argued that "first philosophy" must be the study of "Being *qua* Being";[6] it is clear that what later came to be known as "metaphysics" was not merely another branch of the philosophical endeavor, but was the source in which all other branches of philosophy were ultimately grounded. In our present century we see a similar attempt to plunge to the very core of philosophizing in Bertrand Russell's essay "Logic as the Essence of Philosophy."[7] It is perhaps needless to point out that Heidegger rejects or would reject both of these suggestions. To discuss all his reasons for doing so would be out of place here. It may, however, be of service to point out that, for Heidegger, since *even logic presupposes the disposition of the logician to attend to the purely formal relations of concepts or propositions, the analysis of how one is capable of such a disposition must be primordial.*[8] And similarly, in objection to Aristotelianism (though probably not to Aristotle himself),[9] one cannot consider an analysis of the nature of objects to constitute "first philosophy" because *objects are already categorized by the mind.* According to Heidegger, the only possible way to develop a "first philosophy" is to analyze the source of such categorizing. Nor can this merely be a self that *knows*, since knowing is only *one* of the possible ways in which we exist. Rather, we must reflect upon the *totality* of the ways in which we exist. The principles, then, that are to dictate the procedures for the various branches of philosophical investigation must originate from this transcendental examination of the existence: this is the fundamental discipline.

Thus, the task of *Being and Time* becomes to establish a fundamental

---

6. Cf. Aristotle's *Metaphysics*, books Alpha and Lambda. The term "metaphysics," of course, was not used by Aristotle himself, who referred to this portion of his work simply as "first" or "primary" philosophy. This particular part of his work was termed "metaphysics" by the librarians, who were referring merely to the spatial location of the books: the works "next to" (*meta*) the *Physics*.

7. *Our Knowledge of the External World* (London: Allen and Unwin, 1929), Lecture 2.

8. Heidegger uses the term "primordial" in a very literal sense, "of the first order." By this he means that whatever is primordial cannot be derived from anything else and is hence ultimate.

9. I make this distinction because there are some modern interpreters of Aristotle who take a different view. Heidegger, however, was rejecting the interpreters of Aristotle then prevalent in German universities. He himself would take a more liberal interpretation of the original Greek thinker.

discipline through a phenomenological analysis of the transcendental meaning of Being.

These considerations render certain difficulties less formidable. One of the most persistent complaints heard from many critics and readers is that Heidegger promises to talk about "Being" and instead he engages in philosophical anthropology—i.e., an analysis of the human person. When one reads that Heidegger considers the question of the meaning of Being (*Seinsfrage:* "to question what it meants to be") as paramount, one is led to expect a discussion similar to that of Thomistic scholasticism or Leibnizian monadology. Instead one finds profound analyses of man: the way in which man finds himself in a world; the ways in which he protects his own subtle weaknesses; the ways in which he plunges to the core of his inward strength. But such analyses in the history of philosophy have usually belonged to those whose interests were *not* metaphysical. They are the interests of a Nietzsche or a Pascal, for whom the title "philosopher" has been assigned, as it were, somewhat generously. And yet Heidegger emphatically denies that he is a philosophical anthropologist: he denies that his interest is in developing a "philosophy of man." His analysis, according to his own evaluation, is an analysis of what it means to be—Being. Many of the more acute critics have been confused by this: how, they ask, can Heidegger claim to be considering the question of the meaning of Being when all his energies are directed toward the description of human being in the world? Some have gone so far as to praise the incredible insights of Heidegger's "phenomenology" and insist that Heidegger's "only mistake" was to describe his work as ontological.

If we are to make sense of this seeming contradiction between what Heidegger claims his work to be and what his work seems to be to us, a certain amount of generous tolerance must be employed toward the limits of both Heidegger's expression and our understanding. For Heidegger, the analysis of man as carried out in *Being and Time* is ontology. Such is the right way to study the question of the meaning of Being. If this sounds strange to our ears, we must realize that Heidegger means it to be strange. For Heidegger is seriously challenging the very meaning of philosophy itself. By critically analyzing, through reason, the very modes of our own existence, Heidegger bridges the gap between the "pure philosopher" on the one hand, who disdains the common problems of existence, and the "living person" on the other, who disdains the "navel contemplation" of the professional philosopher. In doing so, however, he is not going to argue that "philosophy must bake bread." For Heidegger, philosophy is its own reward, its own justification. But it is not thereby separated from existence. Hence he is not a pragmatist, for whom the justification of thought lies in the realm of action; for Heidegger refuses to believe that something *other* than philosophy should justify philosophy. On the other hand, Heidegger is not a contemplative who feels there is a greatness only to thought, or who would argue that values and choices of human existence are sheer emotionalism, unconcerned with rational inquiry.

The only way in which Heidegger's analysis of human existence can provide a foundation for the question of Being is that the term "Being" be read within the context of his thought. The German term is *Sein*, which is the infinitive "to be." The *Seinsfrage* is: to question what it means to be. (Hereinafter I shall use the phrase the "question of Being" to mean: "to question what it means to be.") Only man can reflect upon what it means to be; hence "to be" or "Being" can be realized or analyzed only through the self-reflective consciousness of human existence. Thus the existential analysis is itself a part of ontology.

But if a study of man reveals the structure of ontology, so too does the investigation of ontology reflect much of what is man. In a later work, *Was Heisst Denken?* (*What Is Called Thinking?*), Heidegger put it this way:

> Every philosophical—that is, thoughtful—doctrine of man's essential nature is *in itself alone* a doctrine of the Being of beings [i.e., what it means for a being to be]. Every doctrine of Being is *in itself alone* a doctrine of man's essential nature.[10]

This point is crucial. Heidegger refuses to *separate* the study of Being—what it means to be—from the study of man. It is not even the case that one *begins* with Man and *ends* with Being, nor does one begin one's analysis with Being and end with man. In the same work, Heidegger continues:

> No way of thought, not even the way of metaphysical thought, begins with man's essential nature and goes on from there to Being, nor in reverse from Being and then back to man. Rather, every way of thinking *takes its way* already *within* the total relation of Being and man's nature, or else it is not thinking at all.[11]

Thus, to the critic who asks: Is Heidegger's *Sein und Zeit* really a theory of Being, or is it only a study of man? the answer is that Heidegger thinks there is no difference; that one cannot have the one without the other.

Such an investigation, then, does indeed reveal a great deal about man.

---

10. Martin Heidegger, *What Is Called Thinking?* trans. Fred Wieck and Glenn Gray (New York: Harper & Row, 1968), p. 79.
11. *Ibid.*, pp. 79–80.

It does provide a picture of what we are, but it is a picture of man always in terms of his awareness of his own existence. If Heidegger is right, no analysis of man is possible without a consideration of how man relates to the possibilities of his own existence. And, following Heidegger's identification of the theory of man with the theory of Being, the reading of *Being and Time* should reveal a great deal about what we, as men conscious of our own existence, really are.

Heidegger's man, however, like his philosophy, reflects the profound revolution of the modern age. It is a man acutely aware of his own possibilities, for whom the responsibility of his authenticity falls directly on his own shoulders. It is a man whose spirit can be stifled by inauthenticity, by the emasculation by machines, and by the failure to achieve a proper understanding of his finitude. Heidegger's man is the man sought in such inquiries as those of Dostoevski, Thoman Mann, Hermann Hesse, and Friedrich Nietzsche. It is man with whom the people of today must feel an affinity, a man whose essence escapes the slick calculus of the technocrats. But it is *not* a man whose basis is found in emotion or in the commitment of a "cause." It is a man whose deepest and most worthwhile characteristics can, through profound and disciplined reasoning, be exposed by philosophical (and not mere "psychological") inquiry. Hence the very study of *Being and Time* is a part of what man is—a being concerned about his own mode of Being.

In reading the existential analysis, then, we should never lose sight of the fact that it is essentially both an analysis of man and an inquiry into the meaning of Being.

II.

HEIDEGGER'S INTRODUCTIONS

sections 1–8

UNTITLED FIRST PAGE

On the first page of the German text of *Being and Time* (page 19 of the English translation), Heidegger has included an untitled page that belongs to neither the Preface nor the Introductions. In spite of its seeming dislocation, it is a very important part of the book. Three points are to be made about it.

. 1. To begin the entire treatise of *Being and Time* with a direct quotation from Plato's dialogue is in itself significant. Although there are several possible interpretations of Heidegger's intention in quoting from the *Sophist*, it seems clear that he was not suggesting that *Being and Time* is merely an extension or reinterpretation of the analysis of Being that occurs in the *Sophist*. For one thing, Heidegger translates Plato's term ὄν [on] by the German *seiend*, whereas the subject of inquiry in

Heidegger's work is not *seiend* but *Sein*.[1] And in later works[2] Heidegger explicitly points out the many ways in which his own view of Being is quite different from that of the Greek thinker. Yet there is surely significance in using a quotation from Plato rather than from, say, Aristotle or Kant. One possible reason may be that, among all the great thinkers, Plato is unique in relating the problems of the individual human being to the immensely speculative reaches of abstract metaphysics. For, as every reader of the dialogues knows, Plato's theory of Forms arose out of such immediately existential needs as love, death, and justice. It may well be that Heidegger wishes to achieve a similar kind of unity between his own ontological description and the immediate and existential awareness of everyday life.

2. By quoting from Plato, Heidegger emphasizes that the problem to which he is directing his attention comes from the tradition of Western thought. So much has been written of the uniqueness of Heidegger's thinking, in both positive and negative senses, that Heidegger's own recognition of the traditional nature of his investigation is often overlooked. To be sure, Heidegger feels his investigation has gone beyond a mere evaluation of the past, but the quest for the meaning of Being is one of the most persistent in Western thought; Heidegger's analysis of it gains in stature because of his recognition of and dependence upon other thinkers.

3. Most important, though, this untitled page emphasizes that a major task of the entire enterprise of *Being and Time* is to awaken the *significance* of the question of Being. Just as in Plato's dialogue, the meaning of Being is difficult to examine because one rarely recognizes that there is a problem. It is precisely the theme of the entire existential analytic that the vague and unexamined understanding of Being is the ultimate source for, and yet an impediment to, a genuine comprehension of what it means to be. For Plato—and Heidegger as well—the unexamined life, the vague and unanalyzed life, is not worth living; and so, in spite of the perplexity of which Plato speaks, to examine Being is the committed task of one who would call himself a philosopher rather than merely a sophist.

---

1. These two German terms are discussed in detail below. I have used the German here merely to allow the discussion of the terms to occur at a more convenient place.

2. Cf. especially *Platons Lehre von der Wahrheit* (Bern: Francke, 1947); and *Vom Wesen der Wahrheit* (Frankfurt: Klostermann, 1943). This latter has been translated as *On the Essence of Truth* by R. F. C. Hull and Alan Crick in *Existence and Being*, ed. Werner Brock (Chicago: Regnery, 1949); the former has been translated as *Plato's Theory of Truth*. This essay is found in *Philosophy in the Twentieth Century* by Henry Aiken and William Barrett (New York: Random House, 1963).

FIRST INTRODUCTION   (sections 1–4)

Heidegger has two Introductions: the first examines the meaning of the question of Being; the second explains his procedure and methodology. Since these Introductions are so different, we should consider them separately.

In certain cases, the introductions to great philosophical works contain the kernels of entire systems of thought, so that a comprehension of the introduction or preface is often a comprehension of almost the entire work itself. Obvious examples of this are the introductions to Kant's *Critique of Pure Reason* and Hegel's *Phenomenology of Mind*. This is also true of Heidegger's *Being and Time*. In the first Introduction, Heidegger states the bold and broad outline of his thought, and it is consequently difficult and demanding reading. Because of the great deal of import placed upon the Introduction, we must review it carefully. The first Introduction should be reread frequently during the study of the entire text.

Heidegger is, above all else in the first Introduction, asking a difficult and unique question. He calls this question the *Seinsfrage*, the "question of Being," or perhaps a better translation would be: "to question what it means to be." We may well ask: Is it at all meaningful to ask such a question?

Although it is true that one must exist in order to know something (for if I didn't exist I couldn't know anything), at the same time it is *not* true that I must be *aware* of my existence in an explicit way before I can know something. In fact, most human experience attests otherwise. In one's normal cognitive experience, what is known is always a kind of object or thing or relation between things. It is a highly sophisticated kind of awareness that recognizes the self, because truly to recognize the self requires that one transcends the normal way of knowing, which is to consider what is known as an object, and reflect instead upon the pervading presence of existence. It is fallacious to argue, as some positivists have done, that since most of our knowledge is a knowledge of objects that can be experienced by sensation and spoken of by an object language (which is true), it therefore follows that all knowledge and language is of this sort (which is false). Yet, even in the case of the question of Being there must be some sort of primary kind of occurrence to which the language corresponds and which it makes explicit, and this occurrence is our own existence. Hence what Heidegger is asking for is: How can we make explicit that vague awareness of our own existence? According to him, the greatest barrier in accomplishing any kind of significant answer to this question is the natural tendency of mind immediately to render the self as an *object*. For the question we are asking is a question of the process or activity of existing, not *what* it is that exists. We are asking, not what kind of thing a being is, but what it means to be at all.

Since the normal way of investigating anything is to consider the object of inquiry as an entity (*Das Seiende*), the first and most important task for the reader is to make clear in his mind the difference between an inquiry about an entity, and the inquiry about what it means to be. Unless this distinction is clear, the whole of Heidegger's work remains obscure. The second major task for the reader is to grasp why the inquiry about what it means to be is "primordial" and why it thereby constitutes the fundamental or basic discipline of all philosophy.

Ontic and Ontological Inquiry

An inquiry about what it means to be is called "ontological," whereas an inquiry about an entity is called "ontic." The terms that describe an ontical investigation are called "categories," whereas the terms that describe ontological investigations are called "existentials." Since Heidegger invents a nomenclature of his own to distinguish these types of inquiry, this chart may be helpful:

Object of Inquiry	Being (*Sein*)	Entity (*Das Seiende*)
Type of inquiry	ontological	ontic
Terms of inquiry	existentials	categories
Status of occurrence in inquiry	factical	factual
Type of self-awareness in inquiry	existential	existentiell

As can be seen from this chart, any scientific inquiry about an entity is ontical, makes use of categories, and is factual. Whereas any philosophical inquiry about what it means to be is ontological, makes use of existentials, and is factical. The meanings of these various terms will become clear in further discussion.

The whole purpose for the development of this elaborate nomenclature is to emphasize strongly that one cannot successfully inquire about Being in the normal or "ontical" way. In order to illustrate this, Heidegger points out quite clearly that if Being is analyzed in an ontical fashion, the entire question of the meaning of Being as such becomes trivial or meaningless. In fact, Heidegger maintains that after Plato and Aristotle, the subsequent history of philosophy accepted an attitude that resulted in a disregard for the question of Being. This disregard is based upon the attempt to consider Being ontically rather than ontologically by studying the particular *things* that are instead of what or how they are.

Within such attempts to consider Being ontically, three major "presuppositions" developed. Heidegger analyzes these three presuppositions, and his analyses are important, for they clarify the *reasons* behind his ultimate rejection of an ontical analysis. The three presuppositions of an ontical inquiry of Being are: (1) that "Being" is the most universal and empty of all concepts; (2) that it is undefinable; and (3) that it is self-evident. It is the second of these three presuppositions that is most crucial, because if "Being" is undefinable, Heidegger's entire project is in jeopardy. In examining these three presuppositions Heidegger makes the following points:

1. Simply because "Being" is the most universal of concepts does not mean that it cannot thereby be further examined. If "Being" were *merely* the "most general of concepts" and had no meaning other than the meaning of the most abstract generalization, there would be no sense and no real possibility of examining the concept further. But Heidegger points out that even Aristotle recognized that there *is* a meaning to "Being" that is primordial, and it is *because* of this meaning that it becomes the most general concept. What this meaning is will be analyzed by this text.

2. The second presupposition, concerning the indefinability of "Being," affords Heidegger an opportunity to make a very important point. The presupposition states that "Being" cannot be defined, since to define something one needs broader genera and species, and there is no broader genus than "Being," hence it is undefinable. The argument is perfectly valid *if* the only way to ascribe meaning is by placing a term under broader terms. But it is precisely this technique of ascribing meaning that Heidegger is to reject.

As every freshman logic student knows, "man" is defined in traditional terms by first placing the term in a broader genus, "animal," and then attributing to it the specific difference "rational." But if we ask about the meaning of "animal," we must then decide upon another, even broader genus, and so on, until we finally come to the widest and broadest of genera, "Being." Since we are now incapable of defining that term by any further use of genera, since there are none broader than "Being," we are left with a problem: *If this broadest of terms has no meaning, how can it serve as the genus for anything else? But if it does have a meaning, how can this meaning be realized or defined?* Heidegger's point is simply that this broadest of terms does have a meaning—as it obviously must—but this simply indicates that the meaning must be discovered through a process other than the classical definition. The point here is well taken, for it shows that a genus-species definition procedure of meaning cannot in principle be complete. A similar kind of argument can be found in Plato's *Theaetetus* (203–209). A corollary of this is, of course, the more important point that not only does this mean that we must seek the meaning of Being in another way, it also indicates that Being itself is not an entity.

Being is not an entity. This may be so obvious that it escapes us; and yet it is of central importance for the development of the analysis to come. With my suggested translation, its meaning is more obvious: "to be" is not itself a thing or being. There is no such thing as a "to be." When I ask what it means to be, I am not asking *about* a thing. But does this mean that simply because the question is not about an entity it has no meaning? That would be true only if "meaning" refers solely to objects, and to assert that is to beg the question. But this raises a more important and serious question: How, then, *is* the question of Being to be asked? Before directly answering that, Heidegger briefly considers the third presupposition of an ontic theory of Being.

3. The third presupposition of an ontic theory of Being is that Being is "self-evident." There are two ways to attack this. One is to point out that as a matter of fact the theory of Being is *not* self-evident; the second argument is to disqualify "self-evidence" as a genuine philosophical criterion. Most efforts to build any kind of lasting philosophical argument on the principle of self-evidence come to naught; for if something were self-evident it would never be inquired about, and since the meaning of Being is here inquired about, it must be because it is not self-evident. If one protests that "self-evidence" needs to be refined, then it is that refinement which awaits the consideration of philosophical judgment, and not the principle of self-evidence simply and blandly stated by itself.

To return, then, to the more important question. If we are to examine the meaning of Being, but cannot do so with the use of genera, how do we proceed? Or to ask the question in another and more specific way: Are we not begging the question in asking for the meaning of Being? Are we not presupposing that Being has a meaning? Heidegger's position here is similar to that of Plato in his dialogue *Meno*. It may be recalled that in the *Meno* Socrates is asked by his friend how it is possible to inquire at all, since if I know what to inquire about there is no need for inquiry; whereas if I don't know what I am inquiring about, I can't inquire at all since I wouldn't even know what I am looking for. Heidegger's answer is not dissimilar to Plato's. I *do* know something vague about the object of my inquiry, but my inquiry is an attempt to make more explicit what I vaguely feel. If I attend to it, I will recognize that I am aware of my own existence, but I do not fully grasp what that existence means. At the same time, though, I also recognize that my existence *does* have a meaning, since I am aware of it. What is known, even vaguely, has meaning. In the asking of any question, then, there is something to be asked about, something interrogated, and something gained by the asking. By an analysis of this common aspect of all inquiry, Heidegger points out that the question of Being is an honest and legitimate inquiry. What is asked about is Being. What is interrogated is a particular being or entity, the human being. And what is gained is the *meaning* of Being.

Why Heidegger chooses the human existent as the object to be investigated requires a consideration of that all-important term *Dasein*. Macquarrie and Robinson have wisely left it untranslated. Basically, in common, everyday German discourse, the term refers to human existence. This meaning is not completely abandoned by Heidegger; but he emphasizes its etymology as well. The term consists of two parts—*da*, meaning "here," and *sein*, "to be." Thus the etymologically derived translation of the term is "to be here." Some translators have chosen to use such phrases as "to be *there*," noting that at times the German term *da* can be translated by the English "there." *Da*, however, must be distinguished from *dort*, which means "there" in the sense of "at that place—not *here*." *Da* basically means "here," as in the simple German sentence *Da kommt er*: "Here he comes." The English language would allow such a sentence to run: "There he comes." Nevertheless, I suggest that to emphasize the "there" over the "here" is distortive.[3]

---

3. There are some reasons to hesitate in using "here" rather than "there" as a translation of *Da*. The term, after all, is not the same as *hier*. To show the extent of meaning applicable to this term, one might reflect that the simple English phrase "here and there" can be translated into German either as *hier und da* or *da und dort*; *da* in the first phrase means "there"; but in the second it means "here." My choice of "here" rather than "there" lies in what I think Heidegger means by the term—i.e., within the immediate environment. Macquarrie and Robinson have used "there"; that term, however, lacks the immediacy of my choice. It has been pointed out to me by J. Glenn Gray that the basic meaning of *Dasein* is "openness," so that my use of "here" as the translation of *da* should be read in the sense of "*Here* I am, open to possibilities!"

In light of this etymology, I think it is likewise incorrect to translate *Dasein* as "human being," because "human being" refers to an actual entity or existent, with reference to its genus and species. To inquire about a "human being" would be to engage in an ontical inquiry. What Heidegger means by the term *Dasein* is that entity which is capable of inquiring into its own Being, and indeed, such an inquiry into its Being is what makes Dasein what it is. Much of the examination of *Being and Time* is directed toward a "definition" of Dasein, so I shall not try to give a capsule definition at this time.

The whole point about Dasein is that it itself can wonder about itself as existing. As will be seen later on, the *meaning* of existence can be significant only to one who asks about his own existence. For this reason, the question of Being itself is possible only because Dasein can reflect upon its existence. The model of scientific (ontic) knowledge cannot *in principle* examine such a question.

The main question to be asked of this section is, Why does Heidegger spend so much time and effort on the problem of explaining his kind of inquiry? Why doesn't he simply accept it as undisputed? The answer lies in the recognition that many philosophers—among them Heidegger's Neo-Kantian contemporaries—do in fact dispute the viability and validity of such an inquiry. In England and America, the more recognizable foes would be the positivists. But both the Neo-Kantians and the positivists would at least momentarily share the same platform in attacking Heidegger here. Their argument in its purest form is as follows: Heidegger has admitted that Being is itself not an entity. If it is not an entity, it does not exist; and if it does not exist it cannot be known; if it cannot be known, any inquiry about its meaning is at best poetic and at worst meaningless.

Heidegger's answer to this objection would be to point out that to say that only entities can be said to exist and hence be known is precisely the point in question, and hence to use it as a premise is a *petitio principii*. *It is a fallacy of a narrow kind of substance metaphysics to assert that existence can be applied only to individuals.* We are investigating, not the meaning of any particular thing—not even the human thing—but what it means to be. How do we know that Being has a meaning? Because it does not violate my logic to ask about the meaning of my existence. In other words, Heidegger begins with the obvious and immediate human condition that one's life and very existence *can* be questioned as to its meaning. (We must remember that we are asking about the *meaning* of Being, not after Being itself.) Poets, artists, and even the humblest of men recognize this to be a genuine question. And it is this *fact* that provides Heidegger with his starting point. Heidegger, then, must show how such inquiry actually occurs. And it occurs, he says, just as Plato had explained it in the *Meno* because inquiry is the making explicit of what is implicitly realized. If the positivist or Neo-Kantian were to object that there is no *object* to be studied in such an analysis, Heidegger would agree. We are not studying an object, but a process. How do we know that such a process actually occurs? Because we ourselves *are* a process, the process of our life and existence. An inquiry into such a process is valid because it makes sense. Heidegger correctly emphasizes by italics his sentence which states that "... *the vague average understanding of Being is a fact.*"

What is the upshot of all this? Two points have been made: (1) "Being" *cannot* be analyzed as an entity, and hence any ontical analysis that makes use of categories—by which we describe entities—is in principle inadequate; (2) it is meaningful nonetheless to inquire about the meaning of Being, since there is another type of inquiry—the ontological. In this latter way, Dasein reflects upon itself as existing. The methodology of such procedure is considered in the second Introduction. But before we turn to that, there remains the final question of the first Introduction.

Why Is Ontology Fundamental?   (sections 3–4)

I have tried to clarify the difference between the ontological and the ontical forms of inquiry. We now turn our attention to the second problem of the first Introduction: the claim that such an inquiry provides the basis and foundation of all philosophy.

Heidegger sees the priority or fundamental nature of the question of Being as exhibited both ontologically and ontically. The ontological priority of the question of Being is due to the fact that all science and forms of inquiry presuppose an "understanding of Being." The ontical priority consists of the fact that Dasein considers the question of its Being as an issue: i.e., as something about which Dasein—any self-conscious human being—is concerned.

What do these two arguments mean? Let us consider them in order, and direct our attention first to the question: Why is the question of Being *ontologically* prior?

Although it is true that a biologist or physicist can make tremendous advances in these sciences without ever questioning the ultimate meaning or nature of the sciences, it is nevertheless the case that these sciences do presuppose certain metaphysical principles. The inner consistency of nature and the principle of cause and effect, for example, are presupposed in the sciences of physics and biology. Now the kind of critical analysis done by Kant in *The Critique of Pure Reason* (trans. Norman Kemp Smith [New York: Macmillan, 1958], or that done by Ernst Nagel in *Structure of Science* (New York: Harcourt, Brace & World, 1961) shows that the inquiring mind can discover what the principles and categories of the various sciences are. But it is also the case that the human mind can wonder how it is possible that a Kant and a Nagel carried out their critiques. Suppose we ask, What would be relevant in considering the question: How are critiques possible?

Since both the activity of the ontical science itself *and* the inquiry as to the *a priori* conditions of the science are ways in which a human person conducts himself, the ultimate or final question must be concerned with the ways in which this person can be said to be. Logic, for example, ultimately presupposes the disposition of the logician to attend only to the formal concepts and relations of propositions. Logic further presupposes the willingness of the logician to sacrifice the wealth of probable knowledge for the paucity of certain knowledge, because one of the ways in which a man exists is to long for the assurance of certainty in *some* of his knowledge. Would logic be of any value unless it carried with it the assurance of *a priori* and necessary inference? It seems not. Therefore, the interest of those who develop logic itself *determines* to some extent what it is that logic is going to be.

A biologist or physicist can carry out his science without going through this reduction; but philosophy is supposed to be aware of its own principles and presuppositions, and hence philosophy must make such a reduction. Both science itself and the philosophy of science are ways of Being, in which Dasein directs its attention toward these various kinds of activity. But the ability of Dasein to do this is itself prior to these particular activities, and in fact greatly determines them. Hence ontologically, an analysis of what it means to be is prior to and affects our ultimate understanding of all other inquiries concerning particular things that are.

Suppose, for example, I don't ask, What is science? but rather, What does it mean *to be* scientific? In the former question I may well be asking for categories and the *a priori* conditions that may be necessary if certain functions are to proceed. But in the latter question I am asking what it means for the *self* to direct its attention to such categories, and hence this disposition of the self to make use of these categories is primary. The categories may be open to question but the disposition of the self to attend to what is formally verifiable in an organized body of knowledge is not. In this sense, what it means *to be* scientific is prior to the question of what science is.

This priority of the question of Being is not merely in terms of the sciences. All inquiries, even those dealing with such "unscientific" questions as ethics and value, are likewise grounded in the primordial or fundamental discipline. Whether I ask the question in terms of how it is possible *to be* a scientist or *to be* moral, the fundamental question is always what it means *to be* at all.

It must be clearly understood that Heidegger is in no way suggesting a psychology. When I ask the question, What does it mean to be scientific or moral? I am not asking for an account of my psychological states, or for motives, or for determinant factors in my environment; such considerations are ontic considerations, and themselves presuppose the kind of analysis done by the fundamental ontologist. The question is, What are the modes of Being that I regard as moral?

There is no major argumentation given by Heidegger that the question of Being *is* the fundamental question aside from the fact that the question of Being does seem to be a valid kind of question in every possible form of inquiry. But the real proof of this must wait the completion of the analysis. Although it is perfectly relevant and significant to show, as Heidegger has done, that the question of Being can occur as a kind of presupposition behind every inquiry, whether this question provides the *basis* for such inquiries can obviously be argued only in terms of each and every individual case. In the actual analyses to follow, Heidegger accomplishes this kind of argumentation for some of the major areas of human concern. That he does not carry this out individually for each science is hardly to be expected; but he does provide us with sufficient analysis to give serious credence to the claim that the question of Being is the fundamental question of all philosophy.

The second kind of priority Heidegger mentions is the ontic priority. The analysis of the ontic priority of the question of Being is easier for us than that of the ontological account—which is only natural since our accustomed way of inquiring is ontic. Human beings are concerned about their existence. This means that Dasein is aware of its Being (i.e., Dasein knows what it means to be), and indeed, to some extent, even explicitly. When Heidegger says: "*Understanding of Being is itself a definite characteristic of Dasein's Being*" (E-32/G-12),[4] he means that one of the determining ways that Dasein can be said to be, is to understand what it means to be.

What does this mean, and what is the evidence for it? The fact is that people understand, to some extent at least, what it means to be. And that because "to understand" is itself a way of Being for Dasein, such an understanding is always self-reflective. Is this true? When poets, novelists, and other artists describe their own experiences, it is often the case that they are giving an account of their own insights into the problem of

---

4. Hereinafter, references to *Being and Time* will be given in this way: the "E" refers to the English pagination, the "G" to the German.

existence. In fact, it seems surely within the experience of almost every intelligent and sensitive person to have at one time or another been seized with the agony of trying to accomplish a true conception of the meaning of existence. In some of his later works,[5] Heidegger notes that the occasional feeling of utter *meaninglessness* of life is itself proof that one is questioning what it means to be at all.

It is this reflection upon the nature of existence that gives *Being and Time* the character that attracts so many of its readers; it thereby makes such areas of concern as death, guilt, and conscience the *sources* from which the fundamental discipline of philosophy can be derived. Thus Heidegger inquires as to the ways in which one faces death and listens to the calls of conscience, not for the sake of establishing an ethics or morality, but as insights into the very structure of what it means for Dasein to be, and from this structure to build the entire edifice of philosophical investigation.

Because we ourselves are beings to whom the question of Being is relevant, the subject to be investigated in such an analysis is peculiarly available. As long as I am conscious, I have at my disposal my own conscious existence to consider and investigate. Thus we can be aware of who we are merely by directing attention to ourselves; and as long as one keeps in mind the fact that one's awareness of oneself is different in kind from the awareness of things other than the self, the inquiry can proceed along the lines of a "transcendental" account. The choice, then, of Dasein as that which is to be investigated is only natural. And it is this "natural" choice of Dasein that provides the ontical priority of the question of Being.

At the risk of oversimplification, it might be summarized in this fashion: To consider one's self as existing is to be aware of oneself as Dasein; and (1) Dasein is ontically prior because it exists; (2) Dasein is ontologically prior because it can be questioned *about* its existence; (3) Dasein is fundamentally—ontologically—prior because the questioning of its existence provides the foundation for all other inquiries.

Certain terms must now be further clarified. By the term "existential analytic" Heidegger means the *preparatory* analysis of Dasein's ways of Being. This preparatory analysis is not a mere random listing of the many ways in which human beings can be said to be. The analysis reveals that there is a kind of common meaning to be found in all of these various

---

5. Cf. especially *Was Ist Metaphysik?* (Bonn: Cohen, 1930). A translation of this work, entitled *What Is Metaphysics* occurs in W. Brock's collection *Existence and Being*.

manifestations of human existence. The submerged question is: Can we ask, not "What does it mean to be in such-and-such a way?" but rather, "What does it mean to be at all?" Once this ultimate meaning of Dasein's Being is found, it is then possible to examine the meaning of Being on a more profound, or ontological, basis (Division Two). Thus the first kind of analysis, the "existential analytic," is merely preparatory. Nor should the preparatory nature of this analysis keep it from belonging to the fundamental discipline. Some authors have been confused about just what constitutes the actual fundamental discipline; a few have gone so far as to suggest that "fundamental ontology proper" is reserved for the unpublished and "mysterious" third section of Division One. Such confusion must be avoided. Fundamental ontology is the transcendental analysis of the meaning of our existence, which provides the ultimate basis for all philosophical inquiry. A part of that transcendental account is the existential analysis of the ways in which Dasein exists. This is only preparatory because it merely brings us to an understanding of what constitutes Dasein's Being; it does not carry out this analysis any further. When we are armed with an understanding that Dasein's essential Being is temporality, the second level of analysis is then possible; this second level is Division Two. The third level, in which not only Dasein's Being but Being itself was to be shown as finite, was never published. But this does not mean that the missing third section was to contain some great "secret store of information." There is, unfortunately, a "mystique" about the missing third section, which does an injustice to the first two sections. It is, of course, regrettable that Heidegger did not publish it, but his failure to do so need not detract from what he did publish.

Finally, to object that a human being is a far richer kind of thing than the mere impersonal Dasein is to have missed the point. Heidegger insists[6] that his analysis is not an anthropology. We are not investigating "man," but that aspect of man which is concerned with the awareness of his existence. "Dasein" does not mean "man"; for the concept "man" is both too broad and too narrow: there are many things that a man is other than Dasein; and there is much to the meaning of "Dasein" that goes beyond a simple understanding of what man is. There are a lot of things one does that do not necessarily reveal one's existence.

But is it really possible to examine what it means to be? What *methodology* is there that would serve to examine this question? To answer this we turn to Heidegger's second Introduction.

6. Cf. especially the last sections of *Kant and the Problem of Metaphysics.*

SECOND INTRODUCTION   (sections 5–8)

There are three points that are developed in the second Introduction: (1) how the analysis of Dasein can reveal the meaning of Being; (2) the need for a reinterpretation of the history of philosophy—the so-called Destruction of the history of ontology; and (3) a discussion of Heidegger's phenomenology. The first two points are fairly clear in Heidegger's work and need but a brief commentary, but a discussion of Heidegger's phenomenology requires considerable study and analysis.

The Analysis of Dasein   (section 5)

In order to avoid a kind of dogmatic statement as to what constitutes the meaning of Dasein, the existential analytic must, according to Heidegger, begin from an account of Dasein in its everydayness. "Everydayness" does not have any pejorative connotation; it is merely descriptive. Basically, it means that uncritical mode of daily life which is lived even by the most profound of men. By keeping in mind the "everyday" self, we are, to an extent, allowing experience to speak out for itself. In this sense Heidegger here is an "empiricist." He wishes to avoid describing Dasein by some narrow-minded or "hothouse" criteria that would reduce his analysis to a mere *aspect* of Dasein's Being. The whole point of the analysis is, after all, to study what it means *to be*, and certainly one of the most frequent modes of our existence is that which one might call "everyday."

The procedure of beginning with the everyday is in keeping with what Heidegger had said about how the question of Being starts from the *fact* of a vague awareness and proceeds through analysis to an explicit and thematic account. If the awareness of Being is indeed a vague *fact*, then the place to begin our analysis is with that fact. But the fact comes from our everyday selves. The awareness of Being is not some mysterious or mystical "insight" given only to a philosophical elite; it is not a kind of psychological experience that requires a certain kind of gymnastic to prepare ourselves for the "happy moment of truth." To be aware of the meaning of Being is as common as to be aware of our left ankle: we are aware of it when we look at it or think about it, and we are unaware of it when we don't. Everydayness as the source for the *data* of the question of Being is not contested; in fact, it is demanded. What must be transcended is the everyday *perspective*. But to go beyond the everyday perspective to a perspective of ontological insight, we must first thoroughly examine the range of the everyday perspective, lest in ascending to the broader perspective we emphasize what is inessential or peculiar. In addition, the ontological inquiry will place everydayness itself in a new light, focusing attention on the role that everydayness plays in the ontological perspective.

One of the ways in which the everyday self looks at itself is to see itself in the world. What must be examined is whether to see oneself in the world demands that we take the world as the primary reality of which we are but a part (and are defined merely as a part); or to take the world as a way of our Being, in which our existence is primary and of which the world is merely a function. Hence the everyday observation that we are in the world is surely not incorrect; its perspective, however, which interprets that world, must be transcended. But even this casual observation of the everyday shows us where our analysis must begin: We note that the first "existential" described in the analytic is "Being-in-the-world."

Heidegger also mentions briefly in this second Introduction the term that shares the title of his work with "Being" itself. In anticipation of the results of his inquiry, he shows what he means by saying that Dasein's Being is time. Again, the actual development of Dasein's Being as time is not carried out in the Introduction, and so I shall not discuss it here; but it may be helpful to make the following observation: In all of the ways in which a human person can be said to be, the understanding of such ways is limited by man's finitude. Even the so-called nontemporal truths of logic are temporal in the sense that they are understood by an agent or mind that is determined by temporal dimensions. Thus, for Heidegger, to grasp what it means to be in time is to grasp what it means for Dasein to be at all. The full significance of this will be made clear in Chapter VIII.

The "Destruction" (Destruktion) of the History of Ontology
(section 6)

One of the most distinctive characteristics of Heidegger's thought is the manner in which he interprets the history of philosophy. Although he refers to his own interpretation as a "destruction," he does not mean to imply that he is going to destroy or do away with the history of philosophy. In later works he refers rather to the "overcoming" (*Überwindung*) of the history of philosophy. In analyzing the thoughts of such men as Kant, Plato, and Nietzsche,[7] Heidegger has exhibited a most creative and

---

7. Heidegger's interpretations of these figures can be found in the following works: *Plato's Theory of Truth*; a two-volume study entitled *Nietzsche* (Pfullingen: Neske, 1961); and several works on Kant—*Kant and the Problem of Metaphysics, What Is a Thing?* (*Die Frage nach dem Ding*, Tubingen; Niemeyer, 1962), and *Kants These über das Sein* (Frankfurt: Klostermann, 1962).

unorthodox reading of the traditional philosophers. The second part of the original plan of *Being and Time* was to have dealt with the reinterpretation of the history of thought about what it means to be (the question of Being); but as the second part was never published, Heidegger's readers have had to be satisfied with the several independently published essays on various thinkers.

Since the analyses of Heidegger's interpretations of these thinkers properly belong elsewhere, I shall not dwell on any particular interpretation here; but mention must be made of the *idea* behind such interpretation, and why the destruction properly belonged to the original design of the treatise.

In his destruction, Heidegger does not "explain" what a philosopher wrote; nor is he interested merely in what the thinker "actually said" in his writings. That is the task of teachers of the history of philosophy, and is a respectable form of education. But, *as a philosopher*, Heidegger feels that one must "do violence to" the history of thought. That is, Heidegger takes his own approach and problem, and under the guiding persuasion of this problem, prods these thinkers with his own questions, reinterprets what the past philosopher had actually said along these lines, and tests, then, the power of the *spirit* of their thought. In this way he intends to engage the past thinkers in a *dialogue* about his own subject, the meaning of Being. But is this fair? If Heidegger were to say that his interpretation actually reflected what the thinkers of the past thought and wrote, it would be very unfair and grossly incompetent. But Heidegger insists that is not what he is doing. So we cannot judge him by the simple criterion of historical accuracy.

But what is its value? Heidegger's claim is that many great thinkers *wanted to* talk about Being but, due to the impediment of traditional meaning, found themselves speaking of "existents" instead. Yet in spite of this failure on the part of the thinkers of the past to speak of Being, precisely because they *are* the greatest thinkers of our era they nevertheless, implicitly, said much to further and enrich the idea of Being. Heidegger sees his task as "breaking loose the ice," so to speak, that tradition has frozen around the ideas of these thinkers. Thus Heidegger's attitude toward every great thinker is always an enigma: In the first place, he must point out the major error that the thinker made in not recognizing the difference between Being (*Sein*) and things that exist (*Seienden*). On the other hand, he must show that much of what the thinker has said is relevant to the question of Being. Thus those thinkers whom Heidegger most critically examines—i.e., Kant and Plato and Nietzsche—are actually the thinkers closest to him in philosophical persuasion. The "violence" of which Heidegger speaks, then, is the force used by the interpreter to make what the past thinker had said *relevant* to the present concern, the question of Being. For anyone who honestly reads his *Kant and the Problem of Metaphysics*, as one prime instance, it is clear that he does a remarkable job of forcing Kant to speak to Heidegger about the question of Being, without losing the obvious Kantian characteristic and spirit.

What Heidegger says so devastatingly about "tradition" is unfortunately all too frequently the case. Heidegger complains that traditions have a strong tendency (possibly because "traditions" are the work of lesser minds) to freeze and hence destroy the creativity of the truly seminal thinkers. The so-called schools of philosophy very often do far more damage and dishonor to a thinker than the most violent antagonist. What usually happens in such cases is that the categories and principles of a great philosophical vision become cogs and wheels of a slickly oiled machine that happily churns out "answers" to all problems large and small.

If Heidegger can wrench from Kant, Plato, and Nietzsche insights into the question of Being that no tradition had seen before, the significance as to whether the thinker had "actually meant" what Heidegger has found becomes trivial. Heidegger obviously does not "change the words" of a philosopher; he forces them to yield a meaning that had not been obvious before. And if these words *can* be forced to yield this meaning, any bland assertion that the past thinker did *not* mean what Heidegger says, merely because it is untraditional, begs the question. Furthermore, the point is that the *ways* in which past philosophers have implicitly dealt with the question of Being have affected our own understanding of it, and are hence a legitimate part of the inquiry as to how Dasein understands its own Being. Part of Dasein's Being is its history (i.e., part of what it means for Dasein to be is *to be in history*), and this history affects Dasein's understanding of itself.

Heidegger, then, far from having no respect for the history of philosophy, honors it as few thinkers have ever done. He insists that it is not a dead display of obsolete opinions but an essential part of our present philosophical perspective. His destruction is not meant negatively. And while one may not be willing to accept all of what Heidegger extracts from the philosophers of the past, one is rarely left without an immense supply of new insights about the thinkers he has interpreted. There is always too the nagging and persistent possibility that Heidegger's interpretations might possibly be correct.

Heidegger's Phenomenology (section 7)

The term "phenomenology," which comes originally from Kant's distinction between phenomenon and noumenon, has had an interesting history of its own. It was employed by Hegel as descriptive of his procedure of investigating the development of the human spirit, for Hegel denied the absolute dichotomy between Kant's two worlds. The term was also used by Husserl to refer to his own methodology of the "eidetic reduction." Heidegger too used the term to describe his methodology. As there is little similarity between Kant's, Hegel's, Husserl's, and Heidegger's usage, however, it may be best to consider Heidegger's use of the term with as little consideration of these earlier thinkers as is possible. In light of the historical predecessors just mentioned, it may have been more fortunate for his readers had Heidegger not used the term as descriptive of his own method. The difficulty is that many phenomenologists argue that Heidegger's "hermeneutic phenomenology" is a contradiction in terms. They maintain, and with a certain amount of cogency, that in the tradition of Edmund Husserl—the father of modern phenomenology—the whole purpose of this method is to achieve a vision of consciousness totally untainted by "systems" or interpretations: to let the facts speak for themselves, as it were. The motto of such phenomenology is "To the facts [or things] themselves!" (*Zu den Sachen selbst!*) But Heidegger's phenomenology is hermeneutic—i.e., it is interpretive. The term comes from the Greek verb *hermeneuein* ἑρμηνεύειν "to interpret." The English term is often used to refer to Biblical exegesis. The problem, then, is acute: If Heidegger's methodology is *interpretive*, and if phenomenology means to let the facts speak for themselves, in whatever sense that can be taken without being ridiculous, then surely a hermeneutic phenomenology is impossible.

Although there can be little doubt that these considerations prove that Heidegger is not an Husserlian, it is not as convincing in proving that Heidegger cannot use the term "phenomenology" as descriptive of his method. After all, Hegel wrote a book with "phenomenology" in the title, and no one would want to argue that Hegel is an Husserlian. In any event, the right to the title "phenomenologist" is in itself a minor dispute.

What is not minor, however, is the deeper issue. Heidegger and other hermeneutic thinkers want to be true to both terms of their descriptive methodology: to let the facts speak for themselves; and at the same time to claim that there are no such things as uninterpreted facts—at least not in those cases where the hermeneutic method applies. Such a thing seems to consist, if not in a contradiction, at least in a dilemma. A closer look at this seeming dilemma will be helpful.

It has often been said of certain philosophers—such as Hegel and Plato, for example—that one cannot separate their method from their content. This is especially so in the case of a thinker like Heidegger, whose method is one that strives to reveal the meaning of Being. When one investigates the structure of hermeneutic phenomenology, it must be kept in mind that this method is meant to apply only to the question of existence. (It *may* be applicable to other questions, but that is, at the moment, unimportant.) In any event, there are certain very important reasons why hermeneutic phenomenology cannot be applied to such inquiries as natural science. On the other hand, it is also the case that Heidegger believes that to question what it means to be can proceed only through a methodology that in turn proceeds from an interpretive phenomenology of the immediate awareness of existence—that to apply metaphysical systematic methods to the question of Being is to overlook the peculiar nature of the existence question. It may well be, then, that just as the question of existence is peculiar, so too is its method. But if the existence question is open only to hermeneutic phenomenology or some similar kind of dialectic, and hermeneutic phenomenology is applicable only to the question of Being, then any attempt to force a similarity to other investigations would be futile.

In what way does this method reveal the question of the meaning of Being? How can the hermeneutic method tell us about existence? From the many ways in which I exist, I am searching for an answer to the question what it means to be. Now I can easily enough impose or force a meaning to my life: through a religious belief, national commitment, or psychological attitude, as do dedicated monks, enthusiastic patriots, and pathological sadists. But the question here is not one of morals or even behavioral modes; it is not What modes of action ought I to impose upon my life? but rather, What is it that my own understanding can tell me about what it means to exist?

I exist. And this existence manifests itself in many ways and forms. If in the consideration of the ways of existing I could recognize a pattern or meaning, then I would be true to the first maxim of the phenomenologist: to let the facts speak for themselves. But surely this is dubious. There are many who argue that facts cannot ever speak for themselves. The weatherman, for example, does not read the facts from the skies; he interprets the facts from the basis of a theory. To paraphrase a saying of Kant's: Theories without facts are empty; facts without theories are blind.

It seems, then, as if there is a kind of cruel choice: I must either commit myself to admitting that facts do speak for themselves, in which case I deny the validity of hermeneutics; or I must admit that one must always interpret facts because facts do *not* have meanings in themselves, in which case I deny the validity of phenomenology. Is there any way out of the dilemma? *The only way out of this dilemma would be if there were a case in which the facts were not in principle separate from the meanings of facts!* That this is not the case in science is clear from the following observation: In physics, the occurrence of fire is indifferent to the multiple theories that explain it. The phlogiston theory renders an account of flame, but then so does the theory of oxidation. The preference of one theory over the other is not in the ability of one to explain the fact, because both theories explain the fact. The preference is based on such theoretical considerations as: consistency with other theories, greater precision, wider application to other phenomena, elegance, Occam's razor, etc. Obviously, then, hermeneutics cannot apply to the structures of science. But can it apply to anything: Is there any case in which—unlike the science example, where the meaning and the fact *are* not separable? Heidegger feels that in the case of one's ways of existing there is no difference between the fact and its meaning. He claims, in *Being and Time*, that "only as phenomenology is ontology possible"; but he could also have said it in reverse: "Only as ontology is phenomenology possible." This latter sentence would, of course, have caused Husserl the greatest amount of agony.

Is it the case that when I examine my own existence, there is no difference between the meaning of the fact and the fact itself: An example may be helpful.

When I am afraid, the full and explicit meaning of my fear may not ever be realized; but it is nevertheless the case that my being afraid is *meaningful*. If it were not meaningful to me, I would not be afraid at all. Thus, ontologically speaking, the factical occurrences within my existence are never without meaning; whereas in a scientific account we can make a distinction between a fact and the theory that explains the fact. But it is impossible to think of being afraid without realizing that "to be afraid" has a meaning for the one who is afraid. Thus fear has meaning in a way different from the way fire has meaning. Hermeneutic inquiry is that inquiry in which the implicit meaning of an *existential fact* is made explicit.

But how do I make explicit the meaning of fear without "imposing" an "artificial" theory? The answer is that I make explicit the meaning of the particular existential fact (in this case, fear) by showing how it relates to the whole of my existence. In other words, I show what it means to be afraid by working out how fear relates to what it means to be at all. And how do I come to realize what it means to be at all? By analyzing the particular ways of existing, such as fearing, as a totality.

Such an account is admittedly circular. In order to understand the whole (what it means to be), I need to know what it means to be in such and such a way; whereas to know what it means to be in such and such a way requires a knowledge of what it means to be at all. But reason does not always reject circularity as negative, as long as it is not a vicious circle. An example of circular reasoning that is acceptable to the mind can be taken from normal experience.

In learning a foreign language, one of the most familiar kinds of experience for anyone with even the vaguest sense for language is the discovery of certain words merely by the context of the sentence. In fact, certain modern methods of language instruction emphasize the contextual structure of language.

But this presents certain students with a seemingly legitimate complaint: In order to know the words I must first know the context; but in order to know the context I must first know the words. The seemingly sophistic answer to this is simply to make it positive: One discovers the context from the meaning of the words, and the meaning of the words from the context. And although this seems a ridiculous bit of sophistry, it is nevertheless true. The mind accepts this description of how we learn foreign languages because the *way* in which the words are learned in the first instance is different from the way in which the words are learned in the second instance, even if it's the same word. If an English-speaking student, for example, sets out to learn German, he first looks up in a lexicon or vocabulary list a few basic German words. At this point, however, these German terms are not really German at all. They are merely sounds substituted for English meanings. They are, in a very real sense, English words. This means that they take their contextual significance from the whole or totality of the English language. After the student has become practiced and facile in the use of these terms, however, the words gradually become real German words—i.e., they take their contextual significance from the whole or totality of the *Deutsche Sprache*. To make my example more concrete: If a novice in the German language picked up a copy of Schopenhauer's book and wondered what *Vorstellung* meant in the title, he would probably look the term up in the lexicon, and find such suggestions as "placing before." And although he might think it strange to title a book "The World as Will and Placing Before," he would nevertheless have some idea of the meaning of that remarkable work. But as this novice worked himself through the language, and became familiar with the many uses of the term *Vorstellung* and actually used it himself, his understanding of it would grow richer. He might, to his own surprise, realize that although he now knew what the term meant, he could not translate the German term back into his own language—an obvious indication that the reference of meaning was no longer English as in his first encounter with it.

The learning of a language, then, being existential, is hermeneutic. It proceeds from a whole to a part, and then from a part back to a new whole. From the whole of the English language, the student proceeds to a "part," the single word, and then to a new whole, the German language. Heidegger claims that our awareness of and the refinement of our knowledge about existence proceeds in a similar fashion. From the "whole" of our total, vague, and unanalyzed existence we proceed to the part (the single existential fact—as in the case of fear), and from such "parts" we then proceed to a new whole—the ontological understanding of existence. This is, however, a rational, nonarbitrary activity. It is a disciplined way of coming to know; and its procedure is open to the critical investigations of metamethodological inquiry. The basis for it is the same as the basis for dialectic—namely, a working back toward the ultimate, necessary conditions of thought. It is not ontological autobiography, because it uses that function of the self which is public and contestable. Hence such an inquiry is possible.

Thus it is through the hermeneutic procedure that Heidegger carries out his analysis of Being, and remains true to his two principles: (1) let the facts speak for themselves, and (2) there are no such things as bare, uninterpreted facts.

With the procedure of the hermeneutic analysis clear in our minds, the meaning of Heidegger's phenomenology is relatively simple to explain. According to Heidegger's rather elaborate and scholarly "translation" of the Greek terms that make up the word, phenomenology means: "to let that which shows itself be seen from itself in the very way in which it shows itself from itself" (E-58/G-34). When one first realizes *how* this is to be done (i.e., hermeneutically), the meaning of phenomenology in Heidegger's sense is obvious.

By "phenomenology" Heidegger means that analysis by which the meaning of the various ways in which we exist can be translated from the vague language of everyday existence into the understandable and explicit language of ontology *without destroying the way in which these meanings manifest themselves to us in our everyday lives!* Not since Plato has any thinker so closely integrated the theoretical with the practical. The claim, sometimes heard among Heidegger's critics, that Heidegger abstracts or hypostatizes Being is inaccurate, unless one thinks that only *abstractions* are capable of being understood. But if understanding can operate in a way *other* than abstraction, to analyze Being need not mean to abstract Being.

The point that is most crucial is that the meaning of Being can be known only through a special kind of procedure: the hermaneutic process. A very serious question may well be asked at this point: *But is such a procedure philosophically significant?* Does it not remain always at best a kind of autobiography?

Such an objection has been made against Heidegger's ontology by William Earle and others. Although various criticisms of *Being and Time* need not be examined, it is useful to consider Earle's objections because they represent a position that brings the whole purpose of Heidegger's philosophy into focus. Earle's objections are based upon principles with which Heidegger is in profound disagreement; and thus a consideration of these objections may well serve as a device for understanding Heidegger's whole approach, and the reasons why many have claimed that Heidegger, with *Being and Time,* has inaugurated a whole new way of doing philosophy.

William Earle's main point in his article[8] is that the works of funda-mental ontologists are "in fact ontological confessions by their authors" and that thus "Their work is ontological autobiography." Earle argues that even by the admission of such diverse thinkers as Hegel and Kierke-gaard, Western philosophy "was vitiated by the universal"; that the whole purpose of philosophy was to discover that which is common or universal to man, and by these principles to build one's ethics and meta-physical systems. "But the universal, the common, that which is true of everything and for every rational mind in its pure rationality is precisely that which is thinnest, has least determination, which is least evolved, least developed, which is merely the potentiality for something concrete." Earle argues that what is of value in *The Brothers Karamazov* is not what it shares with any other novel, but its uniqueness; that which makes it *peculiarly* one of the great novels of our time. In short, Earle claims that Heidegger's writings are merely profound statements of his own individ-ual human existence, not human existence as such, and that their value is that they offer us a *possible* manner and way of existence. But Earle insists that there is no way in which that which is so terribly important for each of us—namely, our own existence—can be described or revealed by any universal or certain principles.

Earle himself recognizes that this is not what Heidegger claims that he is doing. It is obvious that Heidegger thinks he is describing what uni-versally belongs to every Dasein, and certainly not that which belongs merely to Heidegger's own private Dasein. Thus Earle's objections con-stitute a very serious challenge: Is it indeed possible to speak universally about human *existence?* While it is obvious that the mind *can* speak uni-versally about such abstract qualities as its logical relations, any *concrete* and *interesting* characteristic is not of the universal mankind, but of the individual man, private and particular.

Heidegger's book provides sufficient argumentation to answer Earle's

---

8. "Phenomenology and Existentialism," *Journal of Philosophy,* LVII (January 1960).

objections. A consideration of this central characteristic of Heidegger's thought should be made clear.

First, in a very serious sense Earle has not really provided an argument *against* Heidegger; he has rather merely underlined the *problem*. For Earle has claimed that one *cannot* give universal dimensions to, or recognize universal principles in, the question of the meaning of Being. Heidegger has said one can. What must be considered, then, is, Whose claim is correct? or, to be less demanding, For whose claim can the greater amount of clarity and philosophical argumentation be given support?

There are two considerations I would like to bring up in defense of Heidegger's position. One is negative, in the sense that it asks of Earle: If the meaning of existence is *private*, what is the *philosophical* value of examining it? There would be, of course, the obvious personal psychological value, but for that one should turn to psychiatrists and certain novelists, not philosophers. As early as the days of Socrates, the purpose of philosophy was formulated in the maxim: The unexamined life is not worth living. Now by what criteria does one "examine" life? According to Socrates and his devoted pupil Plato, it was reason that gave man the wherewithal to make his existence meaningful. But reason is universal. Is Earle claiming that universal reason has no effect at all on the analysis of the meaning of our existence? If so, then isn't the entire investigation of Socrates misguided and invalid? Earle claims that Heidegger has rendered a profound *possibility* of Being which we can *choose*. But by what criteria can we choose? Is there not something in Heidegger's account that we recognize to be true and valid, and not merely psychologically ontically relevant? It seems, in other words, that unless we want to admit a most devastating kind of relativism, there is a universal validity to some statements about the meaning of existence. This does not, of course, suggest that all of Heidegger's observations are correct; it merely rescues the entire enterprise from the meaningless milieu of psychological autobiographies that entertain and titillate, but do not give any truth.

But this is a negative argument. Far more valuable, though far more difficult, are those arguments that do not seek out and destroy, but which, through speculative power, build edifices of reason from which greater vision can be enjoyed. It was Kant, originally, who pointed out a great truth that Earle's argument overlooks: Reason is not limited to the cognitive functions of logical and scientific analysis. Unless one refuses to read past the first section of *The Critique of Pure Reason*, one finds that Kant has shown that reason, operating transcendentally, can reflect upon itself, achieving through this reflection not only the very roots of its freedom, but also the respect and awe that it must have for itself, thereby yielding the principles of ethical judgment. Now I do not claim that Earle or anyone else must accept Kant's transcendental philosophy; but surely Kant has shown that reason—that common basis by which one recognizes the shared bond among men—is by no means limited to that which is "thinnest" or has "least determination."

For this is the whole purpose and impact of *Being and Time*: to show that it is indeed possible for reason, through the hermeneutic analysis, to render an understanding of the meaning of Being. That the methodology employed is not similar to that of the sciences is only to be expected. Such a methodology, though, does not reveal what is merely private or particular to one individual Dasein; rather, it reveals those insights and principles that are true for every individual who reflects upon his own existence.

To expect otherwise would hardly be rational. Surely one recognizes that many of the important aspects and dimensions of existence are shared by other men. Earle claims that it is the *particularity* of *The Brothers Karamazov* that makes it the object of our respect; but one could equally argue that it is in fact the *universality* of its insights and sensitivities that excites the reader and makes it one of the truly great works of Western culture. It is true that an author as sensitive and profound as Dostoevski is *rare*; but that does not mean that what he talks about is any less universal. In fact, it would seem that the reason one praises the book so highly is precisely because it speaks of those qualities and characteristics of the human spirit that are shared by everyone.

The question, then, that every student of philosophy should at some time ask is: Is it possible for my reason—that function of my consciousness which is shared by all men and through which I can ultimately communicate with them—is it possible for this reason to inform me of the meaning of my existence; or am I left to those resources of my understanding that are private, particular, and ultimately noncommunicable? Heidegger, of course, thinks the former is possible; but he goes further than merely to state his belief. In some of the most important sections of *Being and Time* (e.g., section 32) Heidegger analyzes ways in which understanding operates in asking the question of the meaning of Being. This is one of the most frequently overlooked yet most important elements of Heidegger's entire philosophy, because without it Heidegger would be unable to explain how an analysis of a *philosophical* (and not merely *psychological*) understanding of existence is possible.

Thus Heidegger thinks it possible *philosophically* (with universal validity) to analyze what it means to be. To see how he develops this, I would direct the reader to the sections of *Being and Time* and this commentary that deal with understanding (cf. pp. 75–109). However, the most impressive and convincing way to show someone that mathematics is possible is actually to perform a mathematical calculation; and similarly, the demonstration that one can indeed analyze the meaning of existence with universal significance is actually to do it. We turn, then, to the existential analytic itself.

III.

EXISTENTIAL
ANALYTIC

I

The World

sections 9–27

NATURE OF THE TASK   (sections 9–11)

The main purpose of the first chapter in Part One is to point out how and why the analysis of Dasein's Being is different from the analysis of the world and its objects. This was already discussed briefly in our consideration of the difference between ontical and ontological inquiries. In this section, however, Heidegger emphasizes the peculiar characteristics of Dasein as an object of inquiry, thus making the distinction more explicit. All three sections of this chapter are directed toward revealing the special nature of the inquiry: section 9 examines briefly why it is that an inquiry about Dasein must be ontological; section 10 shows how the inquiry is essentially different from the ontical inquiries about Dasein, anthropology, psychology, and biology; section 11 shows how the existential analytic cannot become an analysis of *primitive* Dasein. For the most part, this chapter, if read carefully, should not present too great a difficulty; but a few comments may nevertheless prove beneficial.

Essence[1] and Existence   (section 9)

It is in this section that one finds the famous (or infamous) phrase: "The essence of Dasein lies in its existence." This sentence has suffered far more than the usual misinterpretation and must be clarified. It is a companion to another important and often misunderstood claim that occurs in the section, to the effect that the Being of the entity to be studied is always *mine*. These two claims are of considerable importance in understanding why the analysis of Dasein cannot in principle be ontical— i.e., scientific—but must be ontological and hermeneutic.

To say that the essence of Dasein lies in its existence is obviously not what the scholastics mean in claiming that God's essence is His existence. For the scholastics, God is necessary, and their claim supports the onto-logical argument. Heidegger by no means wants to make the absurd claim that Dasein is necessary. As we shall see, Heidegger insists that man's finitude is an essential factor in his freedom.

Yet the parallel between the scholastics' claim that God's essence is existence and Heidegger's claim that Dasein's essence lies in its existence can perhaps be pressed advantageously. The former claimed that the very meaning of God is that He exists, which makes it impossible to think of a nonexisting God; for if I tried to think of God not existing I would be violating the *meaning* of God, which is something that must exist. In Heidegger's case the argument is similar, though the conclusion is quite different. The very *meaning* of Dasein is one who reflects on one's existence. This means that I cannot think of Dasein except in terms of possible *ways* of existing. Just as the phrase "necessary God" is to a certain extent redundant for the scholastics, so too is the phrase "to be Dasein" somewhat redundant for Heidegger. I can know what it means to be, though not fully, and insofar as I can know this, I am Dasein. The important implication of all this is that Heidegger's term "existence" (*Existenz*) has a different meaning than the scholastics' term "existence" (*existentia*). The traditional meaning of existence has the implication of something occurring in the universe, or something one encounters or comes across in the world. Heidegger uses the term "present-at-hand"

---

1. "Essence" is here used as a translation of *Wesen*. Heidegger has expressed dissatisfaction with this translation, pointing out that the verbal rather than the substantive meaning should be emphasized. There is a German verb *wesen*, used mostly in poetry, meaning "to do" or "to be." "Nature" is a possible translation but, in spite of the imperfection, I prefer "essence." (Of course, "being" would never do, since it conflicts with the translation of *Sein*). The reader should bear in mind that "*Das Wesen des Daseins liegt in seiner Existenz*" means something like: "In order for something to be [*wesen*] as Dasein, it must have existence."

(*Vorhanden*) as characteristic of this kind of existence. (A fuller discussion of *Vorhanden* occurs below; cf. p. 61 f.) For the sake of the present discussion, it is sufficient to point out that *existentia* is the existence of entities, whereas *Existenz* applies only to Dasein.

We must avoid not only the scholastics' meaning but also the existentialists' meanings. Heidegger has specifically repudiated[2] any similarity between his claim and that of Jean-Paul Sartre. According to Heidegger, when Sartre makes the claim that man's existence is prior to his essence he is merely taking the traditional *metaphysical* proposition that man has a nature or essence that precedes man's existence, and turning it around. The result is just another *metaphysical* claim, which has nothing to do with fundamental ontology. Now if Heidegger has gone to such explicit lengths to deny any similarity between his view and Sartre's, it surely seems unfair not to accept his denial. We must search elsewhere for the meaning of Heidegger's claim if he himself has cut off both the avenue of the existentialist interpretation and that of the scholastic.

What, then, does Heidegger mean by the claim that Dasein's existence is its essence? A look at the etymology of *Existenz* may prove beneficial. The term comes from the Latin *existere*, which, in its root meaning, signifies a "standing out." In later works Heidegger has drawn attention to this etymology by hyphenating the term (*Eksistenz*). The point being that only Dasein can stand back from or "out" from its own occurrence in the world and observe itself. Indeed, it is the ability of Dasein to consider and be aware of its own occurrence that is uniquely characteristic of it, and hence is its essence. Thus *Existenz* does not refer to Dasein's being alive or functioning, but rather to its awareness that it is.

The claim that Dasein's essence lies in its existence is, then, significant primarily in terms of the role of fundamental ontology. This discipline is presupposed in any metaphysics because it examines how it is possible that one can reflect upon oneself at all. Metaphysics makes claims about what we are; fundamental ontology examines how such claims are possible. Thus Heidegger has disassociated himself from the existentialists (specifically Sartre), who tell us what man is like (e.g., that he is free, dreadful, lazy, or absurd), and, instead asks for an examination of those *a priori* ways of our Being that allow us to become aware of the metaphysical in the first place.

Now one might protest that Heidegger has abused the meaning of the term "metaphysics." These objectors may argue that metaphysics actually includes what Heidegger calls "fundamental ontology" and that

---

2. Cf. *Letter on Humanism*, in Barrett and Aiken, *Philosophy of the Twentieth Century*, p. 280.

hence ontology cannot in principle be prior to metaphysics. This is surely a mere verbal debate. Heidegger himself finally[3] abandoned the term "fundamental ontology" for precisely this reason. Attention should be paid to the function and purpose of the inquiry, not to its name.

In sum, Heidegger is not to be associated with either the scholastics or the existentialists, in spite of the similarity of many terms and phrases. Heidegger's point is not to argue that man is characterized by dread, anxiety, and boredom; but rather, he wishes to point out that one can significantly examine and inquire about existence, and that this ability of man's reason to reflect upon itself is its most amazing function. Heidegger's use of such moods as dread and fear does not constitute a brooding or nihilistic view of man; they are simple factual moods that do occur in man, and thus can be analyzed as descriptive of his existence. But then, so too can such moods as joy and ecstasy.[4]

The "Mineness" of Dasein   (section 9)

This emphasis, then, upon the internal reflection of man upon himself leads one to the second major claim of section 9: that the entity to be analyzed is in each case *mine*. Is this subjectivism or even solipsism?

If one recalls what was said in our discussion of the hermeneutic it should be clear why Heidegger claims that the entity we are studying is "in each case mine." There is no solipsism implied here; rather, from the internal and self-reflective awareness of *my own* existence I discover principles, which, being of a rational nature, are universal and hence applicable to all Daseins. Hence the first meaning of the claim that Dasein is always *mine* simply indicates the availability of the object of inquiry and points out that the procedure of analysis must be hermeneutic self-reflection.

But there is a further and more important meaning to the claim that Dasein is in each case mine. It is a significance that is almost totally lost in translation. Whatever is mine is my *own*, and the term "own" is *eigen* in German. And from *eigen* comes *eigentlich*, which is translated by Macquarrie and Robinson as "authentic." Now the term "authentic" is used by Heidegger in a very special sense, and its connection with "my own-ness" should never be forgotten. What the term ultimately means is the mode of Dasein's existence in which one is aware of one's *own* existence, whereas the counterterm, "inauthentic" (*uneigentlich*), is that

---

3. Cf. *What Is Metaphysics?*
4. To be sure, Heidegger does not carry out the analysis of joy and ecstasy along these lines, but he admits in *What Is Metaphysics?* that such an analysis could be made.

mode in which one is *not* aware of one's own existence. If the strong and close etymological connection between *eigen* and *eigentlich* is not kept in mind, the argument becomes weak. But if one is aware of the etymology, the argument has a great deal of power. What Heidegger means by "authentic" is the awareness of one's *own* self; by "in-authentic," the awareness of the self merely as others see it, or perhaps to see one's self as having a meaning or essence that is prior to and hence "other" than one's existence. Thus, by claiming at the very onset of the existential analytic that Dasein is in each case mine, Heidegger is laying the groundwork for his later development of "authentic being."

This distinction between authentic and inauthentic is fundamental to Heidegger's entire existential analytic, but it is often misunderstood and even more frequently misapplied. From the very beginning critics have insisted on seeing some form of indirect ethics or value system in the dis-tinction, which is unwarranted by the text. It is admittedly difficult, how-ever, to resist using Heidegger's analyses to indict thoughtless people of inauthenticity, or to set a new goal for oneself, achieving authenticity. We use these terms like new intellectual toys, feeling elevated with the latest conceptual terminology, reducing them by the very frequency and commonality of usage to vulgar notions. But the two terms are meant as purely philosophical ideas, in the service of truth only, not at the serv-ice of popular jargon. How, then, are we to understand these fundamen-tal terms as they operate in Heidegger's thought?

Given any field of thematic, rational inquiry it is always necessary to discover a formal, operating disjunct that allows us to establish the intel-ligibility of the endeavor by making discriminating judgments within it. The difference between true and false sentences is fundamentally presup-posed by all logicians, so that in the absence of this distinction the entire discipline of logic becomes impossible. "Good" and "bad" must be pre-supposed if we are to make ethical judgments; "fact" and "fiction" are assumed by the scientist, "appearance" and "reality" by the metaphysi-cian. Our courts presuppose the notions of "guilt" and "innocence," our businessmen the difference between profit and loss. In all of these cases there is a primary, assumed disjunct—something positive and something negative—that gives the enterprise its capacity for coherent judgment and ultimate evaluation.

The distinction between authentic and inauthentic is to the existential analytic exactly what the distinction between true and false propositions is to logic. That is, the distinction provides the thinker with a polarity or pair of opposites without which the discipline would deteriorate im-mediately into a random series of disconnected insights. As a philosopher and *not* as an advocate of social or moral change, Heidegger needs to distinguish between the ways in which the meaning of our existence is revealed and the ways in which it is concealed or covered up. As an inquirer he is indifferent to whether his reader conceals or reveals; rather the distinction is made in order for the reader to *understand*: its goal is to reveal the truth, not to change the person or preach a new religion.

It is the formal, disjunctive nature of the distinction that is important. Heidegger has before him the following task: to make sense of our existence. He cannot use moral terms, distinguishing "good" existence from "bad" existence; nor can he use scientific terms, separating "factual" existence from "fictional" existence. And so he describes his disjunct in terms of what is our own and what is other than our own: authentic and inauthentic existence. This distinction must be able to apply to *every single possible way in which we exist*. Thus, for example, if we accept the claim that speaking is a way of existing, it must be the case that we can speak authentically or inauthentically. If we can speak authentically we can discover in our speaking something about what it means to exist; if we speak inauthentically we are kept from such discovery. The distinction is as fundamental, and as simple, as that. And readers are well advised to remind themselves frequently that this is the proper meaning of these two terms.

Unfortunately, Heidegger is so skilled and artful in his analyses of the various ways we exist (both authentically and inauthentically) that his insights seem like revelations of extraordinary power in and of themselves. We are fascinated by the man's power to penetrate so deeply into the ways we tend to deceive ourselves; we are impressed by the exciting dimensions he uncovers when he reveals what it means to be authentic. And as a consequence, we are unfortunately led to believe that Heidegger's philosophy is *about* such insights. But this is entirely mistaken; for Heidegger, as a true philosopher, is unpacking these insights solely to isolate the question of the meaning of Being. He is concerned with showing that the ways we exist *can* be thought about, that they *can* be seen as either authentic or inauthentic. Thus, what this distinction reveals about the meaning of Being is crucial; not that Heidegger somehow wants us to follow his insights as signposts along the path of personal redemption. The very brilliance of his analyses thus curiously works against his purpose. It is a fault we can celebrate, a *felix culpa*, for the insights are indeed worthy resources of our desire to understand ourselves. But the primary purpose and function of the authentic-inauthentic distinction must never be lost. The distinction remains, primarily and fundamentally, a device of formal disjunction that allows us to *inquire at all* into what it *means* to exist.

The claim that Dasein is mine has led some observers to regard Heidegger's analysis in *Being and Time* as merely autobiographical. We have discussed this in the previous chapter. It may be helpful, though, for the reader to consider the following state of affairs. When I add the numbers 3 and 5, my reasoning tells me that if I adhere to the definitions and procedures of arithmetic, I must come up with the answer 8. Because I feel compelled to admit the correctness of the answer, there is a sense in which I have no control over it, as I might have control over which meal to order in a restaurant, or which woman I choose to marry. The very fact that the principles of reasoning by which one can establish a system of universally valid systems are public and essentially communicable does not, however, destroy the fact that it is still I who am doing the thinking. One may question whether it is correct to say that it is through my *own* reasoning that I can figure out the Pythagorean theorem, or whether one ought not properly to say through the use of universal (not *my*) reason. But it seems to me that the universality of logic does not destroy the "mineness" of my reasoning when I apply my mind to such a problem. After all, I am the one who becomes *aware* of the necessity of the inferences. If this is true, then it seems there should be no objection to accepting Heidegger's observation that although the entity examined in fundamental ontology is always mine, this does not imply that fundamental ontology is autobiographical or unique to the subject.

Heidegger also mentions in this section the important characteristic that to be or not to be is an issue for Dasein. This means that for Dasein, it matters to be. This seems so trivial at first reading that its full significance is overlooked. If one were to ask you: "Does it matter to you that you exist?" your first reaction might be to wonder whether such a question makes sense at all. If the question simply inquires about the importance one puts on living, or if it suggests a veiled threat, the answer would be easily determined by one's psychological attitude toward life and death. But it should be obvious that this is not the meaning behind Heidegger's claim. His claim means that one's existence can be and is the subject of genuine concern and inquiry. It means that the ways and dimensions of my existence are of interest to me, even if this interest is on the lowest level of avoiding pain and hoping for pleasure. Nor are the states of extreme boredom or apathy arguments against this claim: for the choice of an *uninterested* existence at least reveals sufficient concern for my existence *that* I am bored or disinterested. The ontological characteristics of this interest in existence is more fully discussed below; but its significance here is to show how the inquiry is possible: It is possible to inquire about existence because as Dasein my existence is an issue for me. Hence the question of existence is not an artificial question brought on by philosophical illusion; it is a genuine question based upon the very obvious fact that man does reflect and wonder about his existence.

The A Priori *Structure of Existence* (*section 9*)

Heidegger claims that "the structure of existentiality lies *a priori*." Since the search for *a priori* knowledge has been one of the most important tasks for philosophers since the time of Descartes, this claim is a very serious one indeed. It lies at the root of the entire Heideggerian enterprise.

What is *a priori* knowledge? According to Kant, for whom the term was essential, *a priori* knowledge is that which is known prior to any experience, and indeed, it is that which makes experience possible. He claimed, for example, that the *categories* (such as cause, substance, etc.) are *a priori*; they are themselves not derived from experience because experience itself depends upon them to be possible. Mathematics and logic are both *a priori*, because neither of these two disciplines requires experience to verify its truths (although mathematics, being synthetic, does require the pure *a priori* forms of intuition, space, and time). For many other thinkers, the term *a priori* simply refers to whatever knowledge is derived from thinking or reasoning. The great import of the *a priori* is that it guarantees *universal* validity and is necessary. Hence skeptical and critical philosophers are always loathe to grant that any kind of knowledge is *a priori* except for the purely analytical functions of logic or mathematics.

In light of the great elegance and high prestige given to *a priori* knowledge, it is surely a serious challenge to claim that one's very structure of existence is *a priori*. How can this claim be justified?

A closer and more critical look at how the *a priori* functions even in the purely scientific process of cognition may be helpful. Let us consider, for example, Kant's position that the category of causality is *a priori*. This means that to think in terms of causality in natural events is a necessary and natural attitude of mind, through which man unifies the many otherwise unrelated data of experience. Thus, for example, if one were to hear a sudden explosion outside one's door, one's natural reaction would be to ask: "What caused that?" Now in spite of the great difficulty in assessing just exactly what the specific causes *are* of many events, the one answer to the question "What caused that?" that would *not* be acceptable to the mind would be: "It just happened." If someone tried to tell me that an explosion outside my door "simply happened" without any cause for it, I would be unable to accept that answer. For if I accepted that answer, I would abandon one of the essential ways in which my mind *connects* the variety of experience. My natural and necessary attitude or disposition toward the world, then, is such that I must assume a cause-effect relationship between the events that occur in the world. Causality, then, is an interpretive disposition *prior* to any experience; it is a way in which my mind *necessarily* operates; and without it a comprehension of the world as it appears to me is impossible.

We may now ask: What are the preconditions or attitudes of mind and necessary ways of thinking that allow one to be aware of one's existing self? If the necessity of causality allows a comprehension of experience to be possible, what is necessary for an awareness of the self? Heidegger calls the necessary ways of viewing the self *existentials* (see chart, p. 19). Like categories, the existentials are *a priori*, and further, like categories, the existentials are necessary ways in which the mind operates. Categories are necessary ways in which the mind imposes order on things *other* than the mind itself; existentials are the necessary ways in which mind sees *itself*.

But how are these existentials analyzable? How do we come to know them? Kant derived his categories from the structures of traditional logic. Since the existentials, unlike the categories, are applicable to modes or ways of Being and not to entities, the procedure of analysis or methodology by which the existentials are made available for rational scrutiny must be hermeneutic phenomenology (see Chapter II, above). Again, the details of how this is done must be postponed until we analyze the procedure of understanding (cf. p. 45).

Comparison to Other Disciplines   (section 10)

For the American reader this section may be surprising. Heidegger here argues that fundamental ontology cannot be accomplished by anthropology, biology, or psychology; and yet in his explanation he speaks of such thinkers as Descartes, Bergson, Dilthey, and Husserl. The reason for this is that the term "anthropology" does not mean the same thing in Germany as it does in the United States. Scientific or empirical anthropology as is taught in the United States has very little to do with the older German discipline. Anthropology in Germany does not merely investigate cultures nor does it gather scientific data from the observation of comparative mores or physiological types. The German discipline is more literally a "study of man"; it is a part of the philosophical rather than the scientific investigation. Heidegger is not arguing against the various sciences as we might know them in American universities, but rather against those philosophers who base their philosophizing on such concepts as the ego, the subject, or the person. His whole point in this section is that such thinkers as Descartes and Bergson have asserted the unique characteristics of the human person without challenging the traditional metaphysical status of man's Being. To argue, for example, that man is a *thing* that thinks, or to assert with Aristotle that man is an animal with reason, is to *add on* to an entity certain "special" attributes like thinking and reason. Heidegger's persuasion is that man *is* in a different way than a thing is. Now the philosophical anthropologist Max Scheler had come close to recognizing this, but Heidegger feels that even Scheler failed to fully accomplish an understanding of the significance of how Dasein's Being determines fundamental ontology.

Perhaps a brief comment should be made about Heidegger's consideration of Descartes. Heidegger recognizes that it was Descartes who initiated the analysis of the existing self through his famous *Cogito ergo sum*. As every student knows, Descartes argues that the awareness of one's self is undeniable and cannot be doubted. But Descartes, in stating his "I think, therefore I am," emphasized that this was an indubitable *fact*, and hence was the basis of *knowledge*. Descartes then discovered that, in asking the question about what kind of thing he was, he was led to assert that he was, in essence, a thinking thing. But Heidegger argues that the *cogito* has two verbs, "I think" and "I am." One could just as well say that I am a "being thing" as well as a "thinking thing." The point is that just as the undeniability of my existence assures me that I can know something for certain, so too does the fact of my knowing something reveal my existence. I am not only a thing that thinks, but I am also a thing that is *aware* of his thinghood.

Descartes's *cogito* served his epistemology, but it should also have served his ontology. What Heidegger has dared to ask is this: Granted that the *cogito* is valid; *how is it possible?*

How is the *cogito* possible? Speaking somewhat loosely, this question could almost be a restatement of Heidegger's whole task in *Being and Time*. I know that I am; the question now is, What does that mean, to know that I am? This is the root question that Heidegger feels Descartes (and the subsequent development) had overlooked.

Primitive Dasein   (section 11)

The scientific anthropology with which most American students are acquainted is more relevant in this section than in the previous one. If one is interested in what it means for Dasein to be, why would not an examination of man in his *primitive* state afford us the kind of evidence we need? Heidegger recognizes that the study of primitive peoples may well add considerable information to the study of one's membership in the human race; but it does not constitute the essence of fundamental ontology. We are asking how an understanding of Being is possible; how it is possible for one to transcend one's occurrence in the world and reflect upon oneself. Until such an investigation is carried out, no examination of primitive peoples will be able to provide us with insights into this question. It is still our own selves that exist, and it is this existence that must be analyzed.

Our analysis of the last three sections has been restricted to a consideration of what the existential analytic is in its form, structure, and purpose. Up to now we have merely been talking *about* the analysis. The next chapter begins with the analysis itself.

TO BE IN THE WORLD   (sections 12–13)

The first *a priori* existential described in the analytic is being-in-the-world, or perhaps better, to-be-in-the-world. Heidegger's Chapter II, which deals with the general characteristics of the existential, is rather short; but we must not underestimate its importance. Much of Heidegger's great sensitivity and insight into the nature of existence are evidenced in these and the subsequent chapters on the existential analytic. Particularly in these sections it must be stressed that my task is not to provide a *substitute* for the actual reading of *Being and Time*. The commentary should be read in close conjunction with Heidegger's work and hopefully clarifies some of its more difficult parts.

To-be-in-the-world is the first in a series of existentials that Heidegger analyzes. The *order* of this analysis is important. Heidegger has not arbitrarily listed a series of ways in which Dasein becomes aware of its existence. Rather, the order of presentation of these existentials reflects the development from the *general* awareness of the way in which the world presents itself to us, down to the specific existential that most adequately reveals to Dasein its own existence: care (*Sorge*). Hence Heidegger begins with the broadest of existential notions: the simple fact that I find myself *in* something—the world. But "world" here does not necessarily mean the sophisticated view of the scientist, who imagines the earth as a sphere or ball hurtling through the vast eons of limitless space. "World," in the sense of this existential, would be found in the self-reflective consciousness even of a rather primitive awareness, for which the limits of the world may well be the limits of a village or county. It is, in this sense, the most general of concepts about existence: the place in which one is. As the analysis then grows more specific and particular, we see Heidegger shifting from the various ways and modes in which "world" has meaning—such as "to be of use"—to the more internal and personal modes of self-existence, such as fear, fateful existence, and the awareness of possibilities.

But one must not lose sight of the careful manner in which Heidegger *develops* these analyses. Thus Heidegger's first step is to consider in the broadest possible terms how the world presents its significance to Dasein.

He then carefully plots the analytic along the lines of that which is *found* in the world: objects within the world, other Daseins within the world, and finally the self within the world. First he reaches the self within the world (which Heidegger calls awareness of the "here" in the world, making use of the etymological basis in *Da* [here]-*sein*); he then proceeds again along lines that develop from broad to narrow: first he accounts for the difference between the authentic and inauthentic awareness of the self, then to the difference between the *determined* character of our occurrence in the world and the *free* character of our occurrence in the world. Finally Heidegger reveals the single existential that most vividly describes Dasein's own particular way of existing: to care.

One may feel, in the first reading of the analytic, that the *selections* of the various existentials may be unfair, in that they naturally tend to show Dasein in the light of Heidegger's opinion. Has Heidegger considered the total range of the existentials? No, I don't think so. He does not, for example, talk of love or joy, which would surely seem to be existentials. What Heidegger has done is to choose those existentials that, because they are the broadest in scope, include all others. Loving is surely a special kind of caring (as are all existentials). By proceeding from the most general existential of all (to-be-in-the-world) to the most characteristic (care), Heidegger has shown the basic existential structure, although it may be a somewhat skeletal structure, which others may wish to flesh out by further analysis. The present chapter, however, can scarcely be doubted as the obvious beginning point; for where else would one begin except with a description of how the world in general presents itself to Dasein?

Basically, Heidegger undertakes two tasks in this chapter: (1) to describe the ontological significance of what it means to-be-in-the-world, and (2) to show that this existential is indeed *a priori*, and what this apriority entails. I will consider these two tasks in order.

1. Heidegger's main emphasis in this chapter, which is only an outline sketch of further development in subsequent chapters, is to point out that to-be-in-the-world must be seen not ontically, but ontologically. To show this, Heidegger emphasizes the element of the phrase that centers on the preposition "in." It should be obvious that the *ontic* meaning of in-the-world is not *a priori*, because the ontic world is discovered through experience. What Heidegger means by the "in" in an *ontological* sense is that which makes possible the feeling of familiarity we have with the world, which makes the world "our home." Scientifically, the fact that I am on the planet earth (world) is not *a priori*: it is learned only through experience. But the fact that, as Dasein, I must have a world to live in, to dwell

in, to call my home, *is a priori*. What is meant by this Being-in, if not the simple space-time location of physics?

What Heidegger means by Being-in in the ontological sense is the *a priori* "ability" to have things that we relate to, care about, and concern ourselves with. A somewhat free phenomenological etymology of the English term "human being" may be helpful. "Human" comes from the Latin word *humus*, "earth." A human being, then, is one who exists in such a way as to belong to this earth—i.e., a *human* being is an earth being in the sense of having a home here. It *belongs*. This does not mean to suggest that one cannot have feelings of alienation or feel as if one were a stranger in the world. For to be a stranger in one place means that there is another place where one is at home, even if one can't find it or doesn't know where it is. Heidegger speaks of "dwelling." We do not say that water "resides" or "dwells" in a glass; only Dasein can dwell. The real meaning behind this existential is that my *surroundings* (*Umwelt*: "environment") are not simply *there*, but they affect me and I them. I cannot think of myself as existing simply as a space-time locus. Hence the categories that account for such location do not exhaust the explanation of my Being-in-the-world. I need, in addition, an *a priori* explanation of how I *can* be at home or alienated. To say that Being-in-the-world is *a priori* is also to say that one can successfully *think* about what it means to be in the world without having to rely solely on empirical evidence. But how is this possible? Suppose I go to the theater with a friend and due to the popularity of the play we are assigned separated seats. I am therefore *next to* a stranger but still *with* my friend. The difference between "being next to" and "being with" cannot, then, be determined by spatial considerations alone. Nor is it determined by pure psychological attitudes or how I feel about my companion, for I can be *with* someone I dislike or even one to whom I am indifferent. I can even be *next to* my friend but *with* my enemy. Since these determinations are neither spatial nor psychological, they *precede* such empirical or physical considerations and are hence *a priori*. But such distinctions as being with (Mitsein) and being next to (or being alongside) are indeed meaningful and, when combined with other modes, constitute the *a priori* structure of Being-in-the-world. This means we can think, reflect, reason, and wonder about their meanings successfully, i.e., with principles of determination that allow a thematic unity to the inquiry. The consequence of this is enormous. For with such an obvious example it becomes clear that Heidegger's fundamental strategy—that it is possible to inquire *a priori* into the ways we exist—has been justified.

2. What is given to us in this chapter, however, is only the briefest of glimpses into the more elaborate description of "Being-in-the-world"

that is to follow. This brief picture is sketched in order to show what is meant by claiming that the existentials are *a priori* and what that entails.

For what reason would one want to claim that "Being-in-the-world," in this ontological sense, is *a priori?* Consider the following. We, as human beings, have relationships both with things and with other human beings. They are relationships of which we are *aware* and which change us. In *this* sense, inanimate objects do not have relationships. Now suppose one is asked: What is the capacity by which one has such relationships? There must be some *prior* capacity within us that allows us to relate in the first place. This prior capacity is the *a priori* existential Being-in-the-world.

To-be-in-the-world is the ultimate presupposition of knowledge. (This puts ontology prior to epistemology—a move that incurs the wrath of all Neo-Kantians and positivists.) The bases of epistemology are the knower and the known: but prior to the distinction between knower and known (or subject and object) is the fact that the subject can relate to a known, which means that the presupposition of the very subject-object distinction is grounded in an already admitted basis of relationship—i.e., that the subject *has a world* in which the object can occur. Knowledge does not occur in isolation from one's world of concern and environment. It is never the case that I simply "know" something. Some bits of knowledge cause me happiness or sorrow; and even the seemingly "purely factual" bits of information satisfy my need for "objectivity." Heidegger points out that it is a natural error to see the world as made up of "objects," which are then known by a "subject." This is because, in our development, the ontic world is discovered bit by bit. Furthermore, our language at least in its early primitive stages is an object language. However, this should not blind us to the fact that there must be something that enables us to learn of the world at all, and to speak at all.

If Heidegger is right, and Being-in-the-world is an *a priori* existential of Dasein, then certain philosophical "problems" are "solved." The mind-body problem, for example, and the problem of the reality of the external worlds are misleading *abstractions* from the necessary characteristic of Dasein's Being-in-the-world. Heidegger does not consider such problems, because for him they are not problems at all. Once one admits the apriority of the existential structure, then such *ontic* considerations as the nature of external objects can never undermine the work of fundamental ontology.

Heidegger's Chapter II serves merely to provide a general grasp of the more detailed analysis ahead. So, in following Heidegger, I shall reserve my commentary on much of the richness of what is hinted at in this section, and discuss the points in the sections that Heidegger develops. One thing, though, that *is* specific is that we now know where our next analysis must begin. What is this "world" that we are "in," *a priori?*

WORLDHOOD (sections 14–18)

In Chapter II of *Being and Time*, it was pointed out that Being-in-the-world is an *a priori* existential; but the description of what this world consists of was for the most part negative. The task of Chapter III is to fill in the positive characteristics of this *a priori* existential. Heidegger develops his description of the existential in three sections; and I shall consider them in the order he has followed. There is no need, however, for me to comment on all of the aspects of the existential to-be-in-the-world. There is a great deal of richness and variation to Heidegger's description, which is self-explanatory. I intend to emphasize only those points that I feel are essential for understanding the basic structure of Heidegger's thought.

The World as Environment (sections 15–16)

Our primordial relationship with the world is to *use* it: i.e., the world for us is available—"ready-at-hand" (*zuhanden*). To think of the world as made up of things independent of their function or use (i.e., to see the world as "present-at-hand": *vorhanden*) is not our *primordial* relationship with the world, but a *derived* relationship. Heidegger points out, for example, that I make use of the doorlatch before I consider its physical or "meta-physical" properties.

The picture of the world that science gives us is one in which the world is seen as a kind of reservoir in which various objects occur. These objects are "simply there." That is, they are seen by the scientist independently of their function, their value, or their use. This attitude is, of course, necessary for science. As a scientist I am interested in the object only as an object. But such a view of the world is not primary. At times it takes a great deal of training and discipline for a man to achieve that level of "scientific objectivity" which is so necessary for his peculiar activity. Prior to such achievement (and indeed, *along with* such attitudes in his daily life), the man who is now a scientist did *not* view the world in an indifferent way. To see the objects in the world *as* objects is a very secondary and highly stylized manner of relating to the world. When the scientist himself goes into his laboratory and picks up a beaker or a test tube, he is not thinking of the beaker or the test tube as a scientific object. He *uses* it. He may be interested in the scientific characteristic of the chemical *within* the test tube, but the test tube itself, the tweezers with which he holds it, the Bunsen burner underneath it, are all *used* without being necessarily thought about. This *use* of objects in the world is one's primordial manner of relating to the universe.

Heidegger defines the attitude of seeing the world as something to *use* as *ready-at-hand*. I see the world as ready-at-hand when I don't think about it as a thing; I *use* it. To see the object as a thing, as something that occurs in the world, is to see the world as *present-at-hand*. To see the world as present-at-hand is, in itself, not an erroneous view of the world, of course. What is erroneous, according to Heidegger, is to see the world *only* as present-at-hand. It is when philosophers or other critical thinkers make claims to the effect that only the methodology or "objectivity" of such a view can constitute a rational description of the world that the essential misunderstanding occurs. Taking the view that the world has only one mode of presentation, the mode of present-at-hand, results in the interpretation of the human existent, Dasein, as just another object in the world of objects. What Heidegger is arguing here is that to see the world as present-at-hand is merely one mode of Dasein's relating to its world. For the scientific attitude of objectivity is still only an *attitude*. As such, it shares its position along with other attitudes of mind. To be sure, the attitude of mind by which one sees the objects in the world as present-at-hand is undoubtedly the best attitude for science; but it is not necessarily the best attitude for philosophy; and furthermore, Heidegger points out that it is not even the primary attitude or mode that one, merely as a living being, has in relation to his world.

Many people often have the feeling of vague unacceptance when they hear a psychologist explain all their actions in terms of environmental factors, or when they hear sociologists explain their life patterns in terms of laws of normalcy and patterned deviations from normalcy. The ground for this vague feeling, according to Heidegger, is that the foundation of the scientific inquiry does not exhaust our modes of existence.

Suppose, however, that we grant that Heidegger is right in limiting the description of presence-at-hand to a mere part of our "world"? Does this in any way affect the subsequent problems that have been analyzed through traditional metaphysics? Whether I originally use the doorlatch to open the door or not, is it not still a problem to question about the "cause" of the latch, whether it is real or imaginary, substantial or phenomenal? Is not the mere observation that I relate to the world primordially in the role of a "user" simply an interesting fact among other facts about men, but a fact that does not alter the metaphysical character of the object?

If Heidegger is correct about how we relate to the world, his insight is of tremendous importance, for various reasons. First, if considerations about the universe as merely present-at-hand are *derived* and not primordial, then what it means to exist cannot in principle be adequately explained by such considerations. Further, if present-at-hand considerations describe the world-objects in a way that does not exhaust the possible ways of viewing the world (which it cannot if it is secondary), then the methodology of such investigation cannot be the methodology by which ontological truth can be revealed. Finally, the very limits to which seeing the world as present-at-hand can be pushed are much narrower than the task of philosophy demands.

It must be emphasized that Heidegger is not claiming any pragmatic theory of truth or meaning. To see the world as equipment (ready-at-hand) is not to claim that making use of something is any more ontological than conceptualizing it as a thing. To use something and to think about something as a thing are two totally different activities of mind, neither of which exhausts one's awareness of the world. Nor does this analysis in any way disparage treating the world as made of things, as long as it is recognized that such activity is merely one of several ways of seeing the world. Actually, there are at least three levels of which Heidegger here seems to be aware: (1) the use of the world as equipment, which is to see the world as ready-at-hand; (2) the "objectification" of the world and its objects by which we see things as independent existing objects, which is to see the world as present-at-hand; and (3) the seeing of the world as an existential in which the modes of present-at-hand and ready-at-hand are but different (and incomplete) ways of seeing. In subsequent sections, the types and ways of seeing will be expanded; as for example, when I "see" the world of my fellowmen, I see them neither as things to use or as objects, but in a totally different way of "seeing" in which I see myself as Being-with.

Definitions of the Modes of "Seeing"

Heidegger makes a great deal of these differing ways of "seeing." The point here is that when I look at the world of objects I am *looking* in a different way than when I am looking at the world of other Daseins; and both of these two ways of "looking" are different than when I look at myself. Heidegger names these three ways of "looking" by the following terms: when I look at the world as environment, I employ "circumspection" (*Umsicht*); when I look at the world of other Daseins, I employ "considerateness" (*Rücksicht*); and when I "look at" myself, I employ "transparency" (*Durchsichtigkeit*). The English terms fail to convey what the German makes obvious. In each term the word *sicht* (sight) occurs. Literal translation of the German terms would yield something like this: "circumspection"—a "looking around"; "considerateness"—a "looking back"; and transparency—a "looking through."

The point of all this elaborate nomenclature is to emphasize that

Dasein relates to the world ontologically in many different ways. I am obviously doing something quite different when I "look at" an object of scientific inquiry—say, a smear of plasma on a slide—and when I "look at," in a manner of considerateness, say, the smiling face of a friend. The smiling face of a friend is *not* a scientific object with a certain amount of emotion *added on*. Nor do I "look at" the face of the friend in the same way that I look at the plasma on the slide, even if I "add on" the emotion.

The persistent and annoying question still remains, however. Does it not seem as if the distinction between presence-at-hand and readiness-at-hand is merely one of psychological or mental states? Surely, one might complain, the disposition or attitude of the subject does not affect the metaphysical characteristic of the object!

Or does it? Heidegger's distinction between presence-at-hand and readiness-at-hand as ways of viewing the world, and indeed the entire ontological claim of the ensuing analytic, can be understood only in terms of the historical development of the subject-object description of knowledge. At the risk of seeming pedantic, I shall sketch a perspective on the history of philosophy that can be seen as the natural basis for Heidegger's analysis.

At the beginning of the so-called modern period of philosophy, René Descartes initiated the *rationalist* tradition, of which the most important characteristic was that mind could apprehend, through reason, *objective reality*. Descartes's substances and Leibniz's monads were alike in this respect: they constituted the real furniture of the universe and were directly apprehended by the intellect. Appearances or "accidents," which were apprehended by the senses, are not necessarily "real" according to these thinkers, but that which was known through thought had to be real. This rationalistic view was soon challenged, in varying degrees of seriousness and effectiveness, by the empirical tradition. Locke's admission that substances were "I know not what" gave way to the final denial of substances by Hume, who saw no basis for the unaided intellect comprehending reality at all. But Hume's ultimate skepticism seemed as unacceptable as the naïve realism suggested by some of the rationalists. Although it seemed to be saying too much to accept Descartes's view that the mind knew the thing-in-itself, it was surely too little to say, with Hume, that the mind knew nothing at all. A creative synthesis was achieved in Kant's analysis, in which he retained Hume's denial that the intellect could directly apprehend the thing-in-itself, but claimed that the intellect or mind could and did apprehend the *a priori* structure of appearance.

Kant's examination gave a new dimension to the whole problem. With Descartes's view, the reality of the object, which was fully grasped by the intellect, did not allow of anything from the subject. The object, so to speak, was all there was to be known. The activity of the subject certainly did not affect the nature of the object as it was known. And although the investigations of Locke did bring out a distinction between primary and secondary qualities, it was still thought that the criterion of a true statement was its correspondence to an objective and real external world. But with Kant, what came to be known was given partly by the object and partly by the mind. Thus, on the level of *perception*, what was known was a *space object*, of which the spatiality was given by the mind as an *a priori* form of intuition; whereas in science, what was known was a *concept object*, of which the concept was given by the mind through its *a priori* categories. What is of great importance in Kant's analysis is that the knowing situation is possible only through a *union* of the activities of the subject with the data presented or given by the object through sensibility. This means, then, that knowledge is always, to some extent, influenced and characterized by the knower. *But if the subject's ontological-metaphysical status is a part of the knowing process, then an examination of that status will reveal something about the so-called objective knowledge situation.* It can be seen, then, that already in Kant, ground had been laid for an undermining of the traditional subject-object basis for the knowing activity, although Kant himself was not willing to give up the dichotomy. But at least one can see that Kant has shown that since by "object" we do not mean the thing-in-itself but simply that which is knowable as an external appearance, *then the subject's own structure does indeed affect the object.* In fact, so defined, the structure of the subject makes the object as an object *possible.* Descartes's substances, then, are not directly apprehended as reality; rather, substance is a category of our mental operation. Kant claimed that, viewing the external appearance of the world, the mind necessarily "sees" things in the mode of substance. For Kant, any other way to explain *a priori* knowledge was impossible.

But if Kant is right, and substance and cause are ways in which the mind views objects, cannot one ask whether there are activities of mind that do not see things as objects, and hence do not use the categories? Such is the point of departure for Heidegger. He rejects Kant's monolithic view of how the knower knows the world. Heidegger may well agree that the mind uses the categories of cause and substance when it views the world *as made of objects!* But there is no *a priori* proof for saying that one must view the world as made of objects. That is only a secondary and limited way in which one relates to the world. For one does not, according to Heidegger, merely relate to the world through the cognitive manner of the schematism; in fact, one does not even relate to the world primordially in this way.

But since, even in the instances of seeing the world as present-at-hand (which would loosely correspond to Kant's view), I *impose* upon data my own concepts to make it intelligible, so too does my own character affect the world in its other modes. For this reason, then, an investigation into what it means to-be-in-the-world must precede any "metaphysical" description of the world in which I find myself.

Heidegger and Descartes   (sections 18B–24)

It should be obvious by now why Heidegger finds Descartes's view of the world unacceptable. It presupposes that Dasein relates to the world only in one way, and it has not even fully challenged the basis of that relationship. For the very methodology of Descartes is to narrow one's view of the world to the mode of seeing it merely as present-at-hand. With so narrow a view, the perspective necessary for seeing the world ontologically is lost; and the subsequent interpretation of the world as made of substances is inevitable. And although Kant obviously recognized the essential role played by the subject in object knowledge, he too failed to recognize that the "world" so described is only one mode of seeing the world, and indeed not the first mode.

The point can perhaps now be analyzed in terms of the following question: If the relationship of the mind to the world is *not* essentially that of the mind generating concepts that interpret the data of the world, then what is the nature of that relationship? Heidegger is going to argue that Dasein's relation to the world is one of care (*Sorge*); and that the various ways of Being-in-the-world are different ways of caring. But before he can argue for this position, he must first sketch out the individual existentials that provide the basis for caring. Certainly *one* of the ways I care about the world is to treat the world as made of indifferent substances, as for example, when I investigate certain phenomena from the scientific point of view. But unless this particular manner of seeing the world is anchored in a firm understanding of the total view of the world, basic ontological errors—such as those found in pre-Kantian substance metaphysics, for example—are inevitable. For any view of the world that bases its entire description on an ontical or scientific description necessarily will overlook those aspects of the world that, though genuine, are not capable of being defined as objects in the world.

Dasein and Space   (sections 22–24)

To be in space is a characteristic of Dasein; but the "spatiality" of Dasein is not an objective scientific space, nor is it the purely "subjective" space as seen by Kant. Rather, it is a space generated by the way in which Dasein sees things as "close" or "far away."

Heidegger has taken an everyday, common observation and has forced it to reveal its ontological significance. The common and everyday characteristic is the recognition that formal and objective space does not correspond to one's "felt" space. Heidegger's example is of the comparison between our "closeness" to a friend approaching us on the sidewalk, and the sidewalk itself. Objectively speaking, the sidewalk is closer to us than the friend; but we feel no awareness of or closeness to the sidewalk at all. Now such an observation in itself is not profound. But its implications are far-reaching. It means that the space involved in our world of concern is primordial to the abstract space of "objects"; this in turn means that to speak of Dasein's spatiality is not a question of whether Dasein is in space (or even whether space is in Dasein), but rather that *to be in space* is a necessary way that Dasein is in the world.

The whole point of this analysis is that the modes of spatial awareness, whether "felt" or "thought," do not presuppose a worldless subject, but rather a "subject" *already in the world*. Formally measured space, the space of science, is, then, merely a mode of primordial space, which is *a priori*. Now Kant had also shown that space was *a priori*, but, unlike Heidegger, he did not argue that this Being-in-space was a part of Being-in-the-world. The subject, which, for Kant, had as its form of intuition an *a priori* space, was worldless. But Heidegger argues that the mode of using the world's objects as ready-at-hand presupposes an *a priori* relationship that makes the tools and equipment *available*—i.e., near. If Heidegger's analysis of the world as ready-at-hand is correct, then there must be something that accounts for the world's objects being available and near to us. This is Dasein's spatiality. Hence to say that space is "subjective" is incorrect; it is rather a mode of one's existence in the world.

The phenomenological richness of Heidegger's account of Dasein's spatiality, and of most of the subsequent existentials, needs little or no commentary. What is significant is their effect on the ontological question. For the most part, the relationship of these existentials to the question of Being requires little comment since, as a description, Heidegger's language usually provides little difficulty. It is important to note, however, that Heidegger feels the proper insight into every mode of human existence is to see or interpret that mode in light of the question of Being. If certain critics protest that Heidegger's psychological insights into the various modes of existence are profound or valuable but without ontological foundation, it might be pointed out that the very success of Heidegger's analyses rests on his interpretation of these existentials in the light of the question of Being. It is not really possible to separate Heidegger's phenomenology from his ontology; and if one notices that a great deal of what Heidegger says about the modes of existence seems to be sound, then one should at least consider the possibility that the question of Being can indeed be illumined by such an interpretation of the existentials.

The main attempt of this section has been to show how Heidegger has interpreted the world as a way of Being—i.e., "a way to be." The primordial relationship to the world is to use it as equipment; and this use of the world as equipment presupposes a kind of space that is *a priori*. Heidegger denies the priority of the abstracted mode of Being-in-the-world, that of seeing the world as present-at-hand rather than ready-at-hand. If Heidegger is right, then any metaphysical theory, such as the substance metaphysics of Descartes or Leibniz, is doomed from its very inception to be incomplete and insufficient. So too is any description of the world based merely on a subject-object account of knowledge. The description, then, of how one exists in the world—what it means to be in the world— is the first step of the ontological analysis that provides the foundation or fundament of metaphysics. For this reason, Heidegger describes his analysis as that of *fundamental ontology*.

THE WHO OF DASEIN   (sections 25–27)

The transition from Chapter III's discussion of Being-in-the-world to Chapter IV, on the problem of the self, is by no means a mere shift from one existential topic to another. We are nearing the heart of Heidegger's interpretation. Chapter IV is far more significant in terms of the ultimate picture of Heidegger's analysis of Being; it is also a far more exciting chapter. Yet its implications are so far-reaching that it is likewise a difficult chapter to assess and to comprehend fully. Since much of what is said in this chapter has a bearing on subsequent sections, a brief look at where Heidegger is ultimately headed may be helpful.

Chapter IV gives a rudimentary description of what constitutes the difference between the inauthentic they-self and the authentic self. This distinction is not to be interpreted in terms of moral or "value" dimensions; for its purpose is to provide a ground for revealing the meaning of Being, which is, after all, the task of *Being and Time*. How does the investigation of the self accomplish its purpose?—i.e., that of throwing light on the question of the meaning of Being. Before we analyze Heidegger's description of the various modes and ways of the self, a consideration of the relevance of such description is advisable.

One of the things that amaze and astonish many sensitive people is the simple fact of their own consciousness. Upon reflection, the very fact that one is conscious at all seems, at times, highly unlikely. For why should I be blessed (or cursed) with consciousness? And what are the implications of the fact of my consciousness? The knowledge or awareness that I exist at all and am conscious of it brings to the fore the *significance* of my being. The question is: Is it significant—does it matter—that I exist?

One way to throw light on the significance of any question or fact is to ask what *difference*[5] it makes that that fact occurs. To realize, for example, the significance of a legal order, one need merely consider what it would be like without such an order. To realize the significance of health or wealth, one need merely conjecture what the circumstances would be like in the absence of either. Suppose I consider the question of the significance of existence. What would it be like not to be? In one sense, of course, the question is absurd. I could never know what it would be like not to be, because if I didn't exist, I couldn't possibly know anything at all. And yet the question is not totally without significance, because it awakens in one's consciousness the deeply disturbing realization that one's existence is not a necessary thing. One's existence can be in jeopardy. Although I cannot know what it is like not to exist (for that is meaningless), nevertheless I can know that it is *possible* that I cease to exist. It is the *realization* of the possibility of not-being, rather than nonexistence itself, that is significant. For I can legitimately ask: Does it make any difference whether I am aware of the fact that I could cease to exist, or not? Surely the awareness of my possible not-being might have significance for some of the ways in which I live. (It might make me cautious, for example.) But then the question arises: Is it ever possible for me *not* to be aware of my possible not-being? Or is it that I only submerge my awareness of this terrifying possibility? In order to answer this question, one must examine the modes of self that do not seem explicitly aware of the possibility of nonexistence. Not to be aware of the possibility of nonexistence, though, is surely to cover up the significance of existence.

But it is not merely the awareness of my possible not-being that is important; it is also essential to recognize that I may exist and not be aware of what it means to exist. This, too, is a kind of negation, in which the *meaning* of existence can be lost or covered up. It is obviously a form

5. "In order for there to be a difference, it must make a difference" is a familiar argument in American pragmatist circles. Much of the early existentials in Heidegger's analysis might remind one of the positions held by James or even Dewey. The similarity is only surface, however. The ontological significance given to these analyses would not be shared by most pragmatists.

of self-deception to live in such a way as to avoid the realization that my nonexistence is possible; but it is even more deceptive to exist in such a way as to avoid realizing what it *means* that I exist. To be sure, the first kind of self-deception may be intimately linked with the second; but for Heidegger's purposes, it is the second form of deception that matters and must be analysed first. For this reason, Heidegger *begins* his analysis precisely with that mode which does submerge or cover up the awareness of the self. Against the inauthentic they-self Heidegger will contrast the authentic self, which is the mode of Being in which one is aware of the significance of Being. As the subsequent chapters will soon point out, since the significance of Being lies in one's recognition of the possibility of not-being (in any of the many particular ways of Being), to *understand* the question of Being is to be aware of possibilities. To be aware of possibilities is to provide the ground both of freedom and of truth. But not only that. The fact that one has possibilities other than the mode of the actual brings up the determinant of why, of all the possible ways of Being, one is in just this particular, actual mode. One cannot account for such determination except through one's own mode of Being: either I am *not* aware of the significance of Being, in which case I am determined in the actual by the persuasion of the "they" (inauthentic); or I myself resolutely determine my *own* Being. (The reader should be reminded that *eigen* ["own"] is the etymological base for *eigentlich* ["authentic"]. In the authentic mode, Dasein is aware of its possible not-being. This reveals its finitude. It is this finitude that provides the ontological foundation for Dasein's *temporality*, and hence one's awareness of time.

This brief sketch of the argumentation that Heidegger is going to follow in the subsequent sections emphasizes the importance of the present discussion of the self. One might note that Heidegger's methodology is phenomenological rather than logical: he does not begin with an analysis of freedom and time, and from this deduce the modes of authenticity and inauthenticity. Rather, he begins from our phenomenological and prior comprehension of the modes of our self-understanding, and from this analysis he develops the ontological base.

One of the main tenets of Heidegger's analysis is his insistence that one cannot begin the analysis of the self from a naked and lonely "I," or pure consciousness. Heidegger argues that the primordially given "I" or self is always and already part of the world; and indeed, a world in which other persons are likewise given. The importance of this view is considerable. For if Heidegger's analysis is correct, then there is no problem of "other minds" (for "other minds" are equally primordial with one's own "mind"); and furthermore, any analysis of the self that strives to achieve a totally independent mind or isolated subject will be without foundation. The highly abstract and purely rational "ego" of the Cartesian metaphysics is a fiction. Neither Husserl's "bracketing" nor Descartes's "doubting" can in principle succeed if the total given is a consciousness or a self already involved with the world.

At the same time, Heidegger's insistence that the self be a self within-the-world and with-other-people does not mean that one is doomed to treat the self without clear distinctions or dimensions. One can, according to Heidegger, achieve a view of the self that is authentic—i.e., its *own self*. But the distinction here is not between a lone, isolated self and others; rather, it is a distinction between an authentic self (part of whose nature is to be with other people) and the inauthentic they-self. Clearly to distinguish the limits and boundaries of the self is, of course, important for any philosopher. Without a clear understanding of such limits, one is without a methodology for distinguishing between the mere subjective influences of any process or action, and the external or objective characteristics. Heidegger does not deny that the self should be so distinguished and clarified; but the *manner* of such distinction and clarification must not be that of a fictional worldless subject separate from an object world. By asserting that the authentic self is a self already in a world and already in association with others, Heidegger is undermining a great tradition in which the self was pictured in its "purity" as totally denuded abstractness. But Heidegger insists the self is never without others. The difference between the inauthentic and the authentic modes of the self is not that the latter is alone and the former involved, but simply that the ways the self *deals with* these others in the two modes of Being differ. In the inauthentic mode, one's dealings with others is such that one loses sight of the self; in the authentic mode one is aware of others as well as the self.

Before we begin to delineate the authentic-inauthentic distinction, however, we should perhaps first trace the genesis of the distinction as it occurs in *Being and Time*.

Following what was said about Dasein's primordial relation to the world as equipment ready-at-hand, we find that this use of the world as equipment contains within it a primordial relationship with other Daseins. For when I deal with the world as equipment, I recognize that, as equipment, part of the world is "of service" to other Daseins. Heidegger notes that even in an innocent walk along a field I expose my primordial sharing of the world with others. For by not trampling the crops I recognize their service to another Dasein, the farmer. Such consideration of the farmer's right and use of his land itself is not what Heidegger means by the existential Being-with (or "to-be-with": *mit-sein*). Being-with is that *a priori* dimension of the self which makes consideration of the farmer's rights *possible*. In order to respect the farmer's rights, I first must be able—possess the capacity to do so; that capacity is then prior

to any particular act of consideration for the farmer that is a manifesta-
tion of my being in the world with him. Hence to object that there are
experiences of extreme loneliness in which one has no relationship with
other human beings is not a telling objection. Heidegger is not speaking
of actual experiences in which one relates to others; he is instead speaking of that prior capacity which makes such experiences possible. Just
as the Kantian categories of cause and substance are not the result of abstraction from experience but presuppositions of the experience, neither
are Heidegger's existentials the result of abstraction from experience.
That I can be aware of Dasein's use of the world as equipment is possible
only because as Dasein I am essentially being-with.

To say that Being-with (or to-be-with) is an *a priori* existential of
Dasein means that one cannot be a self unless it is within one's possibilities to relate in a unique way to other Daseins. Hence to be Dasein at
all means to-be-with. But this further implies that others are not completely external—i.e., to be with others is a possibility of every *self*. It
is not, therefore, a non-self characteristic, but an existential of the self.

It seems incredible that some critics have argued that, through this
analysis, Heidegger has "reduced" other human beings to mere "tools."
He has done no such thing. To be sure, it is through the analysis of
Dasein's use of the world as equipment that we come across the realization that there are other Daseins who also use the world as equipment.
The world as equipment is *for the sake of*. Of what? Not always myself.
Therefore, there must be some *other* Dasein that this piece of equipment
serves. Hence other Daseins are conceived, not as pieces of equipment,
but rather as that *for which* something is a piece of equipment. This demands that, as Dasein, my mode of being, my *ontological relating*, to another Dasein is basically different from my relationship to the world as
equipment. The *a priori* possibility of such a relationship is called Being-
with.

Heidegger asks a tremendous question on E-150/G-115. Is it not possible, he asks, that the "who" of everyday Dasein is simply *not* the "I myself"? The seemingly conflicting question is even more startling when one
realizes that Heidegger will answer it in the affirmative. In one sense, in
my everyday self, I am not I. This does not mean that I become somebody
other than myself, for as Heidegger cleverly puts it: "[Others] are those
from whom, for the most part, one does *not* distinguish oneself—those
among whom one is too." What, then, does Heidegger mean by saying
that in the everyday mode, I am not I? The answer to this lies in the consideration of the distinction between the authentic and the inauthentic
modes of the self. I do not lose my "I" to some other Dasein; instead
I lose it to the "they," which is a mode of the self.

The They-Self (section 27)

It is certainly not an original thought of Heidegger's that one has a tendency to lose oneself in the babble of the crowd. Every sensitive person is aghast at the terrible loss of independence brought about by uncritical living. In fact, the prime maxim of the most revered person in philosophy, Socrates—"know thyself"—seems to bear this out. But if the observation that one can lose one's identity in the prattle of daily busy-work is not new, surely the interpretation given to this observation by Heidegger is far from orthodox. A consideration of Heidegger's phenomenological clarity here is rewarding.

Everyone will readily admit that daily concerns can take one's mind off the awareness of the self. But if this is true, it means that since one does manifest different modes of Being, then it is necessary that there *be* different modes. The task, then, of one who is pursuing the analysis of the self is to render an *account* of the phenomenon that does indeed occur—namely, that sometimes I lose the awareness of myself in my concern for daily affairs. In order to make the analysis easier, we give names to these modes: the one in which I am aware of the self I give a name, the "self-mode" (i.e., eigen*lich*: "authentic"). The other, merely for convenience's sake, I call the "non-self-mode" (uneigen*lich*: "inauthentic").

Now given an awareness of these two different modes, the next step is to describe them accurately. Here Heidegger reveals extraordinary sensitivity in his descriptions. But brilliant though these observations may be, their individual worth is secondary to the overall interpretation. For in analyzing these experientially grounded modes of Being, Heidegger recognizes and interprets them according to how they reveal one's relationship to possibilities. As we will see later on, the awareness of the possibility of not-being (in death) is one of the most vivid and important moments in the mode of authenticity. But at this stage Heidegger wishes first to show that the mode in which one loses the view of the self is, in fact, a mode of the self, and *not* of others. (Thus we can blame only ourselves for our own inauthenticity.) One should never mistake the meaning of the word "they" (*das man*) for "others." The "they" is a characteristic of the self that determines a mode of existence; "others" are relationships that occur in both the authentic and inauthentic modes. A cursory and undisciplined reading may give the incautious reader the idea that Heidegger is here very selfish and relativistic. Such an interpretation could not be further from the real meaning of Heidegger's words.

Heidegger in Chapter IV does not yet stress the point that the chief characteristic of authentic existence is awareness of possibilities. The reason for this is programmatic. Heidegger has not as yet laid the groundwork for introducing the term *Verstehen* ("understanding"), which is that by which Dasein is aware of possibilities.

Heidegger's analysis of one's everyday existence has revealed an understanding of two modes: the authentic and the inauthentic. The inauthentic mode is characterized by a loss of self-awareness and an abandonment to the impersonal prattle of the "they"; but as we shall see in the following chapter, it is grounded in the *actual*. The authentic mode, of which Heidegger as yet has said very little, is characterized by the self and is grounded in the *possible*.

In hermeneutic phenomenology, one first describes the characteristics as they reveal themselves to the inquirer, and only then can one turn one's analysis to the grounds that lie at the bases of these characteristics. This is the reason why Chapter IV, which points out only the *characteristics* of the inauthentic self, must precede the next chapter, which deals with the *grounds* of the two modes of the self. If the order of presentation in *Being and Time* were deductive rather than phenomenological, these two chapters would be reversed.

One might perhaps expect that a section dealing with authentic and inauthentic existence would be rich in insights and observations about the human condition. Except for a few acute observations about the ease in which one loses oneself, there is little of this to be found in the present section. The reason is that Heidegger is not here making any claims about how to achieve authenticity or avoid inauthenticity. He is merely making use of the rich supply of insights into the human condition in order first to elicit a phenomenological account of such modes, so that he may then discover the ontological bases that underlie the two modes. Many works, of popular as well as academic literature, that interpret Heidegger's account of the authentic and inauthentic modes have, I think, seriously misread his intentions. Heidegger has not constructed an ideal mode of existence called "authenticity" to which he then points as the goal of some spiritual or philosophical exercise. Nor is he arguing, Nietzsche-like, to "be yourself"! Such would not be an existential *analysis*. It is rather the case that, *taking* the distinction between authentic and inauthentic existence, which is something that most sensitive, reflective, and intelligent men recognize, he first analyzes what these mean, and then *from* this analysis he seeks out the ontological ground.

IV.

EXISTENTIAL
ANALYTIC
II

Understanding

sections 25–38

Our discussion of Chapter IV of *Being and Time* centered upon the distinction between the authentic and the inauthentic modes of existence. It was pointed out that the inauthentic mode was one grounded in actuality; whereas the authentic was grounded in possibility. By this it is *not* intended to suggest that the inauthentic cannot be seen as a possibility, or that the authentic can never be actual. *Authentic existence*, by definition, is being aware of the meaning of existence; *inauthentic existence* is being unaware of the meaning of existence. The question that must be asked now is, How is such awareness possible? To see oneself as having possibilities is, according to Heidegger, the only genuine way in which one can be aware of the meaningful self. To see the self merely as an actual entity is always to see it as an object, and hence basically as something else. For this reason—which admittedly requires considerable thought and commentary—it is said that the ground of authenticity is possibility, the ground of inauthenticity is actuality. The language of Heidegger's Chapter IV, however, did not give much indication of such an interpretation, since Heidegger's chief task in that chapter was to provide phenomenological evidence for the authentic-inauthentic distinction. His fifth chapter goes beyond the previous chapter in spelling out the manner in which Dasein is aware of its *actual* determined existence and its *possible* free existence. In the present commentary literature there seems to be an extraordinary lack of serious discussion of these most important points. It is my opinion, however, that this chapter, with its subsequent effects, is one of the most important of the entire work.

To understand this chapter, one must fully grasp just what the problem is. A clarification of the *problem*, then, should perhaps be made before we begin our analysis of the chapter itself.

THE PROBLEM

Speaking purely speculatively, it seems obvious that one is aware not only what one *is*, but also what one *could be*, in the sense of being able to be what one is in fact not. Thus, although I realize that I am now sitting at my desk, I can, with relative ease, imagine myself vacationing on the Riviera. To put it in another way, it is meaningful for me to utter contrary-to-fact sentences. But suppose I ask, How is it that I can exist in such a way as to have possibilities? and, How does this differ from my existing in such a way as to be actual? It is important to realize that I am not asking merely a logical or linguistic question. For I am not asking about the logical or semantic differences between indicative sentences and contrary-to-fact conditionals. I am, instead, asking two closely related questions: How is my *actuality* meaningful to me? and, How is my having *possibilities* meaningful to me?

At the risk of seeming either pedantic or overemphatic, I would like to stress this difference. To a political prisoner awaiting a trial, the possibility of his liberty is far more important and meaningful than his present *actual* state. On the other hand, to a man who has just won an important battle, his present actual state is more important than his earlier sense of uncertainty, which allowed for possible defeat. For a scientist it is *facts* and not possibilities that affect his concern and excite his interest. Nor is possibility significant only in a futuristic sense. A man who has just committed a morally reprehensible act may realize that his previous position included the possibility of his refraining from such an act, so that the torturous and guilt-ridden question, "Why did I do it?" is more real to him than the simple fact that he did do it. In short, our lives are meaningful not only because of what *is*, but also because of what *might have been* and what *might be*.

But herein lies the great difficulty for philosophy. The language and the edifices of thinking that constitute a description of the actual facts of the world are woefully inadequate to describe the realm of the possible. Once I limit my description to those elements of the world that are revealed exclusively through the faculties that respond to facts, I cannot go beyond them to suggest or describe anything that does not exist, but that may exist. On the other hand, if I concern myself with those faculties of mind that tell me only what is possible, there is nothing in such activity of mind that can separate what is simply *possible* from what actually *is*. Now since the human person lives a life in which both possibility and actuality are important (and indeed, it is a life in which the various moments and situations at one time emphasize the actual, and at another the possible), it seems obvious that the only truly complete philosophy would be one in which both the actual and the possible are duly accounted for. This, however, is easier said than done. The history of philosophy has many instances in which thinkers have tried to reduce the function of one mode to that of the other. We have examples of thinkers who try to show that the machinery through which we describe facts can provide us with sufficient descriptive fluency so as to reveal the structure of the possible. Most empiricist theories, which of course reside on the persuasion of the facts, have attempted such reduction. On the other hand, many rationalist theorists have gone so far as to suggest that the faculties of possibility somehow can determine the limits of facts. Both of these attempts, however, have shown themselves extraordinarily weak in their reduction; though, to be sure, the tremendous attraction and seduction of such theories stem from their obvious ease and ability in describing the mode they have chosen as primary.

The logical and sensible conclusion from this is, of course, to construct a view that will take care of both the realm of the possible and the realm of the actual. But here we have a new difficulty. The moment we separate the faculties of *possible* thought from those through which one understands the *actual*, there appears a numbing dualism. For it is obvious that I do not simply have a possible life as well as an actual life; rather, I have one life in which both the actual and the possible are significant. Hence it is not enough merely to describe two totally distinct and separate functions; I must, indeed, also show how they relate. The moment I realize that there is a relationship between the actual and the possible, the task becomes to find and describe that relationship. Now one can, of course, begin one's description with a "soul" or "given unity"; though such description must be very careful not to rely solely upon the language of fact, or on the language of mere possibility, for it is not a possible soul that has possible life, and an actual soul that has actual life, but one soul that has both. Such "rational psychology" is extremely vulnerable to critical attack, however. For it must contain, in the given factual entity called "soul," powers that go beyond any possible verification by evidence that is available solely to experience. This is the meaning of Kant's famous paralogisms, in which he showed that the traditional arguments for a substantial soul were based on faulty reasoning.

But to show that rational psychology does not answer the question is not to have solved the difficulty. For it is still the case that the mind is aware of both actuality and possibility; and further, that one's life is genuinely affected by such awareness.

Heidegger's approach to this problem is consistent with his description of his thought as "phenomenological." If we are going to avoid excluding either mode (actual or possible), we must begin our analysis by letting these modes reveal themselves in the fullness of their own significance. Heidegger insists that the two modes are equally primordial (E-171/G-133); and that means that neither can be descriptively accounted for by the other–i.e., the one cannot be "reduced" to the terms of the other. Only *after* such descriptions can any attempt be made to *unify* the two under a more general concept. This ultimate existential is going to be called "care" (*Sorge*); but we cannot *begin* with care if we proceed phenomenologically. Care as the ultimate existential must be revealed. The analysis must begin, though, with descriptions of two ways of Being, the one in which one's actuality is revealed (state-of-mind: *Befindlichkeit*) and the other in which one's possibilities are revealed (understanding: *Verstehen*).

As we shall soon see, for Heidegger possibility is more significant than actuality. To be sure, the existential that informs Dasein of its possibilities (understanding) is *equiprimordial* with the existential that reveals its actuality (state-of-mind); but since the authentic mode is grounded in possibility, there is neveretheless a kind of priority for possibility over actuality. It is to some ramifications of this doctrine that I would like to turn briefly, even though the following remarks do not apply directly to any one chapter or section. It must be discussed somewhere, however, and it is perhaps best to consider these remarks now, since they will apply in a general way to most of the subsequent analyses.

THE PRIORITY OF POSSIBILITY

In Aristotle's *Metaphysics* (9. 8. 1051) the claim is made that actuality is prior to possibility as far as metaphysical reality is concerned. For most metaphysicians, such a claim is essential to their theories. Heidegger's counterclaim, that possibility is prior to actuality, might at first seem a direct violation of this tradition. Nevertheless, there are many figures in the history of philosophy who have held positions that tend to support Heidegger's view, even though these figures do not necessarily adhere to the principle in its severest statement. A consideration of a few of these positions may perhaps be helpful.

It is often a common complaint against Plato's *Republic* that the "ideal state" as so described does not and cannot *exist*. It was Kant, however, who pointed out that the greatest *asset* of Plato's theory was that the ideal state does not actually exist. What kind of reasons can be given to support these two idealist thinkers? Kant's own analysis of Plato's *Republic* is here valuable: If the "ideal state" actually existed, it would be limited by its existence. If it actually existed, it would no longer be *ideal*. Why? Because an idea is precisely that which does *not* arise from experience, but precedes it. Both Kant and Plato utilize these ideas (and ideals) for *moral* purposes (though Plato, unlike Kant, gives creative powers to the ideas; Kant restricts them to a regulative use). In terms of morals, the priority of ideas over facts (and hence of possibility over actuality) is quite powerfully felt. Many philosophers argue that the *ought* cannot be derived from the *is*. As long as one restricts oneself to consideration of existing facts, there can be no ground for establishing any kind of morality except one based upon the extremely narrow limits of alternatives afforded by chance happenings. In the case of the problem of freedom versus causality, Kant again argues that inquiries into the nature of freedom cannot be based upon a system of scientific facts, since all facts necessarily fall under the influence of the principle of causality.

The priority of possibility over actuality is not restricted to moral considerations, however. Transcendental philosophy, in both its epistemology and its value theory, places possibility in a higher place. Epistemologically, possibility is seen as the *a priori* forms that come *before* any actual event, as in the philosophies of Kant and Schopenhauer. Nietzsche too, in his demand for a transvaluation of values, emphasizes possibilities above and beyond actualities.

For Heidegger, the principle that possibility is prior to actuality becomes almost a guilding theme. Through this principle he explains how a philosophy of existence is not dependent upon a dreary repetition of actually experienced occasions; he uses the principle to show how history is possible (and it is in his analysis of history that he speaks of "the silent power of the possible"). Most importantly, however, for Heidegger, as for Kant, Schopenhauer, and Nietzsche, possibility—for which an actual experience is not required—is that by which the transcendental perspective is achieved. For there must be a mode beyond the limits of the actual, if there is to be an understanding and indeed a conceptual use of the actual existing entities. Possibility, whether articulated in terms of freedom (Kant), will (Schopenhauer), or the will to power (Nietzsche), alone can provide the perspective of the self necessary to explain the occurrence of the philosophical activity.

The priority of possibility over actuality is rampant in Heidegger's thought. It may be his most persistently used principle in describing the various existentials. It not only deeply affects his own internally developed problems, but affects to a great degree his general attitude toward mankind. As we proceed to examine the various existentials, this principle will be made more clear and will be discussed in greater detail.

Taken from a strictly metaphysical view, of course, one must admit that actuality is more real than possibility. To say that, however, is merely to reveal the ultimate basis of metaphysics: it deals with beings (*Seiende*) and not with what it means to be (*Sein*). If we restrict the term "reality" to mean the sum total of all existing beings in the world, then actuality is "more real" than possibility. Possibility, however, is more *meaningful* than actuality. (For a discussion of "meaning," cf. p. 97.) It must be kept in mind that Heidegger's inquiry is into the *meaning* of Being (what it means to be); and in such an inquiry, possibility is prior to actuality.

In claiming that possibility is prior to actuality, Heidegger is not denying the import of the actual. In fact, to be aware of the actual is also part of authenticity. Surely one would not consider someone who was blind to reality to be authentic. To say that possibility is prior in existential meaning to actuality is not to say that actuality is totally without existential meaning, nor does it say that awareness of actuality automatically constitutes inauthenticity. (It *does* suggest, however, that to place actuality above possibility in one's values may be inauthentic, as we shall see below in the case of various existentials.)

Both actuality and possibility are needed, however, to explain Dasein's awareness of itself in the world. Heidegger begins his analysis of what it means to be *here* in a world with a consideration of that mode of awareness by which the *actual* is made significant.

STATE-OF-MIND (MODE OF THE ACTUAL)   (section 29)

Macquarrie and Robinson translated *Befindlichkeit* as "state-of-mind," and they have remarked in a footnote that their choice only approximates the German meaning. I am sympathetic with the difficulties of translators, and in this case I can find no ready substitute. It must be stressed, though, that the German term is more akin to the awkward "the state in which one is to be found." Heidegger means by the term the *a priori* existential by which Dasein has its moods. Of course, Dasein is always in a mood; so the reader must not take "moods" as those occasional attitudes of mind that belong to the study of psychology.

What does it mean to say that I "find myself" in such and such a way? If I look about me and wonder, not about the things that *might* be in terms of self, but rather about the things that *are* in terms of my self, I realize that I find myself in a world without having first asked to be in it. I did not choose to be born. Nor did I choose to be in the circumstances under which I was born. If I were of a truculent nature I might even complain that it hardly seems fair that I was thrown into this world and this particular situation totally without my preferences being heard. But thrown I was, and now that I'm here I am going to have to make the best of it. There is much that is unalterable about my existence; and I can, in certain moods, either overlook it or meet it in one of many ways; but it is always there. Much of what is unalterable, though, is met in terms of pro or con attitudes toward it, so that what *is* does indeed matter.

Heidegger calls this mode of awareness of the actual, state-of-mind. He points out three characteristics of this existential: (1) The disclosure of our "thrownness" (*Geworfenheit*)—a term used by Heidegger to stand for our being to some extent determined by conditions and circumstances beyond our control. This rather graphic term is employed because it suggests the attitude one has toward these limiting characteristics of one's existence. There is no "metaphysics of abandonment" implied, for Dasein has countercharacteristics that tend to resist and offset the influence of his thrownness. (2) The disclosure of Being-in-the-world-as-a-whole. (3) The disclosure that what Dasein encounters in the world *matters* to Dasein. A word or two must be said about the term "disclosure" (*Erschlossenheit*), which appears in each of the three characteristics. Heidegger insists that "'To be disclosed' does not mean 'to be known as this sort of thing'" (E-173/G-134). Hence, when we speak of state-of-mind disclosing Dasein's actual here (*Da*), we do not mean that moods totally expose and reveal all there is to know about Dasein's given circumstances. State-of-mind discloses or reveals the *fact* that Dasein is in the world; but not why or for what purpose. Hence there is always something *unknown* about one's actual state in the world.

One can reflect on one's own self-awareness to see if this account is true. Our moods do reveal a great deal about our attitude toward the inevitable in life. But our moods never reveal the full meaning of our existence. In fact, it is very often the case that moods actually confront us with the disturbing *lack* of comprehension that we have about the "givenness" of our conditions. Such unlikely concepts as "fate," "fortune," and "luck" (which Kant recognized as "unsurpatory" concepts[1]) cannot ever be utilized in any rational inquiry but are nevertheless genuine attitudes of mind that we take to describe the inexplicable. Although "fate" cannot be meaningful to us in terms of a rational inquiry into causes, it *can* be significant for us in terms of what it meant to exist. Fate is significant as a characteristic of the way (or one of the ways) in which I exist.

One of the most troubling questions that can be asked is the one that

---

1. *Critique of Pure Reason*, A85/B117, p. 120.

confronts those attributes of our existence over which we not only have no control but about which we do not even have any understanding. "Why me?" One person is blessed with a happy life, another cursed with an endless series of cruel fates. Sophocles is said to have been among the happiest of men, living to the ripe and wondrous age of ninety-four, succeeding in almost all that he did, enjoying the great pleasure of seeing his own children succeed as well. Another man is stricken at an early age with a painful paralysis, is abandoned by his wife and family, and in his wretchedness cannot even find solace in belief, as his is not a religious or spiritual nature. Does Sophocles *deserve* his good luck; does the poor victim of paralysis deserve his bad luck? To say they deserve their fortunes is to deny that it is mere fortune. But if we cannot control our fates, then how are we to make sense of them? The truth, of course, is that we do not and cannot know why one man is blest and another cursed. We simply do not *know* why fortune smiles on the favored and frowns on the wretched. But, though we cannot know the causes or the why of such things, we can and must *think about what they mean*. In order to do this, we must understand that what it means for us to exist is intelligible only by the recognition that we are both fated and free; or, to be more exact, we are free as fated beings and are fated as free beings. The very way in which we exist in the world is characterized by our fitting into the current either easily or uncomfortably. This has nothing to do with our free and moral conduct, nor is it a matter of our deciding one way or another. It is rather a kind of "tuning" in on the world, a realization of how we fit into the whole. Since this way of being is not chosen or decided in any way, it is rather like a mood; that is, it is a part of the way we find ourselves disposed to what is meaningful or trivial. Heidegger uses the word "*Stimmung*" (mood) as well as the word "*Gestimmtsein*" (being attuned), and by these terms he means to focus our attention on the truth that what it means to exist is to be, in part, without control or influence. What is peculiar about moods is that, even as they account in part for how we fit into the world, we simply cannot make a certain mood happen. No matter how self-controlled I am, I cannot simply decide one day to be in a good mood or a bad mood. Moods by definition are independent of my selection and control. Though we should indeed control our actions even when our moods are gloomy, what is meant by "being attuned" or "being in a mood" is that the way we find ourselves in the world at any given time is not ours to determine. Thus we "find ourselves" already in certain modes or states: this is called *Befindlichkeit*, (state-of-mind), i.e., how we find ourselves.

As an observation into the human condition, this insight is surely brilliant and profound. Few thinkers spend enough time and thought on what it means that we, as human beings, are both destined by powers beyond our control and, at the same time, are conscious of ourselves as free and responsible agents. To ask, "Why me?" is to confront the agony of this realization. To be able, as Heidegger does, to isolate the principles that make this intelligible is a philosophical gift of great rarity and power. He argues that what makes our half-determined, half-free existence intelligible is the realization that these modes are *a priori*, that is, they are simply *not* accountable by any other principle or force; rather they are the fundamental givens by which we must make sense of our being in the world. It is their very unintelligibility that makes our existence intelligible. To ask, "Why me?" as if there were some kind of determinate answer, such as "God is testing you" or, even worse, "It is determined by some inevitable dialectic," is to ask an improper question. The proper question is not, "Why me?" but rather "How must I think about what it means?" and Heidegger here gives us the fundamental principles that are available to us to do just that.

He insists that how we find ourselves already in the world (*Befindlichkeit*) and how we project possibilities that to some extent *are* in our control are equiprimordial; that is, they are both fundamentally necessary to make sense of who we are. A third, equally fundamental existential, which rounds out this tension, is talk or language. Thus, we make sense of our existence as being in the world by recognizing the influence of our own projecting; the givenness of our own fate or circumstances, which, though still our own, is not our selection; and the influence of our being able to articulate this meaning through speech. Each of these three, state-of-mind, projection, and talk, are ways of being myself; that is, as characteristics *essential* to our existence, they are *ours*; and hence they are made discursive by being either my own, or not my own—i.e., authentic or inauthentic.

Because moods are, to some extent, always with us, it is not possible to define authentic existence as "moodless" and inauthentic existence as "mood-dominated." To be totally unaware of the inevitable, or "fallenness," could scarcely be called "authentic." Nevertheless, state-of-mind is that existential which discloses Dasein as submissive to the world. Authentic existence cannot completely eradicate the influence of its states-of-mind, but it can go beyond them. What Heidegger wishes to emphasize strongly here is that such phenomena as moods or states-of-mind cannot be "added on" to an account of man under the dubious genus "feelings." State-of-mind, as an existential, is a primordial term, and belongs to the essential character of Dasein. As such it stands equal in importance to the traditionally more lofty aspects of man, such as cognition and reason.

What does this analysis of state-of-mind come to? Only when one realizes the purpose and strategy of Heidegger's analysis does it make any sense at all. There are four points that should be made clear.

1. One of the purposes of the analysis of state-of-mind as an existential of Dasein is to show that when Dasein becomes aware of itself in a world (i.e., its "here") it always does so to some extent influenced by the unalterability of facts. This means that no Dasein relates to the world without at least some awareness of the unavoidable influences of the way in which the world is. But if this is so, then—

2. State-of-mind cannot be shuffled off into a mere "psychological account" that renders such awareness as a mere feeling. Rather, state-of-mind becomes an all-important factor even in such seemingly tranquil moments of human existence as the dispassionate activity of scientific investigation. (For tranquillity is, after all, a mood.)

3. Given the realization that both actuality and possibility are significant for Dasein, there must be an account of how Dasein's existence becomes aware of possibility and actuality. Dasein's awareness of *actual* existence is due to Dasein's state-of-mind. (Dasein's awareness of possible existence or modes of existence is due to understanding.) Hence state-of-mind is not merely the mode of Being in which inauthentic existence is recognized; it must be present also in authentic existence.

4. State-of-mind is the basis for the world mattering to Dasein. This last point is, in some sense, the most important of the four; and it is a point about which I have not as yet made any comment. I shall discuss it now, for it leads directly to the consideration of the phenomenon of fear.

At the beginning of this chapter I pointed out that both possibility and actuality were significant to one's existence. The way in which the world *is* affects me just as much as the way in which the world *can be*. The existential that grounds the significance of the world as it *is* is state-of-mind. What Heidegger means by this is that unless there were *prior* to the occurrence of any fact a mode of human existence that would make that occurrence significant *as a fact*, then no *fact* could matter to Dasein. Since such a mode must be *prior* to the fact, it is an existential; and as an existential it is *a priori*. The existential, state-of-mind, does not merely *reveal* Dasein as it is insofar as it is in a world, but it reveals this Dasein as concerned with the world. Moods, taken in this very broad sense that Heidegger here employs, reveal my concern for the facts as *facts*, not as possibilities.

Heidegger seems to recognize that, abstractly stated, the role of state-of-mind may not lend itself to immediate comprehension. So he takes an example, and discusses it in terms of how state-of-mind functions in a more concrete and immediate instance. His choice of *fear* as an example is by no means arbitrary; for he will later contrast fear with anxiety. But as it is given in this section, his analysis of fear is meant to provide an example of how state-of-mind reveals the *actual* mode of the "here."

FEAR   (section 30)

Fear is simply one of the ways in which Dasein relates to the stark givenness of its world. The phenomenon of fear can reveal, to the sharply inquiring investigator, one of the modes in which Dasein lets the actuality of the world become significant for it. As a mode of state-of-mind, fear cannot be something that comes to us totally from the outside. Fear is not learned; it is discovered. The point is this: How can we be threatened by anything unless we exist in such a way that we are intimately connected with the world, and that this openness to whatever threatens is an integral part of the way in which we exist? Heidegger explains that fearing (E-180/G-141) "has already disclosed the world, in that out of it something like the fearsome may come close." Actual occurrences of fearing, then, reveal what has always been there—i.e., a way of Being in the world so that a part of it can threaten us.

Heidegger's analysis of fear, brilliant though it is, must not be taken out of context. By no means is he suggesting that fear, any more than joy or exultation, is a predominant mode of human existence. He is not, through this analysis, opting for pessimism or a pathological and uncertain view of man. In fact, he is merely showing the reader the advantages of the existential analytic. By showing that such a thing as fear can be interpreted as an essential mode of how Dasein finds itself in a world, the occurrence of fearing need not be dealt with in an extraneous manner. In this way such humanly recognizable aspects of fear become significant for the investigation of ontology. Fear is not, then, reduced to a mere and occasional moment of weakness. Fear is rather an important revelation of the truth that to be is, for Dasein, an issue. For it is not possible to explain fear unless it matters for Dasein to be. Now Heidegger goes to great length, in the description of fear, to show that seeming objections, such as "but one can fear about something other than oneself, as a house or a friend," are not really arguments against his interpretation. But these remarks are, I think, easy to follow and do not need further commentary.

Heidegger, then, is not giving a psychological account of fear. He is instead asking the question: How is fearing possible? And his answer is that fearing is possible because Dasein has, as one of its existentials, state-of-mind. Fearing is possible because my existence is determined by a concern for what is, and *what is* is a mode of my existence.

UNDERSTANDING (MODE OF THE POSSIBLE)   (section 31)

Heidegger's analysis of understanding (*Verstehen*) is one of the most important of the entire book. Unless one fully grasps how understanding operates in Heidegger's interpretation, the very foundation of fundamental ontology must remain merely assumed and unexamined. It is easy enough to see, though, why a close and careful reading of understanding is difficult. Heidegger himself does not point to it explicitly as the major section to be read. Indeed, the topic heading is listed merely as one among many aspects in the existential analytic. But it is in this relatively short section that Heidegger explains *interpretation*; and he insists on seeing *Being and Time* as an interpretation of the question of existence. This is the reason why this commentary regards section 31 as the key to *Being and Time*, and the discussion in Chapter II, above, regarding the Introductions presumed it.

Understanding is crucial for three reasons: (1) it provides an account, within the existential analytic, of how Dasein is aware of possibilities; (2) it provides the basis for Heidegger's theory of interpretation; and (3) it provides the basis for Heidegger's theory of freedom, which is developed as a central theme in *Of the Essence of Ground (Vom Wesen des Grundes)*, a work published two years after *Being and Time*. Heidegger's theory of understanding is also in conflict with many traditional epistemological theories, in that it opts for the priority of possibility over actuality.

A close look at some of the terms that Heidegger uses may be helpful. Heidegger claims that understanding is an existential. Hence as we have seen, this means that it is *a priori* and that it reveals the manner in which Dasein exists. Already, then, it should be obvious that understanding is not something restricted to the mind's cognitive activities. It not only tells us how we think but how we are: indeed, thinking is merely one function of Being. Understanding first reveals to Dasein its existence-structure, and only through such revelation can Dasein use this existential in its purely cognitive function.

How, then, does understanding reveal to Dasein its mode of existing? By making Dasein *able-to-be*. The term that Macquarrie and Robinson translate as "potentiality-for-Being" is, in German, *Seinkönnen*, which literally means "to be able to be." Again, in this case, I think the more literal translation would have been preferable. In any event, the word "potentiality" in this translation must *not* be read in an Aristotelian sense. What Heidegger means by the term is more important than how one translates it; and its meaning requires greater analysis than a mere word substitution. Let us just consider this phrase: "to be able to be." As a human existent, my ability to be is something of which I am aware. Hence it is not merely the case that I am a thing present-at-hand in the universe. My own existence is a possibility stretching out before me, about which I concern myself, and over which I have some control. I not only exist, but my *ability to exist* is a part of my mode of existing. Now one might here object that such a claim borders on the monstrous. One might argue that it is meaningless to say that anything that exists can exist. By the very fact that one exists, the *ability* to exist has already been made supremely trivial. One does not talk about an existing telephone or washtub as being able to exist; for since everything that is actual is necessarily possible, to speak of the possibility of an actual thing is about as silly as painting the sign "This thing is here" on an obvious object.

The point is, of course, that neither washtubs nor telephones are conscious of themselves, and that to reflect upon my ability to exist does *not* simply mean that I recognize the *logical* possibility of myself as entailed in my actual existence. It is important, though, to ask: Granted that I am *aware* of possibilities, how is this awareness possible? Heidegger's answer is significant: I know of possibilities because I *have* possibilities. According to Heidegger, understanding is rooted in one's ability-to-be: *Seinkönnen*. It is not the case that the cognitive "mind" first abstractly considers possibilities and then "applies" them to the living situation; for one can always ask: How did the possibilities come to be known? Heidegger insists that I cannot "know" possibilities without "having" possibilities. He does not deny, of course, that having possibilities *cannot* occur without some kind of awareness of them.

Heidegger describes the function of understanding as projection (*Entwurf*: "throwing forward"). In order to understand this term, a reanalysis of how Heidegger has interpreted the "world" may be required, for he makes use of a very important concept—i.e., the aspect of for-the-sake-of, which occurs in one's relating to the world and which in turn explains "projection."

If we recall Heidegger's description of the first-order awareness of how Dasein relates to the world, we will remember that he describes this relationship as ready-at-hand. By this Heidegger means that one first relates to the world in terms of seeing the world as something to use. This means that Dasein sees the world *for Dasein's own sake*. If I "see" the door handle merely as a moment in my activity of opening the door, such a "seeing" reduces the door handle to something existing for my sake. In order for the world to be of such service to me, however, it must be seen as presenting itself to me for the sake of what I am about to *do*. The doorlatch is significant to me basically only in terms of my projected opening of the door. Hence, so seen, the world is significant as it presents itself to my projects, my plans, my possibilities. Even to see the world not as ready-at-hand but as *present-at-hand* is likewise *for my sake*; such an attitude is assumed for a reason—i.e., to increase my knowledge.

But if Heidegger's analysis of the world is correct, then the world presents itself to us not as simple, actual things; but as possible ways of service. The world is my project—it is, in one sense, always a kind of future world, yet to be realized.

Understanding operates, then, by projecting before Dasein its possibilities. It can do this because Dasein is such as to have possibilities. The world does not, as we have just seen, present to Dasein an aggregate of indifferent objects; rather, it presents to Dasein a series of service possibilities. The world, then, presents to me not so much actualities as possibilities. Rather than being free because I consider possibilities, I consider possibilities because I am free. The great import of this analysis is that the ability to have possibilities is not *added on* by some special faculty to a "world" made up of indifferent actual objects present-at-hand.

What Heidegger is claiming here must be understood in its full import. His theory of understanding is a very serious challenge to traditional epistemology, which sees the cognitive functions of mind operating independently of such considerations as one's freedom and capability of choice. Heidegger is insisting that the purely cognitive functions of understanding are generated from the existential awareness of possibilities, and that this awareness itself is based on being able to exist in various ways.

Can this be argued for in any way? Since the task of the existential analytic is merely to describe the manner in which the existentials function, Heidegger does not give any *arguments* for showing that the cognitive functions of understanding can be traced to the existential properties. But such argumentation is easy enough to consider. The reader may wish to exercise his acumen on how one uses that sacred principle of all reasoning: the law of noncontradiction. How do I know, for example, that proposition p is not inconsistent with proposition q? If I can think p and think q together without any violation of reasoning, I say p is not inconsistent with q. "*If I can . . .*" means that the very determination of the logical principle is based upon my having possibilities. This may be made clearer in a more concrete example. Suppose, in order to illustrate the meaning of the terms "contingent" and "necessary" to an undergraduate class, I ask them the question: "Is it *necessary* that this wall be painted blue?" The answer, of course, is no. It could be painted green. Thus we say the color of the wall is a contingent fact, not a necessary one. But how do we know that the blueness of the wall is not necessary? *Because I can think of it otherwise.* It is *in fact* blue, but it *need not* be blue, because I am capable of thinking in a way that is *not* determined by what *is* the case. On the other hand, I argue that a circle necessarily has 360 degrees because I *cannot* think of a circle in any other way except that it has so many degrees. The limits of what I can do determine the laws of logic. The term "can," indeed, means "to be able." In fact, the analysis of how reasoning operates logically shows that the *ability* of what I *can do* with my cognitive powers comes before the determination of the principles of reasoning. To be sure, such "abilities" do not occur without cognitive awareness.

Understanding operates by projecting possibilities. For Heidegger, projection is itself an existential. This means that to throw before ourselves our own possible ways of existing is an essential characteristic of what we are. It is as if understanding were like a searchlight, illuminating what lay before Dasein. But in one sense the searchlight image is wrong, for that which is illuminated and projected before Dasein is Dasein itself. This may seem a bit confusing at first reading, but there is no inconsistency here. Heidegger specifically argues that Dasein is more than what it *factually* is, but not more than what it *factically* is. The latter term refers to Dasein's ontological existence, the former term merely to its ontical present-at-hand existence. Ontical presence-at-hand is limited to the actual—i.e., what determines ontical cognition are facts seen independently of their possibilities. But ontological considerations must always take into account possibilities. Hence the factical (ontological) account of Dasein's existence must consider how Dasein is significant in terms of its projects. Phenomenologically, of course, there seems to be a great deal to such an analysis. Surely what I am right now makes sense to me only in terms of my looking ahead. When I begin this sentence, the completion of the sentence is more significant to me than the few words I have already written. A more obvious example of this is the melodic pattern of notes that becomes significant in terms of its expected resolution. The beauty of a fugue simply cannot be accounted for without consideration of the listener's expectation and even surprise. (Surprise, of course, is meaningless without first having an expectation of something other than what occurs.) When one claims that a "particular note" in a piece is one's favorite moment in the music, it is obvious that one is not referring to the simple *sound* of that one note, but rather to the fact that the note occurs in a pattern of other notes; and that, indeed, the very *expectation* of the composer's resolution is what thrills the mind. It is the choice the composer makes among many possible choices that is significant and has meaning. At times, indeed, it is the unplayed suggested note that is the most beautiful.

In speaking of expectation and pattern, of course, one feels the need for an analysis of how the temporal elements operate in the existential analytic. In section 68 Heidegger completely reexamines these functions of understanding in terms of time. But for the present, Heidegger's analysis is merely a phenomenological account of how understanding operates through projection. The ontological basis of such operation in the various modes of temporal experience can be discovered only after the entire phenomenological account is complete.

One of the most philosophically important claims made by Heidegger in this analysis is that possibilities are known because of our being possible. Such a claim places knowing and existing in much closer relation than is found in most philosophers. It is because the traditional way of describing the knowing process has usually maintained some sort of subject-object explanation that Heidegger's account sounds so strange. At the risk of disturbing much of the delicate subtlety of Heidegger's account through oversimplification, I would like to present his view in the following way:

If one considers what might be called "pure cognition," there is an epistemological difficulty. "Pure cognition," if it does not have an object, cannot tell us *about* anything, for if it did, that about which such cognition would tell us something would be in addition to the cognitive act, and hence the act would not be "pure." This is a Kantian doctrine. Kant asks: Where are the objects of such concepts as God, freedom, and immortality? We have no sense experience of them; hence they cannot be proved to exist. (They may, according to Kant, nevertheless be *useful* and even, in a moral sense, necessary.) Suppose we take, not the Kantian ideas, but the simple procedure of the mind's ability to consider possibilities. If possibility is due to sheer cognitive functions without any experience or objects, then they cannot be *known* in the strictest sense. Yet, as we have seen, possibilities lie at the very foundation of thinking and knowing, as in the case of the law of contradiction. If one tries to argue that possibilities are somehow *extracted* from experience, such an argument misleads the inquiry. For experiences are always actual, and what must be asked is how such abstraction is possible. What are the *a priori* functions of mind that enable one to abstract from a given, concrete experience a mode of thinking that somehow hovers or suspends itself in indefinite enlightenment over a fact?

For Heidegger, possibilities become available to the inquirer neither through pure cognition nor through experience. Rather, they become available to the inquirer through the *existence*-structure of the inquirer himself. Possibility is not something experienced (for we experience only actualities), nor is it something purely thought (for possibility is not the *result* of thinking since thinking itself presupposes it). Rather, possibility is part and parcel of the very existence of one who thinks. To be able to think of what can be, one must *be able to be*, as such. The results of such a doctrine are, of course, many. Above all, though, we must recognize that if Heidegger's account is accurate, a purely cognitive account of epistemology cannot be made. The always difficult problem of how mind relates to body, or of how ideas and ideals relate to facts, has now been grounded in existence. Plato, Kant, and other idealists have often pointed out that pure unaided reason can tell us what *ought to be*, while reason along with the senses can tell us what *is*. But their answers to how one relates the two realms are always somewhat murky and obscure. Kant's solution to the problem is hope and the teleological judgment. Heidegger's "solution" is existence. Of course, for Heidegger there is never any problem in the first place, since even pure reason is impossible without existential significance: I think of possibilities because I have possibilities and because I find myself to be a nest of possibilities.

The oft-heard protest against the lack of significance that philosophy has for "life" is, in this account, simply without basis. Built right into the very philosophical account of one's mind is one's own existence. There is no "step" to be taken between what is abstractly conceived in mind and what is concretely felt or lived in existence, for "existence" is already included in the account of how thought is possible. Heidegger, in laying the groundwork for his analysis of what understanding means, points out the German use of "understanding" that means "to have control over."[2] What one has control over in this case, he points out, is one's own existence. (One can see why "determinate resoluteness" will ultimately be the chief characteristic of authentic existence. One can also now understand why Heidegger provides the seed from which such later "existentialist" phrases as "the courage to be"[3] and "the freedom of self-deception" took root.)

There is much more, of course, to be said about understanding. But before we proceed, perhaps a brief summing up of some of the more salient points may be helpful.

1. For Heidegger, the cognitive faculties of understanding are based on and are secondary to the existential aspects.
2. Understanding operates through a projection of possibilities. What is projected is the entire range of Dasein's *own* possibilities.
3. I can think possibilities because I have possibilities.

2. Cf. *Being and Time*, p. 183, note.

3. *The Courage To Be* (New Haven: Yale University Press, 1952) is the title of a book by Paul Tillich, which is greatly influenced by Heidegger. "The freedom of self-deception" is a phrase used often by Sartre in his analysis of *mauvaise foi* in *Being and Nothingness* (trans. Hazel Barnes [New York: Philosophy Library, 1956]).

4. Dasein is always factically more than what Dasein factually is. (I am more in terms of my possibilities than in terms of my actuality.)
5. One of the chief results of this analysis is a much closer relationship between thinking and being. This result will be one of the bases for the way in which Heidegger's own philosophy can be accounted for.

Let us go back for a moment to the general location of this analysis in *Being and Time*. Heidegger is explaining how Dasein becomes aware of itself in a world. What must be analyzed is the *Da* ("here") in Dasein ("to be here"). Dasein finds itself in a world in two ways: (1) Through state-of-mind, a mode of existence that reveals to Dasein its *facticity*. In this mode, Dasein becomes aware of the givenness of the world and the thrownness of Dasein. (2) Through understanding, a mode of existence that reveals to Dasein its *existence*. In this mode, Dasein becomes aware of possibilities. These possibilities, however, are always Dasein's own possibilities. Hence the existential meaning of possibility is prior to the cognitive meaning.

Heidegger claims that Dasein's awareness of its facticity through state-of-mind and its existence through understanding are equally primordial. That I am in a world as it is, and that I exist in such a way as to have possibilities, are equally primary in my awareness of myself as a person in the world. The one cannot be reduced to the terms or dimensions of the other. No matter how free I am, nor how rich my comprehension of my ability to be in various ways, I am still *thrown* into the world, and I am still faced with the inevitable and unchangeable. On the other hand, no matter how oppressed I am by this thrownness and givenness, I cannot avoid my own freedom or deny the genuine reality of possibilities. (Sartre expresses this idea by saying that I am a slave of my freedom; I am *bound* to be free.)

What has Heidegger done in analyzing these two elements of the "here"? The analysis thus far is as yet wholly phenomenological. All Heidegger has done thus far is to *describe* his interpretation of the manner in which one's self-reflection reveals the two modes of existence. In so doing he has avoided, as yet, the ontological grounds for such analyses. These grounds will be analyzed in Division Two, where time will be seen as the determining factor in this account. We are not as yet ready, however, to turn to the more ontological account.

The reader may perhaps feel somewhat unsatisfied with Heidegger's rendition of understanding as a projection of possibilities. For one might well ask, Is that all there is to understanding? Surely when I "understand" something I am doing more than merely projecting possibilities in terms of something. Heidegger has shown that the *existential* characteristics of understanding are prior to those of the cognitive. But how does understanding operate *cognitively*? Surely the simple account of the existential basis of understanding as the projection of possibilities does not tell me how I come to understand a problem or a series of events. Or to put the problem another way: the simple *ontological* account of understanding, which may indeed be primordial, does not in itself render a satisfactory account of the *epistemological* role of understanding.

In one sense, of course, one must not overemphasize the break between epistemology and ontology, for that would be contrary to the whole spirit of the Heideggerian enterprise. It is nevertheless a meaningful question to ask of Heidegger how understanding operates as a vehicle of the knowing inquiry. His answer to this is his description of understanding as interpretation.

UNDERSTANDING AS INTERPRETATION (section 32)

One of the first things Heidegger emphasizes in turning to the question of interpretation is that one must not see the "interpretive" function of understanding as something "extra" or as something that understanding does only under certain special circumstances. In fact, he seems to say that without interpretation, understanding is not complete (E-185/ G-148). This suggests that there is never a case in which one is capable of having possibilities without being somehow aware of them, or conversely, capable of being aware of possibilities without having possibilities.

The procedure of analysis that Heidegger has followed in his account of understanding is typical of the entire existential analytic, and it reflects his methodology. Earlier we noted that the existential analytic is possible because Dasein is aware of its existence, and that fundamental ontology is based upon a hermeneutic inquiry into the modes of one's ways of Being, or better, ways to be. We now see this clearly revealed in the case of understanding. Rather than beginning with an account of how one *knows* possibilities, and from there proceeding to an account of how these possibilities *apply* to one's existence, Heidegger has begun with an account of how one's *possible ways to be* reveal themselves, and from there he proceeds to the account of how this manner of existing becomes manifest as meaningful assertions. In other words, my existence precedes my "knowing" of it. This is why an account of interpretation must come *after* the account given in the preceding section about being possible.

The term "interpretation," then, means the function of understanding that makes explicit what we, as existing beings, already *are* simply because we do exist. Heidegger points out that understanding functions through the projection of possibilities. In interpretation, understanding *works out* this projection. What understanding projects, interpretation works out.

Being and Time, is, according to Heidegger, an interpretation of what it means to be. Thus the procedure he outlines for interpretation in general reveals much of the manner and procedure of his own thought. In fact, in a later section (63) he explicitly uses the outline of interpretation in general and applies it directly to the question of what it means to be: the Being question. In following the structure of *Being and Time* I shall likewise delay the application of these general characteristics of interpretation to the specific question of what it means to be; but the reader should be warned in advance that the general description given in this section will be used later to reveal how one can render an interpretation of the question of Being.

Interpretation is the "working out" of the possibilities projected by understanding. This means that the chief function of interpretation is to *make explicit* what is already within the range of human awareness. This corresponds to the normal English usage of the term "interpretation," for one usually speaks of interpreting things that one has already seen or heard. The German term is *Auslegung*, which is literally a "laying out." One cannot "lay out" what one does not already have in some way. Hence Heidegger's account of interpretation is an account that focuses on the ability of the mind to make explicit and to reveal what is somehow already within one's experience. We have already discovered the mode that provides us with the data, so to speak, to be interpreted: it is the world as we see it as environment; the world as it is available to us. In short, what is interpreted is the world, already given to us in the mode of ready-at-hand.

There are three basic considerations that make up Heidegger's account of interpretation: (1) the as-structure, (2) the fore-structure, and (3) meaning. All of these considerations are used by Heidegger to reveal how Dasein, through understanding's projection of possibilities, makes explicit to us what is to be interpreted.

The As-Structure   (section 32)

If one claims that a furnace *as* a furnace must give off heat, one is *interpreting* a furnace, or more exactly, one's *relation* to a furnace, which is all that the term "furnace" really signifies. This means, then, that interpretation is making explicit the *as*. If we consider the furnace example, it should be clear that when one does make explicit the as-structure of something, one is pointing out the purpose or usability of that thing.

When I argue, for example, that a particular device is not really a furnace, because it does not function *as* a furnace—i.e., it does not give off heat—I am making explicit what is understood in the everyday and primordial way in which one deals with furnaces. No matter how much a certain object may look like a furnace, or be in a location suitable for furnaces, unless it can function *as* a furnace it cannot properly be said *to be* a furnace. Such obvious insights should not lose their ontological significance merely because they seem so basic. The main point of this is that the as-structure of our understanding is based on our seeing the world as ready-at-hand, and *not* as something present-at-hand. Heidegger speaks of the in-order-to that is present within the world. For example, we say that a furnace is built *in order to* make heat. This in-order-to (*Um-zu*), however, obviously comes from the world as ready-at-hand. It is only because I am quite familiar with doorlatches as something with which to open doors that I can interpret a doorlatch *as* a doorlatch in terms of its in-order-to-open-a-door. One does not take an object abstractly and uncaringly, and *add on to it* a peculiar kind of meaning. I do not take a piece of brass and decide to bestow it with the significance of opening doors. As Heidegger points out, the more I just look at an object and do not use it, the *further* away I become from its proper meaning. Thus when I interpret something, I do not add on to an experience an external meaning or significance. Rather, I simply *make clear* what is already there. Furthermore, what is *already there* in the case of the World's objects is the manner and purpose for which I make use of them. Interpretation, then, is simply articulating or emphasizing the in-order-to of a particular object, which is to see the object *as* that object.

The Fore-Structure   (section 32)

To interpret means to expose or clarify the as-structure. As we have seen, this requires that there be aspects of that which is interpreted already in advance of the actual moment of interpretation. Every interpretation is grounded in a fore-having (*Vorhabe*), a foresight (*Vorsicht*), and a fore-conception (*Vorgriff*). Heidegger explains these three elements in unusually terse and economical terms. His entire analysis of all three terms takes up less than a page. Since later on he will make use of these terms to describe his analysis of the question of Being, I explicate them more fully here.

When one is in a hurry to get from one place to another, let us say from one's home to the university, the use one makes of an automobile in such cases is simply to relate to it as a means of conveyance. In such an activity, the various parts of the automobile have little or no independent meaning. Although it is surely true that the spark plugs are terribly important for the successful operation of the machine, the hurried driver is simply not aware of their existence. In fact, as long as nothing goes wrong, the driver probably does not even consider the car *as* a car. His mind is elsewhere. The total involvement that the driver has to all the many parts and functions of the automobile *as tools* of his conveyance are summed up in this account by the term "fore-having." What I have in advance of my interpretation at all is the total range of ways in which I relate to the object being interpreted in terms of its particular in-order-that. This becomes clearer when these relationships are made explicit by circumstances that force one to consider their as-structure. In the case of the automobile, for example, when the hurried professor or student on his way to the university discovers that the machine won't start, he directs his attention to the possible sources of trouble—to the *lack* of proper functioning, which would never attract attention if it were working properly. But the battery, ignition system, and the linking wires between these systems all make sense only in the context of the general purpose of the automobile: to provide transportation. When the hurried driver comes to consider the battery or ignition system explicitly, *it is already in context.* The context within which the battery is significant is the broader context of the car's significance. (The car's significance is, of course, further contained in an even broader range of significance.) The entire, given situation of the hurried man, his concern for being on time for the lecture, his estimation of how long it will take him to get there, etc., all focus upon the ability of the car to get him there. The battery in the car takes significance from this ability. The water level in the battery takes its significance from the ability of a battery to provide electrical power, and so on. Interpretation, which is the awareness of the as-structure, does not occur unless something forces one to *become aware* of the as-structure. The battery *as* battery is forced upon one's attention through the failure of the automobile to operate. Certainly one could not repair the stalled automobile if one did not realize that the purpose of the battery was to supply the necessary electric impulses. What Heidegger means by "fore-having" is that, in interpretation, such prior awareness as to the function and purpose of the parts is necessary in order for the as-structure to become explicit.

If we return to the example of the hurried student confronted with a stalled automobile, we can see further that, even within the very general and broad range of conveyance, as soon as he recognizes that the automobile won't start, his attention is directed toward more specific functions within the machine, which are based on his knowledge of how the machine operates. Thus, when the car won't start, he turns his attention to the general ignition system, in which the starter, the battery, and the connecting wires all have significance. This first step in the isolation of the possible problem area is called "fore-sight" by Heidegger. He describes it as taking the "first cut" (E-191/G-150) of the fore-having. An alternative translation of *Vorsicht* might be "point-of-view." One must not make the mistake, though, of seeing the fore-sight as something that occurs in a special manner after one has reflected on the fore-having. The fore-sight and the fore-having are both in advance of one's focusing on the explicit as-structure. Even before I turn my attention to the solution of the problem of the stalled automobile, I have a previous point of view or fore-sight that allows me to direct my attention to the electrical system. Fore-sight, as a moment in the development of interpretation, is a part of what is generally had in advance, and through which the articulation of the as-structure is possible.

The same can be said for fore-conception. A fore-conception is that by which one tends to interpret the phenomena. The function of the fore-sight is to direct our attention to the specific problem area, whereas the fore-conception functions in terms of a conception by which the as-structure will be made explicit. In the example of the stalled automobile, the fore-conception would be that attitude or disposition in the mind of the driver which would lead him to interpret the failure of the car to start as an electrical problem. That is, the as-structure is, in the fore-conception, made explicit. (The car is not functioning *as* a car because it won't start. The starter, *as* a starter, is not functioning, either because of its own disability or because the battery *as* battery is not providing it with enough power.) The really important factor in this analysis is that the fore-structure comes from Dasein's involvement in the world as ready-at-hand; *not* as a purely calculative function of the present-at-hand.

In every interpretation, then, there is a fore-having, a fore-sight, and a fore-conception, based on Dasein's *use* of the world as ready-at-hand. This is true of the interpretation of the question of Being, which Heidegger spells out in section 63. Interpretation is the articulation or the making-explicit of the as-structure projected by the understanding. This structure, then, will be very important for the reader when Heidegger spells out how an understanding and interpretation of what it means to be is possible.

Meaning (section 32)

It was pointed out that a furnace, *as* a furnace, has to give off heat. We now can say that the *meaning* of a furnace is to give off heat. Meaning, then, is understanding becoming aware of the as-structure. When one understands the meaning of an act, one understands that act *as* that act—i.e., in terms of its purpose or its use. If one understands the meaning of a kiss, one understands the kiss *as* a kiss—i.e., in terms of its purpose: to demonstrate affection. Such an analysis of meaning seems terribly oversimple and naïve. But it is deceptive in its simplicity. And for Heidegger, it is crucial to his whole investigation. For such a rendition of meaning places the focal point of meaning not in the words, but in Dasein.

There is a large and impressive tradition, especially in English-speaking countries, that would take serious issue with this claim of Heidegger's. It is usually thought or argued that only words or propositions have meaning. In order for an act or occurrence in the world to have meaning attributed to it, it must first be articulated in some form or another. Heidegger, however, denies this. His claim is that word-meaning is a derivative form of meaning. In the subsequent section (33) of *Being and Time* Heidegger spells this out quite clearly. In light of this dispute, it must be made clear exactly how Heidegger makes use of the term "meaning" and what it signifies.

The locus of the term is important. The heading of the general section under which the discussion of meaning occurs is "The Existential Constitution of the 'Here'" (section 29–34). Meaning, then, is a part of Dasein's "here" in its general "Being here in the world." In words less tied to the jargon, this means: Dasein is a person in the world, with constant and often uncritical use of its elements and parts. A part of this familiarity with the world (and hence not *separate* from it) is the fact that I can at times focus upon the ways in which I make use of the world. When such focusing occurs, the specific manner in which that part of the world becomes available to me (the as-structure) is made explicit. When such explication occurs, I say that the way in which I make use of the world is *meaningful*. Meaning, then, is a mode of my Being here in a world.

If we examine even more carefully the locus of meaning in the existential analytic, we find that it is, specifically, a part of understanding as projection. It is not something "added on" to understanding when one puts the projections and interpretations into words; rather, it is the *a priori* characteristic of meaning that allows such putting into words in the first place. One does not first express one's interpretations in words, and then find meaning in the words; rather, one first has meaning, and then expresses that meaning verbally.

A consequence of this teaching is that only Dasein—i.e., only that which is aware of possibilities and sees the world as ready-at-hand—can have meaning. When Heidegger says that only Dasein has meaning, he is including the negative form of "meaning," which is "meaningless." Dasein, and Dasein alone, is either meaningful or meaningless. Dasein, though, can never be absurd. The world other than Dasein can be absurd. This may at first seem like verbal playing, but the terms have almost technical significance, and should be kept clearly separate. "Absurd" (*widersinnig*) means totally outside the realm of possible meaning (literally, *wider*: "against," *sinn*: "meaning"—against meaning). Only something other than Dasein can be absurd, because Dasein is always the ground for its own explanation. One can, and often does, violate one's sense of self-awareness, but such an act is merely senseless or meaningless, it is not absurd.

Heidegger italicizes his interpretation of meaning. Altering slightly Macquarrie and Robinson's translation, we read: "*Meaning is the 'upon which' of a projection, and is structured on the fore-having, fore-sight, and fore-conception, in terms of which something, as something, becomes understandable.*"[4] Let us look more closely at this view of meaning.

Meaning takes its structure from what is *already* there (the fore-structure), Dasein's relating to the world as available for its use (the world as ready-at-hand). For something to have meaning, then, means for something to be made explicit in terms of its service toward Dasein. But the "something" in this case, since it is in the mode of ready-at-hand and not abstractly conceived as present-at-hand, is a mode of Dasein's *using*. Hence *a particular use by Dasein is revealed to Dasein by Dasein in terms of its function for Dasein.*

Abstractly stated it may seem a bit difficult to swallow. Consider, though, an example. Suppose a young man, named Peter, has a friend named David. After one particularly friendly kind of shared activity, David shakes Peter's hand in a gesture of friendship. Peter feels and enjoys the warmth and pleasure of this, and on his way home he reflects: What did the handshake mean? The handshake, we say, was a gesture of friendship. This is its *meaning*. It is an activity engaged in *by* Peter; it was through Peter's already existing friendship that the meaning was revealed *to* him; the significance of the act was interpreted *by* Peter; and the act was done *for the sake of* Peter. We do not say that the handshake *is* the friendship, nor do we claim that the term "handshake" can be analyzed by itself to reveal the meaning of what happened. We do say that the meaning of the handshake is structured on something already there, and that it is interpreted by making explicit that which was already there. Only *after* such an interpretive reflection can words be utilized to *express* the meaning. There are, of course, certain actions and words that themselves function as a kind of relating that do not need a prior activity to justify them or explain them. The so-called performative utterances ("I hereby promise that . . .") would be a case in point. But even in such cases

4. Cf. *Being and Time*, p. 193.

what has meaning is not the word but that *upon which* certain possibilities are projected. (For we often say: "When you promise me something, that means that *even if* it is difficult, you will fulfill your promise." Thus the *meaning* of promising is a kind of projection of possible activity—i.e., the conditions under which one will do or not do what one has said one will do.)

Meaning, then, for Heidegger cannot be analyzed solely within an epistemological inquiry. Nor does it apply primarily to words or sentences. Instead meaning is a way of existing, a mode of one's being able to be. Meaning is thus located within the ontological inquiry. We have seen Heidegger leading up to this throughout the entire existential analytic. But it is with Heidegger's interpretation of meaning that his break with the epistemology of the Neo-Kantians is complete. That some of the English-speaking linguistic analysts are in basic disagreement would be a mild truism.

The chief characteristics of Heidegger's theory of meaning, then, are these:

1. Meaning refers to a condition of Dasein, not to words or sentences.
2. Meaning is the result of the projection of possibilities in terms of the as-structure.
3. Meaning takes its ultimate ground from the world as ready-at-hand (*zuhanden*) rather than present-at-hand (*vorhanden*).
4. Verbal meaning is a derivative form of existential meaning. This last point is made more specific in the following section of *Being and Time*.

Heidegger next reflects upon a possible objection that may be made against his account. He asks: If meaning is structured on what is already present in Dasein's relating to the world, then don't we have a vicious circle? Are we not interpreting what is *already* known, and so why interpret? A similar complaint was made of Socrates in Plato's dialogue *Meno*:

MENO: And how will you inquire, Socrates, into that which you do not know? What will you put forth as the subject of inquiry? And even if you find out what you want, how will you ever know that this is the thing which you did not know?

SOCRATES: . . . you argue that a man cannot inquire either about that which he knows, nor that which he does not know: for if he knows, he has no need to inquire, and if not, he cannot,

> for he does not know the very subject about which he is
> to inquire.
>
> Meno, 80b

Like Plato, Heidegger does not feel that the problem of circular reasoning
is an idle protest. He takes the circular structure of interpretation seriously. He does not feel that it is a vicious circle, to be sure; but that it
is a circle he insists upon. There is a rather easy solution, of course: Although I am aware of what I inquire about or interpret, the inquiry or
interpretation makes clearer or more explicit what I was only vaguely
aware of before the inquiry. The only difficulty with such a "solution"
is that it merely locates the problem. The question then becomes: How
does this "making explicit" take place? That, of course, is the problem
on which Heidegger's analysis of interpretation is meant to throw considerable light.

In no less than three separate sections Heidegger comments on the circular nature of his interpretation.[5] The circularity of interpretation is of
great importance when Heidegger applies this structure to the specific
problem of what it means to be (cf. p. 173). The application of the structure of interpretation to the specific question of *Being and Time* is, of
course, one of the main reasons why Heidegger places such emphasis on
grounding his analysis firmly in his account of Dasein. At several points
throughout his discussion of interpretation in general he drops hints of
its application to the question of Being. This should not be lost on the
reader. The structure of *Being and Time*, however, requires that the existential analytic be completed before the ontological grounds are considered.

The consideration of Heidegger's theory of meaning and interpretation, requires that the following question be posed: Why does Heidegger
ground interpretation and meaning in *readiness*-at-hand rather than
presence-at-hand? Heidegger shows that meaning and interpretation take
their significance in readiness-at-hand because he wants to argue that at
no time does Dasein understand the meaning of something independently
of Dasein's existential awareness. If by "objective meaning" one means
a significance totally without *any* subjective, existential influences, then
Heidegger would deny the possibility of such meaning. Thus the scientific
model of knowledge as the paradigm case of how we know is misleading,
if not downright inaccurate. Furthermore, by grounding both interpretation and meaning in readiness-at-hand, Heidegger has paved the way for
an account of how the meaning of "to be" can be interpreted. For if all

---

5. Cf. *Being and Time*, pp. 152, 314, 432.

forms of interpretation consist in the explication of the as-structure of how one exists in particular modes, then the theme of existence as such is likewise available for interpretation. For the "as" is simply shifted from a particular instance of existence, to the question of existence *as* existence.

The task of *Being and Time* is, after all, to elucidate what it means to be (*Sinn von Sein*). In order for such elucidation to be made clear, a proper understanding of the existential, meaning, must be fully grasped.

ASSERTION AND INTERPRETATION   (section 33)

Heidegger's purpose in this section is to spell out explicitly what has now become almost a central doctrine of the existential analytic: truth cannot be realized by a simple listing of "true" propositions. To be sure, the thematic analysis of "truth" has not up to this point been made explicit. And even in this section, the reader is clearly informed that Heidegger is not yet ready to examine fully the phenomenon of truth. Nevertheless, we have already seen that meaning is not primordially a matter of judgment or propositions, but of existence. That "truth" will likewise find its primary ground not in sentences but in existence will not, then, come as any kind of shock.

Judgments, however, *do* have meaning, if only in a derivative sense. One can derive assertive or propositional meaning from existential meaning. When one does this, however, an important shift occurs, and what becomes interpreted in the as-structure is no longer the world as ready-at-hand, but the world as present-at-hand. This shift from ready-at-hand to present-at-hand is a change from seeing something *as it is used or available*, to seeing something *as it is known merely theoretically*. The first "as" Heidegger calls *hermeneutical*, the second, *apophantical*. The hermeneutical "as" occurs, for example, when I "see" or "interpret" the hammer *as* something to drive a nail into wood. The apophantical "as" is to "see" or "interpret" the hammer *as* an object that is simply there in the world, with certain "characteristics" that can be attributed to it. The danger lies in the fact that when judgments or propositions are analyzed, they are often treated solely in terms of the apophantical "as," which leaves the existentially significant hermeneutical "as" without any possible opening to the critical inquiry. If one limits oneself to the strictly apophantical use of language analysis, one's very starting point excludes the possibility of fundamental ontology. Some attempts may be made to add on certain existentially meaningful characteristics, but such "adding on" does not belong to the cognitive meaning, and they are usually treated as emotional additives, unworthy of philosophical accuracy.

If Heidegger's analysis is correct, however, the existential significance comes first. On what does he base such a claim?

A close look at Heidegger'a analysis of "assertion," taken together with what we already know about meaning and interpretation, reveals why Heidegger insists existential meaning is primordial. Assertion, which Heidegger seems to equate with judgment (and which seems to include the modern logical sense of "proposition"), has three significations. Assertion means: (1) pointing out; (2) predication; and (3) communication. Taking these three together, the term is formally described as "a pointing-out which gives something a definite character and which communicates."[6] Heidegger's analysis of each of the three elements in his "definition" reveals some important points. (1) In showing that the primary meaning of "assertion" is to point out, Heidegger argues that what is pointed out cannot be a representation, but the thing itself (*das Seiende selbst*). For when I "assert" that the hammer is too heavy, I'm not talking about my *concept* of the hammer, theoretically conceived; but rather, I am talking about the hammer *as I use it*, which, as we have seen, is the primary meaning of the hammer. (2) Heidegger also points out that "predication" means to give something a definite character. In doing this, however, I am still "pointing out," but in a narrower and more specific way. Assertion, then, not only points out, it points out a specific or determining characteristic. Again, what is determined by the predicate is not a *representation* of the thing, but the thing in its primary meaning as ready-at-hand. (3) Finally, assertion communicates. But what is communicated is how one can be said *to-be-toward* what is asserted. The abstract theoretical concept is not communicated, but how one relates to its readiness-at-hand. Thus, when I say: "This hammer is too heavy!" I *point out* the hammer, and I focus specific attention on the fact that it is too heavy by the *predicate*, and I *share* or *communicate* with my listener my inability to handle the hammer with ease. What I do *not* do is simply join (by the *copula*) the theoretical and indifferent character of "hammerness" to the theoretical and indifferent character of "heaviness."

As Heidegger describes the basic meaning of assertion, it is still within the primordial realm of ready-at-hand. But when the assertion gets expressed in theoretical terms, it shifts from the hermeneutical ready-at-hand to the apophantical presence-at-hand. Such theoretical activity is, of course, useful in its own right, and is essential for science. But it must never be taken as isolated from its existential roots.

This view of assertion seriously challenges those who would claim

6. Cf. *Being and Time*, p. 199.

that propositional logic somehow is primordial. The full significance of Heidegger's analysis, however, will be made more clear in discussing his theory of truth (cf. p. 127, below).

LANGUAGE (section 34)

If someone were to say to a mother, "Your son is ill," the meaning of that particular moment of human expression could not be analyzed merely by a consideration of the logical and grammatical properties of the particular sentence. Who is saying it, under what conditions, to whom it is said, the personality of the hearer as well as the speaker, all together go to make up what really happens in such a circumstance. An accurate account of what was communicated between the speaker and the hearer must be based upon the existential situation rather than the purely linguistic or even purely logical situation. Heidegger maintains, then, that the basis of language is neither grammar nor logic, but *talk*. Talk (*Rede*), as opposed to language (*Sprache*) in the formal sense, is existentially significant. Talk is essentially a characteristic of human beings interrelating with each other, intrigued by the commerce of things in the world and the many subtle relations with other humans. To maintain, as Heidegger does, that such activity or mode of existence is the basis of language has tremendous consequences for any theory of language. If Heidegger is correct, then any purely formal analysis of language is in principle inadequate. Furthermore, if his account is correct, the locus of truth must be shifted from propositions to the existential basis of such propositions.

The most important aspect of Heidegger's theory of language is this: Sentences are merely the formal expression of the existential manner through which Dasein relates to the world, and as such, sentences are derived and do not carry with them the foundation of human communication. Sentences, in fact, are not even in a secondary position; they are in what might be called a tertiary position. The existential ground is talk. The expression of talk is language. But language is ready-at-hand, it is used. When *it* becomes interpreted theoretically, however, it becomes present-at-hand in the form of words and sentences.

Heidegger's analysis of talk and language is calculated to emphasize what has already been noted in the previous sections concerning meaning and interpretation—i.e., in every case, one must seek out the underlying mode of existence before any adequate discussion of formal relations and theoretical meaning is possible. In this section, Heidegger is determining the very structure of theoretical and formal analysis: language itself. It is, indeed, somewhat alarming that even logic is always based upon a purely abstract and formal consideration of relations that are meaningful only in terms of articulated sentences. But truth does not reside in such formal relations; rather, these relations are made to make explicit what is already there in truth. What Heidegger's account is meant to do is to focus on the existential basis of language (talk) in order to reveal that the purely formal characteristics of human intercourse are indeed derivative. As in the case of his analysis of meaning, this account is also laying the groundwork for his theory of truth.

If talk is the basis of language, then such activities as "hearing" and "keeping silent" belong essentially to the description. For it is in the give-and-take of actual talking that human communication occurs; and such talking also involves listening. What is heard, of course, is not noise that is later "interpreted" as something "meaningful." To describe a moment of hearing as a purely abstract noise is a highly sophisticated kind of "theorizing." When someone speaks to me, I do *not* hear *words*; I hear a message. I can, of course, upon reflection, abstract the words in a theoretical manner, thereby changing the ready-at-hand character of language to the present-at-hand character of words. But in so doing I have left behind much of what occurred in the communication. (A child or uneducated adult is rarely aware of how many "words" there are in a sentence. The sometimes comical spelling of oft-heard phrases demonstrates that a child does not hear isolated words, and more importantly, he does not understand them in such present-at-hand theoretical manner.)

Language is a communication; but it is a communication that is *already there*; it is something we use to make explicit our talking. Talking is a sharing which is always more than what is represented by the explicit verbalization of word language. This does not mean that one cannot communicate with words that which is felt in talking. The point is that a reader of a well written dialogue, for example, does not read only the words. He contributes his own "talk" when he reads. This means that he involves himself, not as a mere viewer of the words on the page, but as a fellow human being for whom the spoken words excite the existential response necessary for talk. Nor is this "emotional." It is only when the existential mode of talking (in the special mode of reading) is achieved that the reader actually understands what is written.

Heidegger's account of talk is necessary, of course, to fill out his description of Dasein as Being-in-the-world. But his account also has "strategic" purposes. By showing that it is not the strict and formal relations between propositions that constitute the basis of language, Heidegger has also explained, to some extent, his own philosophical procedure. If Heidegger's account is correct, of course, no philosophical position based purely on propositional language can challenge Heidegger's existential account. This is not to say that Heidegger has made it impossible for someone to point out logical errors or even to come up with a superior view. But such a superior view will have to render an existential and not merely a linguistic account. This, of course, is predicated on the belief that philosophers are interested in truth; and the locus of truth is a very important philosophical problem. Heidegger's main point is that truth does not reside in the purely formal or logical characteristics of propositions. This will become more fully explicated in the discussion of Heidegger's analysis of the phenomenon of truth.

With Heidegger's analysis of talk, his interpretation or analysis of Dasein's "here" in the world is complete. We have seen that Dasein has significance both in terms of its actually "thrown" state and in terms of its possibilities. Dasein is never simply actual or simply possible, but both possibility and actuality are equally significant to it. Its awareness of it in terms of these two ways are state-of-mind and understanding. The significance of both modes can be made explicit in language, the basis of which is existential talking. Heidegger, however, is not yet ready to abandon his consideration of everyday Dasein. Before he turns to the final and unitary existential, care, he first exposes more fully the mode of the self that prompted the entire analysis, the "they."

EVERYDAYNESS AND FALLING   (sections 35–38)

A few sections of *Being and Time*, though very important and far-reaching, need little explanation. Sections 35–38 are a case in point. Heidegger's fine phenomenological account provides little difficulty and I shall simply give a brief explanation of the major terms and present a few remarks.

Fallenness   *(section 35)*

Fallenness (*Verfallen*) is the general characteristic reflected in more specific detail by idle talk, ambiguity, and curiosity. As Heidegger emphasizes, it must not be seen as anything reprehensible or "sinful." Its existential significance is that one quite frequently loses one's awareness of oneself by one's absorption in the inauthenticity of the anonymous "they." The greater ontological significance, however, lies in the fact that this very mode of inauthenticity can, upon analysis, reveal that from which one has fallen—i.e., the authentic awareness of the self. This aspect is not developed in the present chapter, of course; but its importance can well be pointed out to the reader. In its simplest form, *fallenness is the nonawareness of what it means to be.*

Idle Talk (*section 35*)

> ... And we sit and drink our coffee
> Couched in our indifference
> Like shells upon the shore
> You can hear the ocean roar
> In the dangling conversation
> And the superficial sighs
> The borders of our lives ....
>
> Yes we speak the things that matter
> With words that must be said
> 'Can analysis be worthwhile
> 'Is the theatre really dead ...
> You're a stranger now unto me
> Lost in the dangling conversation
> And the superficial sighs
> In the borders of our lives.[7]

The lyrics of this beautiful song by Paul Simon depict a conversation, or an attempt at one, that could only be called inauthentic. Idle talk is like this conversation; though idle talk also refers to those modes of expression that are less obviously inauthentic: the chattering enthusiasm of those who find everything in the world "interesting" but never relevant. The noncommittal and hated "That's interesting!" often suggests a kind of unconcern that is far more unpalatable than a direct statement of dislike. Idle talk also refers to those who constantly present a great number of facts and statistics as substitute for rational inquiry, as if through some magic a more exact statistical rendering of what is an obvious fact will somehow generate of itself an *understanding* of what the problem is or what ought to be done. All of these are examples of what Heidegger calls idle talk (*Gerede*), and it is the manner in which the inauthentic they-self articulates its subtle smoke screens, which hide the genuine skill of language to expose the workings of what it means to be.

(It is perhaps in the mode of idle talk that the methodology behind Heidegger's interpretation of fallenness is most obvious. For when we listen to "Dangling Conversation" we immediately realize that so often we do not even *talk* to one another. But this awareness is not simply an interesting fact. It awakens a longing to get to a genuine conversation. The

---

recognition of the falsity of one mode of our language tells us *that there is another* mode, a mode in which conversation will become discourse. One is reminded of Ivan, in Dostoevski's *The Brothers Karamazov*, who argued that if there is evil there also has to be good. All Heidegger wants to insist upon is that one must first fully understand what is inauthentic— for that is immediately available to us—before the structure of the authentic can be revealed.)

Curiosity *(section 36)*

The attitude toward the world, its objects, and its people that is articulated in idle talk is curiosity *(Neugier)*. Here again we find examples similar to those in our analysis of idle talk. People whose attitude toward the world is one of bemused, curious, but ultimately indifferent observation can be said to be inauthentic in their relationship to the world. Heidegger titles such an attitude curiosity. It is, of course, more than merely an "attitude"; it is an existential. This means that it is not simply something due to a psychological influence or a passing whim. It is an essential manner in which one relates to the world. It can, and perhaps should, be overcome. But its existential influence on Dasein cannot be denied. The extreme example of such an attitude might be instances of human behavior in which severe human suffering can be casually observed either as a curiosity or even as "scientifically interesting." In many respects, the Nazis' indifferent "interest" in the victims of Nazi science strikes us as more terrifying than the actual crimes themselves. But it is perhaps not wise to give such an extreme example, for curiosity, as a mode of fallenness, is far more frequent and hence far more elusive in its less spectacular moments. We all are acquainted with people who accept all human events with equal significance. In fact, it is sometimes even seen as a praiseworthy attribute to enjoy a second-rate work of art as much as a great one. This is "democracy" pushed to its most ludicrous extreme. And it is, according to Heidegger's analysis, essentially inauthentic.

Ambiguity *(section 37)*

To those well trained in idle talk and curiosity, the ability to hide oneself behind these inauthentic outlooks is almost a necessary consequence. The reader must not read "ambiguity" *(Zweideutigkeit)* as a low-keyed schizophrenia (though Heidegger's analysis throws a great deal of light on that psychological phenomenon). Again, as in the cases of idle talk and curiosity, we are talking about an average and everyday phenomenon that is a necessary mode of one's Being-in-the-world. The chief characteristic of this mode is tranquillity. By saying this, Heidegger is not suggesting that one should be very dynamic or intensely excited in all of one's actions. Nor is he denying the importance of scientific objectivity. But he is pointing out that when one interprets one's self as a purely cognitive and passive calculator, such a mode is inauthentic.

Summary

Heidegger's rich phenomenological account of these modes leaves little to the commentator's task. Before proceeding to the next chapter, however, attention should be directed to these four points concerning the fallenness of Dasein:

1. In explicating the modes of the everyday they-self in the manner in which we articulate this inauthentic existence (idle talk), and in the manner in which we inauthentically look about us in a world of interesting but indifferent objects (curiosity), and finally in the manner in which our own self-awareness is clouded by such limited ways of seeing and talking (ambiguity), Heidegger has shown that the phenomenon of inauthenticity is not merely a vague and general feeling of alienation, but a very specific mode of human existence, which is open to inquiry. Hence one of the important aspects of this section is simply to show that such an analysis *can be done.*

2. Heidegger's account of the inauthentic modes of the self—i.e., the they-self—does not suggest that such a mode should be seen as something evil, which is to be overcome at all costs. In one sense, of course, an awareness of how the inauthentic functions is important, for one is concerned about achieving authenticity. But it is not something that is shunned or that assails us with shame or guilt.

3. By showing (E-222/G-178) that tranquillity is the mode of inauthenticity, Heidegger is again undermining the model of knowledge suggested by the dispassionate and coldy neutral investigator. Authentic knowledge, then, would not be the facile and terrible accurate knowledge of the computer, nor the stunning brilliance of the encyclopedic knowledge of one who knows all the facts. Most people, of course, have a vague feeling that the "whiz-kids" and college-bowl champions, even with their tremendous investure of human knowledge, somehow fall short of true wisdom. Heidegger has done more than merely point this out. He has shown *why* such attitudes toward knowledge are inauthentic. The man who knows only "all the facts" is out of touch with the most central question (What does it mean to be?) and hence is inauthentic. This again brings to the fore the observation that not all the ontic knowledge in the world can render an understanding of ontological meaning.

4. Finally, of course, it must be kept in mind that inauthenticity is

by no means any less *real* than authenticity. It is for this reason that Heidegger began his analysis from the ground of the everyday Dasein.

Heidegger's account of fallenness is a gold mine of suggestiveness; probably from no other section of *Being and Time* have there been so many quotations and citations in behalf of the new theology and the new changes in religious consciousness. This is, to be sure, a commendation both of Heidegger's creative genius and the sensitivity of the more recent teachers of religion. However, such emphasis on a mere aspect or part of the existential analytic can be distortive. As exciting and personally satisfying as this section is, especially for those struggling to extricate themselves from the vague enslavement of the "they," it must be seen in its proper perspective. Heidegger is not "moralizing." He is simply using his extraordinary insight into the human condition to show how such inauthentic moments reveal the structure of how one avoids the confrontation of the ontological question. This is done for the sake of exposing the dimensions of the Being question (*Seinsfrage*: what it means to be). The psychological benefits one may receive from reading this section may be helpful, but they must be seen as incidental to the main task. Heidegger has taken great pains to emphasize the supportive role of his analysis, but inevitably there will be those who insist on reading him as an existential moralist. In light of all the warnings against such an interpretation both by Heidegger and by his more astute critics, when one is confronted by such intransigence one must only conclude that not all the protesting in the world will affect those unwilling to listen.

V.

CARE,
REALITY,
AND
TRUTH

sections 39–44

In the sixth and final chapter of that section of *Being and Time* concerned with the existential analytic, Heidegger completes his "preparatory analysis" with a consideration of three important philosophical concepts: care, reality, and truth. From the point of view of the existential analysis, the most important of these three concepts is care (*Sorge*), for it is in care that all the existentials are unified into a single structure, thus providing the analysis with the logical synthesis necessary for fundamental ontology. In order for the reader to grasp the importance of this unification, it must be understood *why* such a unification is necessary in the first place. Further, it must be made clear why dread (*Angst*) is used to reveal the unifying function of this existential.

Why does Heidegger, as he draws to the end of the existential analytic, feel a need to establish a single, unifying existential that lies at the basis of all others? There are two reasons. The first is that without a unifying existential, the entire analytic would simply be a mere random sampling of various kinds of existential moments. The pattern of beginning with the broadest of existentials, Being-in-the-world, and proceeding on to those existentials most peculiar to the self, would have no logic at all unless there were to be one mode of existence that describes Dasein *as*

Dasein. Without a peculiar or particular existential that focuses upon Dasein *as* Dasein, there would be no proper meaning for Dasein at all (recalling that meaning, for Heidegger, is the focusing upon the as-structure).

The second reason for seeking a unitary phenomenon within the existential analysis, however, is far more important. Heidegger is bent on finding a single unitary existential because *if there were no unitary existential, there could be no basis for going beyond the simple enumeration of existentials, and there would then be no possible link between the mere analysis of everydayness and the ontological ground that lies at its foundation.* Unless there was a single unifying existential, one could not go any further than Division One of *Being and Time*; it provides the possibility of Division Two.

For what purpose, after all, was all of this careful interpretation of human existence made? It was not carried out merely for its own sake. Heidegger himself consistently refers to the analytic as "preparatory." For what was the analysis preparing? Not merely to reveal the *existential* account, but to expose the ontological ground.

The ultimate ontological ground of Dasein's existence, as Division Two demonstrates, is time, conceived as temporality. (Heidegger makes a most serious distinction between temporality and time; but in speaking generally like this, I prefer to use the term "time" in a generic sense that covers both "time" in the stricter sense and "temporality.") But before time can be revealed as the Being of Dasein, Dasein must be grasped essentially in terms of its existence. There must be some characteristic of Dasein that can be shown to lie at the basis of all the existentials and that, in a single unitary phenomenon, can be exposed to the same kind of inquiry that occurred with the other existentials.

The significance of this ultimate existential cannot be overestimated. Throughout the entire analysis, the various existential inquiries were always formulated on the structure: What does it mean *to be* in such and such a way? Thus we asked: What does it mean *to be* in the world? What does it mean *to be* with others? etc. If all of these different inquiries are to have any *common* meaning, if all of the existentials are to have significance beyond themselves, the most important question is: What does it mean *to be Dasein*. In an important sense, of course, one might well point out that each of the existentials helps do precisely that. They all demonstrate what it means to be Dasein. But always the analyses have been in terms of a *particular* mode of existing. The present task, however, is to show that the previous analyses do in fact allow for a consideration of what it means *to be Dasein as Dasein*. Unless this unique characteristic of Dasein (its own as-structure) can be isolated and examined, we can never know what it means to be Dasein; and subsequently, if we cannot know what it means to be Dasein, we surely cannot analyze the ontological ground of what it means to be.

The isolation of the unifying existential, then, is of supreme importance for the whole business of doing fundamental ontology. How does Heidegger ferret this difficult concept out of the full range of possible existentials? He simply examines the phenomenon of dread and from his analysis shows the unifying existential to be care. The more important question, though, is, Why does Heidegger use the analysis of dread to show that care is the primordial existential? A consideration of Heidegger's argument will reveal that his choice was by no means arbitrary.

Dread is interpreted both as a turning away from, and as a confrontation of, the self. But what we want to know about is the meaning of the self. Why examine that one phenomenon which turns us *away* from the very thing that we are so interested in finding out? Heidegger's answer is that our turning away reveals *that from which we are turning away.* Now before the reader throws up his hands in despair, he might consider that such a state of affairs is by no means beyond one's normal experience. Consider the following:

Suppose I have a friendship that makes a particular demand on me. The nature and closeness of the friendship are such that I recognize I am obligated to do something for my friend; something, though, that is very difficult for me to do. Suppose in a moment of weakness I turn away from this obligation. Most of us have experienced situations somewhat similar to this—it is within the range of most human existence. Now if one were to ask me what it was I was turning away from, I would be most acutely aware of the answer. In fact, it is because I know *only too well* what my obligations are that I tremble before them. I do not turn away from my commitment to my friend because I *don't know* my obligations, but because I *do* know them. It is only one who has felt the terrifying *burden* of a solemn oath who shies away from ever taking another. Those who almost gaily enter into solemn commitments rarely have a deep understanding of what commitment is. It is the young and inexperienced who happily take the terrible oaths of military duty. It is the more experienced soldier, who has felt the agony of his call to duty conflicting with his moral conscience, who might hesitate to renew that terrible pledge. Thus within one's normal experience the idea that turning away might reveal that *from which* someone is turning away is not uncommon. Heidegger, though, wants to emphasize something even more profound. In such cases as the ones mentioned, it is sometimes true that the genuine character of something comes to the fore *only* in those instances when we actually do turn away from them. Love, as we know, is often like this. It is only *after* we have turned away from loving that we become explicitly aware of the immense commitment required. Our own failure to live up to such a commitment alone truly reveals its enormity.

Such is the way that dread, upon existential examination, reveals the authentic structure of the self. It is knowledge of the self that we shun, and this shunning is "dread-ful." Thus a careful reading of dread, which is a turning away from the self, paradoxically, though nonetheless soundly, reveals our first real glimpse of the unique characteristic of the self, because in dread also we come face to face with ourselves.

Heidegger's general strategy, then, is this. First he examines phenomenologically the phenomenon of dread. This examination reveals that the primordial existential of Dasein is to care. Once this is grasped in its existential structure, the inquiry is ready to be shifted from the everyday viewpoint to the ontological viewpoint, which is time.

Before time can be shown as the ontological ground of caring, however, the two concepts "reality" and "truth" must be existentially analyzed. Once they are considered, though, the preparatory level of the inquiry is complete.

There is always a danger, in the reading of such immense investigations as *Being and Time*, that one will "lose the forest for the trees." This rather cursory outline of Chapter VI is an attempt to offset that danger. As long as one keeps in mind *why* Heidegger has chosen to analyze dread and care, Chapter VI, though not without difficulties, remains essentially readable. The fact that structuring the inquiry of dread on the question of Being somehow throws greater significance on the phenomenon of dread itself is also not without philosophical significance, for it *suggests* the aptness of the methodology. But this must not be seen as the major task. Heidegger's main task, at this juncture, is to isolate that existential which uniquely manifests Dasein *as* Dasein.

DREAD (ANXIETY: ANGST)   (section 40)

Within the experience of most reflective and serious people can be found instances of a weird and uncanny feeling, in which the whole familiar world seems to lose its normal significance. In such instances those things that usually affect us with familiar and intimate significance seem to take on the property of oddness and unfamiliarity. Our room, for example, suddenly seems to be a room in a strange land or even on another planet. Our mind tells us that it is the same room in which we have always felt quite at home. Yet in an uncanny way, the very logic that assures us of our familiarity with the room seems in such circumstances to emphasize our alienation with it. We perform familiar actions; yet under the influence of this state of mind we seem merely to see ourselves performing these actions as one sees a marionette performing the antics of an alien script. Most of us have experienced such moments in our lives. Sometimes, in becoming aware of such experiences, we often find ourselves reflecting on our own existence. Plucked out of the stream of our daily concerns, we seem forced to reflect upon our existence as if it were a totally new revelation. We observe ourselves, suspended from the concerns that occupy our consciousness, almost as if we were strangers to ourselves. Perhaps we even become aware of ourselves as something independent of our daily concerns.

Such experiences are not pleasant, but many feel them to be valuable for various reasons. It often seems that such experiences are not really "experiences" at all, in the normal sense of that term. For they are not moments occasioned by some external activity, as for example, the experience of a symphony is occasioned by the actual playing of the music. These uncanny "experiences," though, seem to be always with us, lurking on the fringes of consciousness, ready to assert themselves explicitly at certain undefined moments. But even when they are subdued or pushed away by other attitudes and "feelings," they seem to exert their influence.

It is difficult to find a term adequate enough to express this state of mind. It is perhaps even more difficult to imagine why an ontologist would want to consider such a phenomenon. Heidegger, however, considers it to be of great importance for his analysis. His choice of term in the original German is *Angst*. Although Macquarrie and Robinson have rendered this as "anxiety," I feel that "dread" is really a more successful choice. No single term, though, can adequately reflect the meaning of the phenomenon; but the role that the term plays in Heidegger's philosophy is central nonetheless. In some of his later works,[1] Heidegger inquires even more acutely into the phenomenon. The reason for all this interest in the experience of dread is that it does seem to remove us from our concern about the things that are happening around us, and in so doing allows us to reflect upon our own stark and terrifying existence. In that it does focus upon existence, its analysis is invaluable for the inquiry into what it means to be.

Heidegger's account is, at first, phenomenological. That is, he renders an interpretation of the phenomenon, describing it in terms of how this

1. Cf. especially *What Is Metaphysics?* in Brock's *Existence and Being.*

experience manifests itself. From this description, of course, he will then seek out first existential and then ontological significance. By that I mean that he first examines the phenomenological description in order to see how it is a way in which Dasein exists. Then he seeks to find if this way of existing can throw light on the question of what it means to be.

One of the first ways in which Heidegger isolates this phenomenon is to contrast it with a similar one: fear. Dread (anxiety) is not the same thing as fear, because fear always has a definite object that is feared. I fear the tax collector, the forthcoming examination, or the snarling dog in my path. But what is it that I dread? I cannot put my finger on one single object. In the case of fear I know exactly what would remove my fear. If my taxes were to be paid by a benefactor, if the examination were to be canceled, if the dog were to be impounded, I would no longer be afraid. But I cannot say what it is that bothers me in the case of dread. In fact, if one were to ask me what bothers me, I would probably say, "Nothing." In saying that I do not mean that I am not bothered at all, but that there is no *thing* that bothers me. What bothers me is my *existence*.

We have just observed that when one is asked what it is that bothers one when one is in a state of dread, the likely answer is that "nothing" bothers one. This seemingly innocent looseness of speech contains for Heidegger a greater literalness than one might imagine. Heidegger asks quite seriously this question: What is this "nothingness" (*Nichts*) about which one has such dreading anxiety? What is the existential meaning of "Nothingness"?

Few terms of any philosopher have suffered as much confusion and even ridicule as Heidegger's rather specialized usage of the term "nothingness." It is a term most offensive to the careful critical analysts, for in normal usage the term has no substantive referent, and hence to treat the term as the object of any kind of inquiry is simply linguistic perversion. Many Heideggerians add to the confusion by distorting its import. The term does have great significance for Heidegger, though, especially in works that come after *Being and Time*.

The existential meaning of "nothingness" is really a rather simple matter. A human being, through the reflection of his own possibilities, becomes aware of his finitude—i.e., he knows he is going to die, to cease to be. The strangeness of this feeling cannot be compared to any other form of human experience, since all other forms of experience are structured in a continuum of time in which the continuation of existence plays an essential role. But in death, or in the awareness of the meaninglessness of existence, one is aware of something quite unlike any experience. To call this "nothingness" might seem an outrage to language—but any term used to designate that which in principle is incapable of being experienced will be an outrage to language. The term "nothingness" is really quite apt; for what is meant is something that is indeed existentially significant, but is incapable of being the object of an experience.

Heidegger insists that there is no such thing as a *Nichts* or a nothingness. No metaphysical properties can be applied to *Nichts*. Yet even the most ardent anti-Heideggerian would not deny that a human person suffers from some kind of strange awareness when the possibility of the complete termination of his consciousness is somehow presented to him. It is absolutely essential that one realize that "death" cannot serve as a substitute for the term "nothingness." It is not the experience of dying, or the pain of having life wrenched from one's body. These things are indeed "experienced," and can be "feared." But to be aware of being able not to be is something quite different. Heidegger uses the term "nothingness" to represent that which has existential significance but cannot have any metaphysical referent.

In the Foreword to *Of the Essence of Ground (Vom Wesen des Grundes)*, Heidegger writes: "*Das Nichts ist das Nicht des Seienden und so das vom Seienden her erfahrene Sein.*" This is a terribly difficult sentence to translate. It means something like this: "Nothingness is the Not of beings, and is hence [the awareness of] to be as experienced from beings." To make it readable, I had to add: "the awareness of"; but in spite of the immense difficulty in translating, the meaning is not too difficult: Nothingness—that is, the awareness of being-able-not-to-be or more importantly, the awareness of Being in a meaningless way, as a nihilist—is the "Not" (the transcendence, or going beyond; the rejection) of beings (things); and as such, this awareness of being-able-not-to-be focuses upon what it means *to be*, even though that which does the experiencing is a being (thing). It is through the rejection or the transcendence beyond mere entities that both Being and not-being can be existentially significant.

That existential which makes us aware of nothingness is dread. Dread is a state-of-mind. This means, as we have seen, that we are made aware of what *is*, as opposed to the mode of understanding that makes us aware of what could be. To be sure, dread also has its understanding elements, but insofar as we see dread as a state-of-mind, it reveals to us how we *are* in a world. And how is it that we are in a world? We are thrown in a world. Dread brings us face to face with this thrownness.

But dread does not merely present us with our Being-in-the-world. Because the world is, in the moment of dread, alien to us—we no longer feel at-home in the world—dread focuses upon us as unique individuals. Dread, according to Heidegger, *individualizes*. This awareness of my individuality reveals to me my own possibilities. In fact, we *now* can see *about* what it is we are dreading. We dread our *being able to be ourselves*. Since dread puts us before ourselves, naked, as it were, we now are aware of our possibilities: either to be genuinely ourselves, or to lose ourselves once more in the comforting chatter of the "they." It is in tranquillity and everydayness that one can *avoid* the confrontation of the self, but in dread one cannot *avoid* one's self, though one can turn away from it. That's what dread is. It is the uncanny awareness of the self as free to be either authentic or inauthentic.

Heidegger emphasizes that the primordial meaning of dread is to feel not-at-home. Now as we have seen in our preliminary study of the inauthentic they-self, the whole persuasion of this inauthenticity is to make one feel comfortable in the unexamined and uncritical life of the "they." That is, in the they-world we *are* at-home. But we lose this feeling of being at-home in dread. Dread is uncanny, and Heidegger emphasizes that in German: "uncanny" is *unheimlich*, which etymologically means "not-at-home." Now, if I no longer feel at-home, I am forced to focus on my *own* Being, not that of the "they."

Because, more than any other existential, dread focuses attention on my own state of Being, Heidegger sees it as a tool to reveal the primary existential of Dasein.

What are we to make of Heidegger's analysis? In the first place, it should be made clear that Heidegger is not relying on some mystic or strange experience. He has not claimed that *only* through dread can one reflect upon the authentic self. He would not make such a claim. He has not attempted to exhaust the psychological account of such an experience. He has merely shown that such an experience is genuine enough, call it what you will, and that in such an experience one does see the difference between the world and the self. Dread, then, is merely an example. It is a phenomenon, the analysis of which makes the determination of the primordial existential somewhat easier. He is not claiming that the "way" to authenticity is through dread. He is showing that dread can reveal something that many other kinds of experiences cannot: consciousness can become aware of itself *as* itself, and not merely as something using the various items of an equipmental world. It does this by forcefully isolating Dasein from its surroundings and confronting it with the choice of how to be. Heidegger does not deny that dread is "rare," but that does not make it any less revealing. To object that one's personal experiences of dreading do not correspond to Heidegger's account, of course, is bound to be something of a verbal dispute. Heidegger has not tried to show that all uses of the term *Angst* reflect his meaning. He has merely shown by careful description the genuine possibility of such an experience. Dread, as Heidegger has described it, is a *possible* experience;

and indeed, if we can accept the words of various people, it is not as uncommon as might be expected.

The ultimate purpose of the analysis of dread, however, is to show that the primordial existential of Dasein is care. A full evaluation of dread cannot be made until its essential purpose has been carried out.

CARE AS THE BEING OF DASEIN (sections 41–42)

On a purely intuitional level the claim that care is the Being of Dasein seems an unobjectionable claim that is easy to grasp. What it means for one to be is to care. This seems supported by the realization that everything one does can be interpreted as manifesting a kind of caring. When I reflect upon myself, I center upon my interests, my concerns, my excitements, my disappointments, etc., and all of these things can be seen as a kind of caring. Furthermore, the claim seems even more supported by the fact that my own existence reveals itself more clearly in moments of increased caring. When I care very deeply, as in love or terror, guilt or courage, my own unique and individual existence seems amplified. Surely Heidegger's whole analysis has exposed this factor.

All of these considerations, which appeal purely to a kind of refined intuition, may be true enough. They are contained too in Heidegger's very choice of terms. By using the term "care," Heidegger was not unaware of these immediate aspects by which one might accept his claim that care is the Being of Dasein. But supportive as such considerations may be, they are not what constitute the explicit grounding of this claim in the development of the existential analytic. Much of the previous analysis has been directed toward this claim. Let us recall a few interpretations of previous existentials.

The analysis of fallenness has shown that Dasein, in the mode of falling, turns away from itself through interest and care in the inauthentic world of the they-self. Thus indirectly, though nevertheless surely, fallenness exposes Dasein's concern for its self. But it has exposed all of this through the recognition that the turning away from the self is a kind of *involvement* in the they-self. That is, it is a kind of caring.

In Dasein's involvement with the they-self, however, there is little or no opportunity for Dasein to reflect upon this involvement. In fact, the whole persuasion of the they-self is *not even to consider* such questions. When Dasein gets into a certain kind of mood, however, in which this involvement with the they-self is no longer an easy, "natural" kind of thing, Dasein seems forced to stand back and reflect upon its role. The feeling at-home with the thoughtless milieu of the "they" is lost. In the midst of such alienation Dasein turns to itself. Dread, as we have seen, individualizes Dasein by forcing it *away* from the uncritical commerce of its inauthentic self and isolating it. It does not, of course, force it to exist authentically. It does, however, present it with the choice of such a manner of existence.

The analysis of dread, then, focuses one's attention on the isolated Dasein, thereby setting the stage for a consideration of Dasein *as* Dasein.

The analysis of Dasein has, to be sure, already been prepared. The first series of existentials (Being-in-the-world, Being-with, Being-in, etc.) deals with the manner in which Dasein relates to entities *other* than itself. Of course, in such considerations the analysis is still focused on the manner in which *Dasein* relates to the world, and not on the world in itself, but they are nonetheless characterized by non-self relationships. As the analysis begins to draw closer to the nature of Dasein as such, three distinctive existentials are dominant. The first of these existentials that reveal the self is state-of-mind, which manifests the way in which one *is* (the mode of the actual). The second existential that reveals the self is understanding, which manifests the ways in which one *can* be (the mode of the possible). The third existential in this series is fallenness, which manifests the ways in which one hides behind the chatter, the curiosity, and the ambiguity of inauthentic existence (the mode of fallenness). Heidegger's discovery of care as the primordial discipline follows this threefold character of the self. At the risk of extreme pedantry, I would direct attention to the fact that in the first paragraph of section 41 (E-235/G-191), Heidegger reviews this threefold characteristic of Dasein; in the second paragraph of section 41 he discusses the role of understanding; in the third paragraph he discusses the role of state-of-mind; and in the fourth he discusses fallenness.

In the first paragraph of section 41, Heidegger writes: "The fundamental ontological characteristics of this entity [Dasein] are existentiality, facticity, and Being-fallen."[2] Facticity, as we know, is revealed in state-of-mind, whereas existentiality is revealed through understanding. Heidegger considers these two existentials, as well as that of fallenness, in terms of the meaning of Dasein *as* Dasein.

1. Understanding. In the analysis of understanding it was pointed out that its chief characteristic is to *project possibilities*. When this is applied to the meaning of the self, understanding projects before itself *its own possibilities*. Dasein is aware of its being able to be. It not only *has* possibilities; it *is* its possibilities. Through the awareness of my own possibilities, I can project before myself the choices of authenticity, in which *my*

---

2. Cf. *Being and Time*, p. 235.

own Being is significant, and inauthenticity, in which not my own Being, but the Being of "they," is significant. Heidegger calls this structure, in which what it means to be is an issue for Dasein, Being-ahead-of-itself. He emphasizes that such a characteristic does not refer to the "not-yet" quality of future hopes and dreams, but to the existing qualities that make the future significant for one.

2. State-of-Mind. This Being-ahead-of-itself is not a random and arbitrary freedom to live any way one wants to live, however. My world has limits. In fact, to a large extent, there is much about what I am that cannot be overcome. Hence, if we recall the analysis of state-of-mind in general, we must add to the above description that one is already thrown into a world in which one has little to say or to determine. The characteristic, then, of Dasein is not simply a Being-ahead-of-itself, but also a Being-ahead-of-itself-in-the-world. All this means is that I not only have possibilities, but that I am also aware of the limits of my actuality. Existing is always factical, Heidegger says. This is because understanding always has a state-of-mind.

3. Fallenness. In addition to the characteristics supplied by understanding and state-of-mind, Dasein *as* Dasein is generally occupied with its daily, inauthentic events. This is what fallenness means, as we have seen. But fallenness is not an occasional attitude. Hence it too must be added on to the general characterization of Dasein *as* Dasein; the term representing this concern with our daily tasks is Being-alongside.

In synthesis, then, Heidegger has characterized Dasein *as* Dasein with the lengthy term: "Ahead of itself Being already in the world as Being alongside entities encountered within the world."[3] Since this is to be seen as a single concept, I suppose one could hyphenate the entire phrase. But there is no need to do that, since it is expressed in a single term: "care." To care, then, means: to be ahead of oneself already involved with entities within the world. Care (*Sorge*) can be more specifically subdivided into caring *about* (Macquarrie and Robinson have translated the German *Besorgen* as "concern") and caring *for* (they have translated the German *Fürsorge* as "solicitude"). Thus I *care about* automobiles, door handles, knives and forks. But I *care for* my brother, my friend, and other people. (I do not dispute Macquarrie and Robinson's translation; I merely wish to show the etymological connection between care (*Sorge*) and its particularization in *Fürsorge* and *Besorgen*.) Of course, all three of these terms—care, concern, and solicitude—should not be taken in the sense of worry, uncertainty, nervousness, etc. The terms are ontologically, and

3. Cf. *Being and Time*, p. 237.

not psychologically, significant. Heidegger adds that a special term to mean caring-about-the-self would be redundant, since all instances of caring include the self.

Immediately after showing that state-of-mind, understanding, and fallenness provide the basis for Dasein *as* care, Heidegger proceeds to argue that care is indeed primordial and that it cannot be reduced to such phenomena as willing, wishing, urging, etc. Rather, he shows that these phenomena are based in care. There is no need to trace all of these arguments, since they are simple enough, as long as one remembers the ultimate strategy of Heidegger's account. The main point to remember is that all of the existentials used to describe Dasein's self find their central locus in care. If that is fully grasped, what Heidegger develops from this should be easy enough to follow.

In a rather strange section (42), Heidegger points out that there are historical precedents to the claim that what it means for man to be is to care. He takes an ancient Latin fable in which "man" is seen as having been formed by "care" and interprets the fable as a kind of primitive understanding of what has been won by the tortuous reasoning of the existential analytic. Although there is no need to comment on this charming little section, it is curious. For what purpose has Heidegger included this fable? He does not, of course, rely upon any argumentative value from the coideration of the fable; although it does show that others have seen the primordial importance of care in the definition of man. Perhaps its greatest significance lies in the fact that as an ancient fable it reflects a kind of thinking unhindered and unimpeded by extreme "theoretical" influences. On the other hand, it may be an appeal to the "intuitional" insights that support the claim that for man, to be is to care. In any event, there is a pleasant charm in the reading of this section, which serves, if nothing else, as a kind of respite from the difficult labors that have preceded and that are to come. This section, by the way, is just about in the very center of the book. Heidegger has at least found support for his claim from another author, and though this author is ancient, at least he presents his case in the unabashed directness of a poetic fable.

PROBLEM OF REALITY (section 43)

Throughout the interpretations of the existence of Dasein given thus far, the distinction between presence-at-hand and readiness-at-hand has remained an important aspect. It was pointed out earlier that the many attempts to construct a metaphysics in which the world was seen as nothing but an aggregate of objects present-at-hand was essentially mistaken. This crucial error is now examined more specifically.

In his interpretation of reality, Heidegger is exposing an error inherent in other thinkers. Thus his style is quite negative in this section; but it is not criticism for the sake of criticism. The whole point of this argument is: If the traditional view of reality is incorrect, then any criticism against Heidegger's view *based* on the presuppositions of the traditional view would be without philosophical value. In the simplest of terms the claim is this: Traditional metaphysics has depicted reality as consisting of objects that are present-at-hand in the world. Heidegger, however, argues that to see the world in this way is to overlook other and indeed more primary ways of seeing the world. He also points out that to see the world in this traditional way necessitates interpreting Dasein merely as another object present-at-hand in the world; in so interpreting Dasein, the traditional theories have been stymied by immensely complex pseudo problems, such as the existence of the external world. Rather than interpret reality as objects present-at-hand, Heidegger interprets reality as care.

This simple statement of the argument needs to be fleshed out, of course. Since it has now become so critical, a closer look at the nature of presence-at-hand may be helpful. Heidegger, in section 19, accused Descartes of interpreting the world in the manner of seeing it as present-at-hand. What does that mean?

In the second *Meditation*, Descartes uses the example of a ball of wax to show what he means by the difference between substance and accident. The essence or the substance of the wax is reduced to pure extension. What the wax looks like, feels like, smells like, etc., are "accidents." Descartes does not even consider in this analysis how one makes use of wax, or what wax *means* to one who pours it into a candle mold or seals a letter with it. But it is in sealing letters and making candles that one relates in the first instance to the wax. The highly abstract view of the wax as a being whose ultimate meaning is simply to take up space is so highly speculative that even many Cartesians feel uneasy in accepting it as true. Certainly for Descartes's servants the wax was simply a convenience in the tasks of adjusting the world to the purpose of their master or themselves. Thus Descartes's view of material substances is purely present-at-hand: substances are entities that are seen in their simple thinghood—i.e., they take up space and thereby constitute the furniture of the universe. By not taking into consideration the purpose, the service, and the function of these entities, Descartes has left the world a rather sterile place. The only way in which such ready-at-hand characteristics as use and purpose can be *added to* this world is to have the other kind of substances, thinking substances, somehow endow these material substances with such significance. Of course, every student of philosophy knows the tremendous difficulty that results from such dualism and inter-action. This difficulty has been given the name the "mind-body prob-lem."

At this point, however, a Cartesian may wish to object in support of a substance metaphysics. The reason, he might say, that Descartes treats substances in so sterile a way is to avoid attributing purely subjective characteristics to an object. The uses and purposes of the world are in-deed added onto the world by the subject. Surely one would want to ob-ject that we cannot accept the interpretations that anyone might want to give to an object or event. The primitive sees the death of a cow as due to evil spirits. A child might think a frayed electrical cord is a toy. In both of these interpretations any sensible man would feel compelled to deny the validity of the *use* put to these objects by the primitive and the child. The Cartesian would continue that by defining the substance purely in the abstract terms of what the mind sees as the essence of a thing, one avoids the fallacy of accident.

The response of the Heideggerrian to this argument would be some-thing along these lines: To attribute purely abstract characteristics to an object and to the world in general is just as much a subjective imposition upon the world as is the child's determination that the cord is a toy. The ball of wax is not an extended substance with the accidents of softness and smoothness added on to it. A ball of wax is something used to seal letters or make candles. Such a description is telling us about the world. Toys are a part of a child's world, and the child's mistaken use of the frayed electrical cord as a toy does not suddenly make his relating to a part of the world as entertainment equipment any less genuine. Surely the child—or most adults for that matter—does not see the cord as sim-ply pure extension. But what if the Cartesian objected: "But that's what it *is*, independent of your interpretation"? How does he know that? He has told us that he arrived at his "essence" by *thinking*! And thinking is an interpretation. In fact, interpretive epistemology is a most highly stylized form of interpretation. As a part of the world I live in, that piece of wax is equipment for making candles or sealing envelopes. Such an interpretation tells me about the world as I am in it; Descartes's interpre-tation merely tells me *how I can think* about it (though I *need not* think about it in this manner).

In any event, Descartes's substances, independent as they are from the world of use and purpose, are present-at-hand. Most philosophers, even Kant, seem to have considered the world as made up of these indifferent things. By the term "world," Heidegger, on the other hand, includes, along with the present-at-hand, far more immediate and primordial modes of relating. For his strongest argument is that presence-at-hand, like readiness-at-hand, is *a mode of how we relate to the world*, and hence cannot be seen as the simple element that exhausts what is in the world. The normal and traditional meaning of the term "reality" is what Heidegger has called present-at-hand. Thus it is that "reality" is discussed almost secondarily, as it were, and it is not seen as the most important philosophical problem.

One of Heidegger's central modes of attack against a philosophy that takes as its starting point the problem of reality is to indicate the pseudo problems to which such an interpretation leads the inquirer. We have seen one such pseudo problem in the case of Descartes and his difficulty with the mind-body problem. The problem that Heidegger chooses to examine, however, is the problem that Kant was faced with in his *Critique*: the so-called refutation of idealism. Kant, as you may recall, argued that the concept of permanence could not come from within, so there had to be a world existing "outside" of us. Heidegger's objection to this argument is not so much that there are logical errors in the refutation of idealism, but that the very fact that Kant even tried to "prove" the existence of the external world belies his acceptance of an isolated subject, which he inherited from Descartes. The whole point is, of course, that the existential analytic has shown that there is no such thing as the isolated or pure subject or ego. Dasein *already has* a world by its very constitution. To "prove" the existence of an external world is to overlook the *a priori* nature of Being-in-the-world. The same kind of argumentation that I have sketched against Descartes can be brought against Kant. Of course, one might well question whether Kant's refutation of idealism wasn't in fact a kind of unfortunate carry-over from his earlier rationalism that is inconsistent with his whole critical approach. The advantage of section 43 is that the reader can see Heidegger's claims contrasted with more traditional theories, and such contrasting serves to sharpen one's comprehension of the general task and character of Heidegger's thought.

Two classical forms of the problem of reality are realism and idealism. Heidegger accepts and rejects both, though he leans toward idealism far more than toward realism. What he shares with the realist is the simple acceptance that there are objects present-at-hand within the universe. But with the whole spirit of epistemological realism he is not so sympathetic. With idealism, on the other hand, he shares the view that one begins the philosophical enterprise with a description or awareness of the self. But he rejects the view of some idealists that this self is isolated, a worldless subject. The self, or the awareness of existence, is already in a world, and cannot be seen in isolation except by highly sophisticated abstraction.

Heidegger's spiritual kinship to idealism, broadly conceived, lies in his preference for possibility. Here we are tracing his rejection of certain doctrines commonly held by many idealistic schools. Heidegger is shifting

the locus of the primordial discipline from the epistemology of the Kantian critique to fundamental ontology. But the transcendental nature of
Kant's teachings is retained. In emphasizing that one should not start
philosophy from the problem of reality, but should start instead from
the problem of existence, Heidegger shares the ultimate perspective of
Kant, who insisted that the nature of reasoning must be analyzed before
the nature of the world we reason about. Heidegger has sought to show
that Kant's continued mode of thinking in terms of reality as present-at-
hand was an unfortunate carry-over from rationalism; that had Kant been
capable of carrying out his "revolution" completely, he would have
abandoned the attempt to prove the existence of the external world.

If Heidegger rejects the view of reality as formally espoused by Descartes and presupposed (though resisted to some extent) by Kant, then
how is reality to be conceived in terms of the existential analytic? If the
real is not made up of present-at-hand objects, what is it? Heidegger's
answer is that reality is referred back to the phenomenon of care.

If we extend the term "reality" to include not only the present-at-
hand, but also the ready-at-hand and the Being of "Nature," it is still
not primordial, for even so broadly conceived, reality can be understood
only in terms of the world. The world, of course, has already been shown
to exist as a mode of Dasein, whose primordial existential is care. Thus,
to direct one's attention to reality is simply to exercise a particular mode
of caring. Reality, then, is based on care.

Does this mean that Heidegger is maintaining that reality is dependent
on man's existence? Yes; but this does not entail that the existence of
the external world is dependent on Dasein. For reality (not real things)
is a mode of human existence and hence it obviously could not exist without man. To put it in clearer terms: since philosophers insist on using
the term "reality" only to refer to objects in their abstract thinghood,
obviously this abstraction depends upon the mind doing the abstracting.
Thus rocks and trees do not depend on man for their location and occurrence in the universe, but reality, which is merely a mode of man's interpretation of the world, does depend on man's existence. The same can
be said for Being (to be). When Heidegger says that only as long as
Dasein exists is there Being, he is not urging any kind of dependent idealism in which the external world somehow depends upon a subject to per-
ceive it. He is simply pointing out that to know what it means to be requires a self-conscious entity capable of this awareness.

The final but by no means least important point to be made about
this section is that, as a result of this inquiry, Dasein cannot be described
or defined solely in terms of substance or reality. Since both substances
and reality come from the ways in which Dasein relates to the world and
to its self, they are derivative. Although this claim was made in the very

early pages of the analytic, the grounds for the claim are now explicitly stated.

HEIDEGGER'S THEORY OF TRUTH   (section 44)

Philosophy has often been described as the search for the truth. What is it, then, that the philosophers search for? What is this "truth" that drives men on to such difficult intellectual activity? Most philosophers of any stature at all include within their system or description an interpretation of truth itself. Heidegger is no exception. His analysis of truth is one of the more important characteristics of his philosophy—indeed, in addition to his consideration of the problem in *Being and Time*, Heidegger wrote two subsequent works that deal directly with the problem of truth: *Plato's Theory of Truth* and *Of the Essence of Truth*. These later works reflect a certain development in Heidegger's thinking, to be sure, but they do not deviate in principle from the account of truth as given in *Being and Time*.

Heidegger's theory of truth is considerably at variance with the "traditional" account; since it is consistent with his own existential ontology, the analysis of what truth means plays an important role in understanding and defending Heidegger's philosophy. The reader should keep clearly in mind that the major difference between Heidegger's account of truth and the many "traditional" accounts is this: Heidegger is *not rendering a criterion of truth*; he is interpreting the essence or meaning of truth.

Such theories of truth as the "correspondence," "coherence," and "pragmatic" can be seen basically as theories about the *criteria* one uses in assessing a true or false proposition. Supporters of the correspondence theory, for example, argue that a judgment or proposition is true *when* (i.e., under those circumstances in which) the proposition corresponds to the facts, or *when* it accurately communicates (and hence "corresponds to") the facts as they really are. In like manner, supporters of the coherence theory maintain that a proposition is true *when* it is consistent and contained within an extensive system of knowledge. Pragmatists argue that something is true when it is practical, useful, or otherwise significant in terms of human values. The point is that in all of these cases, even granting a great deal of sophistication possible in each case, the traditional theorists have asked when (under what conditions) something is true. They have not asked what truth itself means. They have not asked what truth is. Of course, the supporters of these theories argue that their views provide not only an account of criteria but also the nature or meaning of truth. It is indeed possible to argue that truth not only occurs when there is correspondence but that correspondence is just what truth means. But even so, this argument *begins* with criteria and *arrives* at meaning. Heidegger interrogates the meaning prior to and independent of, the criteria. But how are we to understand this existential approach to truth? In the following paragraphs I shall first sketch out the overall perspective before focusing on the individual sections.

The first point to realize about Heidegger's approach to truth is that it is not so much a theory as an analysis. That is, he examines what *happens* in an event in which truth occurs. But to understand truth in this way already has enormous consequences, for truth is no longer a mere relation between the subject-knower and the object-known but rather something that *happens*. And what happens is that the meaning of the event is revealed to us. This way of thinking is at once a brilliant discovery and at the same time an obvious, almost irresistable insight. Whether one begins with a sentence, a meaning, or an event, the truth of it is the manner in which it is made available to us; thus for something to be true is for it to be revealed. The activist language alone illuminates the point: truth is not *seen*; it is *shown*.

Heidegger gives the example of a picture hanging askew on the wall. Why "askew"? Because the very crookedness of the picture jumps out at us, it "announces itself," it provokes our attention, saying, "Look, there's something wrong here!" What is the difference between saying merely that there is a picture on the wall and saying that the picture is crooked? The latter tells us something, the former is merely what it is: what is said about it is reduced to what is the case. Because of this remarkable philosophical shift, Heidegger succeeds in rescuing truth from the static formality of a thing merely *being* what it is to the dynamic sense of a thing *revealing* what it it.

Suppose one were to object that surely both sentences, "The picture is on the wall" and "The picture is askew on the wall" are true. Perhaps. But why would we say (or even notice) that a picture is on the wall, unless something provokes us to say or notice it? If I ask, "Where is the picture?" of course, *then* the response would be the truthful one, "It is on the wall." But this simply shows that it is the question and not the answer that directs our attention to the location of the picture. This directing is thus a part of our understanding the claim, and is thus an *active* occurrence rather than a mere static relation.

One obvious advantage of this account is that it makes truth about the meaning of Being possible. In later works, Heidegger more emphatically emphasizes the difference and hierarchy of the three levels of truth. From the lowest to the highest, the development is as follows: (1) *Propositional Truth*. This is the traditional understanding in which truth is seen as the correct correspondence between a proposition and what is the case: "The picture is askew on the wall" is true because the picture actually is askew on the wall. But this correspondence is itself possible only because of (2) *Ontic Truth*. This is what is meant by the picture announcing itself or revealing itself *as* askew; this is the first level of unconcealedness or manifestness. But the picture can announce itself to us as truly askew only because of (3) *Ontological Truth*. This is the highest—or "truest"—sense of truth, in which what it means to be is revealed. In the present example, one must first *be able to exist* so as to let the askewness matter and be noticed; thus in revealing its askewness the crooked picture also reveals to us something about who we are, i.e., our own meaning.

Thus this single analysis not only accomplishes an understanding of truth in the traditional sense but also shows us how truth about Being is possible. However, this example fails to tell us much about this more fundamental sense of truth, and so we must now consider such instances of revealing directly.

The proper way to comprehend a philosopher is to search within one's own awareness to see if there is a kind of experience or attitude one has that will support the philosopher's claim. Only after such a claim is understood in this way can it properly be accepted or rejected. Heidegger's claim is that the essence or nature of truth is disclosure (*Erschlossenheit*). He points out the etymology of the Greek word for "truth," *aletheia* (ἀλήθεια): "unhiddenness." Is there any kind of experience or awareness that seems especially supportive of such a claim?

Most of us have had experiences in dealing with other human beings (or with ourselves, for that matter) in which the other hides himself behind the little masks of deceit and role-playing. When this person is the object of our affection, such deception is irritating and frustrating, for we want to get at the true picture or the true understanding of that person. It seems not to be a violation of language usage to say that when someone hides behind such masks he is not giving a *true* picture of himself. On the other hand, we say that our understanding or awareness of someone is true if there are no masks, and we see him as he is. In this sense, then, "truth" means something like "exposure," "nakedness," "disclosure," "opening up." The question to which we must now direct our inquiry is this: Is this meaning of truth as disclosure the primordial meaning? Do the other varied uses of truth have their roots in this meaning, or is it that this meaning is derived? It must be kept in mind, of course, that if Heidegger's theory is correct, then truth does not reside only in propositions. If Heidegger is right, propositional truth is a derived and limited kind of truth.

Before reviewing Heidegger's argumentation, it might be important to ask: What else could the essence of truth be? If we do not ask about the criterion but the essence, what other kind of answer could we expect? There are, of course, other answers that are possible. One might suggest that truth is what is in the mind of God. Such is not a theory about the criterion of truth. The disadvantages of such a theory are many, though. In the first place, the existence of God must first be established in order to support the theory. Furthermore, if such is the proper way to interpret truth, then truth will never be available for us, for we cannot get into the mind of God. Or suppose one suggests that the essence or meaning of truth is the Good. All this suggestion does, however, is to shift the problem from one arena to another, and the new question, What is the essence of the Good? must be posed. I do not intend by this line of inquiry to suggest that Heidegger's claim is the only sensible solution. But I do wish to underline the critical difference between asking a question about the essence of truth and asking a question about the criterion of truth, between asking about the nature of truth and the ways in which we can recognize it. The latter question is by no means unimportant. But according to Heidegger it is derivative.

There are two major tasks in this interpretation of truth: (1) to find out what Heidegger means by his claim that truth is unhiddenness and (2) to find out how Heidegger argues that such a view is primordial. In a strictly logical account, the first task would be taken up before the other. But there is a pedagogical advantage in treating the two tasks in reverse order. The traditional view of truth is one of correspondence, and such an interpretation may be quite resistant to change. Furthermore, if one can show that correspondence is itself based on something more fundamental, the task of describing the nature of truth rather than its criterion would be made easier. In any event, Heidegger begins his analysis with the traditional theory, and I shall comment on his account in the same order.

The Traditional View (section 44)

The general strategy of this section is to show that the traditional theory of truth—correspondence—is only *derivative* and that its ontological foundation is truth as unhiddenness. A very close reading of Heidegger's interpretation is advisable.

Heidegger points out that starting with Aristotle's view that the soul's passions are reflections of things, and Aquinas's view that truth is the correspondence of the mind with the thing, the traditional view of truth has been to locate truth in judgments. Even Kant can be shown to have accepted the view that sees truth as a characteristic of judgments in which there is a correspondence between the knower and the known. There is a difficulty in such a view, however. How is this correspondence to be interpreted? It surely cannot be a one-to-one correspondence. My idea of a cat, as a mental activity, does not have whiskers. The cat is heavy, my thought of it is not. Hence a simple one-to-one correspondence is ruled out. In certain traditions it was argued that there was a *representation* that serves as a kind of bridge between the idea and the thing known. In a previous section, however, it was pointed out that propositions, as assertions, do not point out representations, but the things themselves. This is so because when I say, in the mode of ready-at-hand, that the hammer is heavy, I am not predicating the concept "heaviness" to the concept "hammerness"; rather, I am complaining about the difficulty I have in using the tool.

Heidegger's example in the present section, is of a man claiming that a picture on the wall, to which his back is turned, is hanging askew. It is not a representation of the picture that the man says is askew, but the picture itself. What, then, is the basis of this correspondence? How is this correspondence brought about? According to Heidegger, correspondence (or adequation) is based upon the phenomenon of confirmation. The "correspondence" or "agreement" that is the basis of the traditional theory of truth comes about because something is confirmed or demonstrated as true. When the man turns around and sees the picture actually hanging askew on the wall, his claim that it was hanging askew is now confirmed as it is. Hence the foundation of the traditional theory is *to show itself as it is*. To have said, before his turning around, that the man's "idea" corresponds to the "fact" is simply to say that, on turning around, the fact would confirm the statement. Confirmation, or "showing itself as it is," grounds the traditional theory of correspondence.

If this is true, however, then "how something shows itself" is a more important and primordial characteristic of truth than the simple criterion of correspondence. Heidegger says that "to be true" means "to be uncovering." Having shown that the traditional theory of truth (correspondence) itself rests on the phenomenon of uncovering, a closer analysis of that phenomenon becomes the next task.

Truth as Uncovering   (section 44)

After pointing out that the view of truth as uncovering has historical precedents among the Greeks, Heidegger discusses one of the more important and challenging characteristics of his theory of truth. Truth, he claims, in the first and most real sense, *refers not to objects but to Dasein*. If we define truth as uncovering, it must obviously be a characteristic of Dasein itself. Only in the sense of being uncovered can one say that "objects" are true. It was pointed out that the examples that best support Heidegger's theory of truth as uncovering are those dealing with human beings. We saw, in the example, that we often speak of "true" and "false" characteristics of human activity in terms of one's hiding behind masks and deceits. The example was apt. For now it has become evident that it is indeed Dasein that most properly uncovers and discloses. In fact, our analyses have already sketched out for us how it is that Dasein is disclosed. In Chapter V of *Being and Time*, Heidegger interpreted the disclosure of Dasein in terms of state-of-mind (thrownness), understanding (projection), and fallenness. Heidegger himself, in pointing out the role that the disclosure of Dasein has for the meaning of truth, recalls the analyses of thrownness, projection, and fallenness. This means that as an entity that uncovers (as an entity "in truth") Dasein reveals itself as factical—limited by what actually is; as existential projection—open to its own possibilities; and as fallen—closed off to these possibilities by its they-involvement. This last characteristic is especially important, for it introduces the concept of untruth. For the most part, Dasein does not expose itself; it remains hidden. As hidden it is in untruth. This is due to its fallenness, which we have already investigated. Heidegger points out that the very etymology of the Greek *aletheia* shows that truth is a kind of violation or robbery of what is normally the case. Truth is snatched from the usual mode of untruth in the they-self. If we recall the whole structure of the existential analytic as proceeding from an everyday and inauthentic existence in which the grounds of authenticity can be spotted, this peculiar language will seem less offensive. We are all aware that we avoid those areas that will expose and reveal our inmost selves, so that a shrewd observer can recognize just where our real selves are hidden by noting what it is we avoid.

Heidegger himself points out the two really important results of his analysis of the phenomenon of truth: (1) that truth belongs primordially to Dasein and (2) that Dasein is both in truth and in untruth. He also shows, in greater detail, that propositional truth is a derivative form of truth as uncovering.

The Being of Truth   (section 44)

From these characterizations of truth it should be clear that truth is an existential of Dasein. Truth, then, is a characteristic of Dasein, and as such does not exist independent of it. This has led Heidegger to say that truth exists only so long as Dasein exists. There is no truth without Dasein.

Is it the case, then, that truth is "relative"? Has not Heidegger's development of the phenomenon of truth left him with a purely subjective interpretation that borders on relativism or even solipsism or skepticism? The point is, of course, that by saying that truth exists only insofar as

Dasein exists, Heidegger is not saying that Dasein *determines* what is the truth. Nor does Dasein have the power of arbitrarily assigning truth values. But since truth is defined as unhiddenness based on disclosure, and since only Dasein discloses, truth can exist only in the mode of Dasein's existence.

This claim is actually not as untraditional as it might seem. For even within the tradition the force of the argument can be felt. According to tradition, truth resides in propositions. Hence if there were no propositions, there would be no truth. But who makes the propositions? Man. Thus there is no truth without man. (Or at least there is no truth without someone who is capable of making propositions.) What it means for truth to be, then, is that truth exists as a mode of Dasein; and this mode is based on Dasein as disclosedness.

It is not too terribly difficult to understand what Heidegger has said concerning the nature of truth. But the question that should be asked is this: What is the strategy behind this interpretation of truth? Why describe truth in this way? The answer can be seen in terms of how this theory of truth affects the existential analytic. For unless truth is of such a nature that it is ultimately tied up with human existence, Heidegger's analysis cannot be "true." By seeing truth as essentially a characteristic of Dasein coming to be aware of itself through its disclosure of itself in its limitations, possibilities, and tendencies toward concealment (i.e., its state-of-mind, its understanding, and its fallenness), the self-reflective activity of hermeneutic interpretation is thereby rendered as possibly *true*, and not merely emotively exciting. For this reason the discussion of truth has come at the end of the preparatory analytic; for the whole analysis has finally crystallized in the awareness that the interpretation of the existential self is the very foundation of truth.

The effect of this analysis might best be demonstrated by applying it, in less universal language, to an example. Suppose a young man has decided to inquire about his own nature, frustrated as he is with the inadequate suggestions of his society and upbringing. As he reflects upon himself, he becomes aware that his existence is in one sense limited by forces beyond his comprehension and control. He experiences the utter impotence at being unable to determine his origin, his color, his sex, race, native language, and social status. (That is, he becomes aware of his *facticity*.) But he is a creative and imaginative thinker, and his self-examination also reveals his rich and almost infinite variety of possibilities. He realizes that to a great extent his whole authenticity is his own affair. He becomes aware of his potentiality to be. (That is, he becomes aware of his *existentiality*.) His analysis does not stop there. He also becomes aware that the analysis itself was possible only through a violence done to his own everyday existence. To search so deeply in himself he had to turn a deaf ear to the pleas of his pleasure-loving comrades, who accused him of overseriousness and even morbidity. He realized, however, that there was an almost natural tendency in himself to avoid such investigations, to yield to the comfortable persuasion of the chatter of the they-self. (That is, he becomes aware of his *fallenness*.)

As the self-examination begins to reveal these characteristics, however, suppose a comrade derides his inquiry as being totally without any cognitive truth value at all. Suppose the claim is made that our inquirer has merely engaged in a romantic activity, which was psychologically invigorating, perhaps, but not of universal validity? To protect his interests, the young inquirer, let us suppose, investigates even further, and asks, Why isn't this kind of inquiry valid and with universal significance? He feels deeply within himself that such awareness is *not* arbitrary; and that if anything can be said to be true, his awareness of his existential structure is true. He feels it is true not only because the issue is so important to him, but also because he himself has experienced the actual stripping of himself, as it were, before his own relentless inquiry. He was aware of himself being exposed, being disclosed. Surely, he might say, that is what truth itself *means*. To be disclosed. To reveal oneself *as one exists*.

There is no argumentative force suggested by this purely fictional account of a make-believe inquirer. Its purpose was merely to show the inner consistency of the strategy followed in the existential analytic. There is a natural attractiveness on a purely intuitional level to Heidegger's claim that truth is unhiddenness. It strikes the reader immediately with a sympathetic ring. But for the sake of philosophical rigor, it is not this intuitional grasp that supports Heidegger's theory, but the painful and tedious working out of the entire existential analytic on the level of everydayness. All philosophers, to be complete in their account, are required to render an acceptable interpretation of how their own philosophizing is possible. Heidegger has achieved this by rendering his account of truth *as a phenomenon*. (The very reference to truth as a phenomenon may have struck one as somewhat peculiar.) The advantage of this is that truth thereby belongs to the existential analytic, indeed as its crowning achievement. The strictly strategic advantage, however, must not override the sounder philosophical one. Heidegger has accomplished an interpretation that not only appeals on an intuitional level, but renders an acceptable account of such derivative uses of truth as those employed in judgments and correspondence. And finally, his account of truth has reopened the possibility of genuine inquiry into what it means to be—a possibility that Heidegger feels had been closed by traditional philosophical accounts of "reality."

With his account of the phenomenon of truth, Heidegger's preparatory existential analytic has come to a close. We are ready now to shift
from this existential account to the more ontological one that follows.
I say "more ontological," for one must not see the preparatory analysis
as being without any ontological significance. The preparatory analysis
does indeed belong to the discipline of fundamental ontology.

We have seen the critical distinction between presence-at-hand and
readiness-at-hand resulting from the first existential awareness: that one
is always already in a world, and that this world does not primarily consist of pure substances, but of equipment ready to use for the sake of
Dasein. We have also seen, in terms of the second group of existentials,
that the self has two modes, the authentic and the inauthentic. Upon reflection of the self it became obvious that the self discloses itself in three
major ways: through state-of-mind, understanding, and fallenness. This
threefold structure of disclosure manifested itself in a single, comprehen-
sive existential called care. And finally, truth was seen as unhiddenness—
an interpretation that rendered the entire analysis open to the claims of
truth. All of this, however, was preparatory. The analysis has laid the
groundwork for the ontological account—i.e., it is now possible for Heidegger to show that the structure of care, and hence of the entire range
of Dasein's possibilities, is actually temporality. This is the burden of the
second major division of the published version of *Being and Time*.

VI.

DEATH

The transition from Division One to Division Two of *Being and Time* is not a mere shift from one kind of subject matter to another kind. According to Heidegger himself, it is a shift from the "preparatory" analysis to a "more ontological" analysis. The importance and nature of this shift can hardly be overestimated, for it lies at the basis of what is the deepest and yet most puzzling characteristic of Heidegger's thinking.

In one sense, the shift from the first to the second division of *Being and Time* is simply an aspect of the formal structure of the work. In this restricted sense, the shift is from an account of the purely existential ways in which Dasein manifests its occupation of the world, to the authentic and ontological awareness of itself that comes from an awareness of the meaning of death. In this restricted sense, the shift does not afford any great difficulties or problems. It is easy enough to see why the author wished to divide his account of the inauthentic they-self from that of the authentic self.

The transition from Division One to Division Two cannot be seen merely as a convenient structuring of a thesis, however. The shift is, by Heidegger's own admission, a turning from a basically *existential* analysis to something *ontological*. Even if we admit that it is an oversimplification to see Division One as purely "existential" and Division Two as purely "ontological," the impact of this transition is deeply troublesome. Once we grant, as is necessarily implied in Heidegger's account of the shift, that an "existential" and an "ontological" account are not the same thing, then the question becomes: What *is* the relation between the structure of existence and ontology? Otto Pöggeler, a competent and worthwhile interpreter of Heidegger, has drawn attention to this. In his work *Der Denkweg Martin Heideggers* he writes: "It remains unclear how the existential analytic and fundamental ontology belong together."[1] To be sure, Pöggeler is talking about the shift from Heidegger's account in *Being and Time* to his later investigations. But the question can be asked of the very structure of *Being and Time* itself.

The extent of the confusion that centers on this transition can be seen in the interpretations given to the role of the existential analytic by several American authors. In my opinion, few if any of these commentators have given proper thought to this problem, for their often conflicting accounts of the structure of *Being and Time* cannot be made consistent with the text. Richardson, for example, considers fundamental ontology itself to be "only a preliminary analysis.[2] This is completely inconsistent with Heidegger's own use of the term "preparatory," for not only does he restrict it to Division One, but when he proceeds to Division Two he asks: "What have we gained by our preparatory analysis?"[3] implying that the preparatory stage is now over with. Richardson is surely right in asserting that fundamental ontology, as found in *Being and Time*, was never *completed*, but this does *not* mean that *both* divisions of the published work should be seen as "preparatory." By Heidegger's own admission only Division One is preparatory. This seemingly innocent misinterpretation by Richardson is a weakness shared by others, which, I feel, has seriously misdirected their energies.[4]

On the other hand, there are those writers who have seen the existential analytic as completely divorced from fundamental ontology. One writer, for example, claims that ". . . no bridge can be thrown from his existential analytic to the *anticipated* fundamental ontology."[5] According to him, fundamental ontology was to appear in the third division, which was never published. This misinterpretation is also refuted by a careful reading of Heidegger's own words. Heidegger refers to the existential

---

1. (Pfullingen: Neske, 1963), p. 176.

2. W. Richardson, *Heidegger: Through Phenomenology to Thought*, p. 40.

3. *Being and Time*, p. 274.

4. Cf., e.g., Laszlo Versenyi, *Heidegger, Being and Truth* (New Haven: Yale University Press, 1965).

5. James Collins, *The Existentialists* (Chicago: Henry Regnery, 1952), p. 175.

analytic as the "present investigation in fundamental ontology": *die vorliegende fundamentalontologische Untersuchung.*[6] This can only mean that the existential analytic properly does belong to the discipline of fundamental ontology.

In pointing out the weaknesses of these popular interpretations, I have not merely tried to show that these commentators have made errors—that kind of argumentation belongs only in the professional journals. I have indicated these errors in order to show the tremendous difficulty and at the same time the tremendous importance of seeing the shift from Division One to Division Two in its proper light.

The following points have, I hope, been clearly established:

1. The existential analytic is indeed a part of fundamental ontology. Even though Division One is preparatory, it still constitutes an essential ingredient of fundamental ontology.
2. Fundamental ontology itself is *not* a preparatory analysis, paving the way for "ontology proper."
3. It is *not* the case that Division One is "existential" and Division Two "ontological"; for Division Two is still a kind of existential analysis, though no longer a merely "preparatory" one; whereas Division One, by Heidegger's own admission, is an essential part of fundamental ontology.
4. Nevertheless, there is a significant change from Division One to Division Two: for it is no longer preparatory, and it is seen as "more ontological."

This approach to the shift from Division One to Division Two also has its effect on the problem of the so-called turning (*Kehre*) from the early Heidegger to the later Heidegger. Although such considerations fall beyond the scope of this present work, it seems to me that the key to interpreting the "turning" lies in a proper understanding of what Pöggeler has claimed was yet unclear: the relationship between existential analysis and fundamental ontology.

To the reader new to Heidegger's *Being and Time*, such considerations may seem highly academic. They reflect, however, the profundity of the question now being considered. If what has been accomplished thus far (in Division One) is only preparatory, what is its relationship to the subsequent account, which is "more ontological"? Notice that the phrase is "*more* ontological," which implies that there was something "ontological" about the first division. What is it about the existential analytic that

6. *Being and Time,* p. 238.

it can be "more" or "less" ontological? How must ontology itself be viewed if it can be seen in such degrees?

The existential analytic continues. But it continues on a "more onto-logical" basis. And as such it is not *preparing for* fundamental ontology, but *is actually* fundamental ontology. Thus a minor difficulty is solved. What Division One *prepares for* is not fundamental ontology, for Divi-sion One is already that, but it prepares for a *more* ontological account. This suggests that fundamental ontology proceeds by stages of ever in-creasing ontological significance, so that the ontological characteristic is always there, but simply made clearer and more precise.

This is, in fact, the only possible solution; and it is a solution which Heidegger himself clearly spells out. We shall see more later about the circular nature of fundamental ontology, but for the moment it is perhaps sufficient to realize that Heidegger has not been careless in those terms that refer to his own analysis. The very structure of *Being and Time*, then, reflects the entire logic of Heidegger's thought: it is only in the ways in which a human being exists that one can discover what it means to be. To question what it means to be (fundamental ontology) is to search out the ground of all philosophical inquiry. The relationship between the study of "the ways in which a human being exists" (the existential ana-lytic) and "what it means to be" (fundamental ontology) is a relationship that can be discovered only in working out the essentials of the way in which one does indeed exist. It is a relationship in which the first question about existence becomes more and more specific until it reveals its true ontological dimensions. We must not see the existential analytic and fun-damental ontology as two separate disciplines, as if one could do the one without the other. Moreover, we must not overlook the fact that there are moments in the existential analytic when the weight of the interpreta-tion reaches a point of new insight so that a "shift" occurs—a new per-spective, as it were—in which the ontological aspects become more clearly revealed.

What is it about the second division of *Being and Time* that somehow focuses attention on a more ontological aspect? Division Two contains three major subject matters: death, authentic existence, and time. The last of these, time, is not merely a new phenomenon to be analyzed: time is seen as *the* ontological perspective. Setting aside "time" for the mo-ment, we have two new phenomena to be analyzed in the second division of *Being and Time*, death and authentic existence. Why is it that the anal-ysis of these two phenomena reveal the ontological aspect (which, as we will soon discover, is the aspect of temporality) in a way in which the preparatory analysis did not? Death, of course, does reveal the terrible temporality of our existence. Because death focuses upon our *own* exis-tence rather than upon the inauthentic they-self (for the they-self does not die), it becomes the ground for authentic existence. Death, then, becomes that important phenomenon which can expose the authentic and ontological basis of human existence.

The "everyday" perspective of the world and the self, basically inauthentic, is characterized by avoiding the ontological question. Experientially, this means that one's daily life is so imbued with trivial distractions that one cannot, from such a perspective, ask the question: What does it mean to be? To ask such a question we must transcend or go beyond the demands for our attention placed on us by daily concerns. Now, in *examining* this state of affairs, the fundamental ontologist must first sketch out the essential limits set upon him by the inauthentic perspective. Once this is done, and the full structure of everyday existence is revealed, that *same perspective*, can *then* reveal the underlying authentic structure. The question then becomes: What is it that allows the inquiry to shift from questions about the ways of existence to what it means to be? Heidegger's answer is: one's awareness of death. But not just any kind of awareness of death. For even in viewing the phenomenon of death the they-self has a tendency to operate its function of covering up and darkening the ontological question.

There still remains the question, however, about the logic, as it were, of the shift from the everyday perspective to the more ontological view. Heidegger admits that the development of the question of what it means to be is circular. Heidegger delays his analysis of how this circle operates until the third chapter of the second division. Since a commentary should follow the author's own development, I delay my analysis until we have reached section 63. But what we should bear in mind is what has already been said about the circular nature of this interpretation: Heidegger admits it is circular, and argues that all true inquiries are in fact circular. To question what it means to be operates in the hermeneutic circle; it begins with a consciousness of what it means to be, and through the analysis of the various ways of existence reveals more specifically and more ontologically the true meaning of Being. This consciousness of Being, of course, is itself a way of existing.

The important thing to bear in mind in turning to the second division is that the new ontological perspective occurs through the analysis of death. What is it about one's awareness of death that provides the unique difference in viewing the question of what it means to be?

THE THEORY OF DEATH

Every man dies his own death. It cannot be shared or be taken over by someone else. All the protections and devices of mind that one uses to avoid confronting the question of dying fade away when death actually comes. The very uniqueness of death—for in spite of its rather frequent occurrence it comes only once for each person—makes it an invaluable object for inquiry. In fact, the perspective given to the human situation by death is precisely the perspective one naturally assumes in interpreting and assessing *life*. We often ask, for example, such questions as, If I were to die today, would I have accomplished a worthwhile existence? That the scope of life is determined by death is made evident even in the most trivial of expressions: "Before I die I'm going to visit the Hebrides!" This indicates that one views death not only as inevitable, but as *common*—such expressions rarely alarm us or make us sorrowful—and not only that, death is seen as the ultimate evaluator, the *terminal* point of a career, the *end* of a life: that which neatly ties up all the loose ends of a personality and binds it up in a nice and sterile package.

We all know that we are going to die. Yet the full impact of such knowledge so easily escapes our awareness that occasional insights into its true character shock us and amaze us. In *The Idiot*, Dostoevski describes the impact of death-awareness on an individual condemned to die. Few accounts in literature can match the phenomenological power with which Dostoevski focuses attention on the terrible *certainty* of ceasing to be. Dostoevski himself was faced with such an imminent death, and from his accounts of this experience, it deeply affected him and completely altered his consciousness. And indeed, we all would agree that to have to go through such an experience would probably have a similar kind of effect on us. And yet how utterly strange that is, for the only difference between Dostoevski's experience and our own is that he knew *when* he was going to die. We know that we will die: we just don't know exactly when. Why is it that this simple indefiniteness as to when death occurs releases us from the poignancy of death? Can it be that the indefiniteness of "when" deludes us into avoiding its inevitability?

Perhaps, though, the fact is that we don't fully realize that we are going to die. Perhaps the love of life, or the comfortable tranquillity of self-deception, keeps us from truly realizing *what it means to be something that will one day cease to be*. The full grasp of this cannot help but have a tremendous significance on the nature of our existence. The purpose of our investigation here is *to find out what it means to be* (*Sinn von Sein*: "the meaning of Being"). Since as human beings we are one day going to die, what it means *to be* is influenced by our awareness of what it means *not to be*.

Each man, as we have said, dies his own death. Yet it is not so obvious that each man lives his own life. In fact, we often say that there are people, perhaps even the majority, who do not really live their own lives. Why is it that one can live another's life, but cannot die another's death?

For whatever reason one cannot die another's death, at least it is clear that in death one does confront one's genuine, true, and authentic self, if only for that brief and revealing moment (if there is such a moment) in which one realizes that one is dying alone. There are certain types of death, of course, when the awareness may not be there—as in the case of sudden and violent death—but such considerations do not disprove anything about what the consciousness of dying can reveal.

The great wealth of existential meaning that can come from an analysis of death has led Heidegger to analyze the phenomenon in *Being and Time*. Before we begin to analyze in detail much of Heidegger's interpretation, let us look briefly at the overall picture and strategy contained in his account.

Heidegger does not investigate the phenomenon of death for reasons resting on a "morbid" sense of life or a Christian-like hope for a "better" life hereafter. As with all other existentials, the analysis of death is made to serve the ontological problem. What the reader must share with Heidegger, if he is to understand what is being said, is the importance of this question: What can death tell us about the fundamental ontological inquiry into what it means to be? According to Heidegger, the most important aspect of the death phenomenon is that one's awareness of death *can* focus one's attention on the self *as it belongs to* the individual Dasein—i.e., the authentic self. The existential analytic, in its preparatory stage, was an analysis of the self only in the mode of inauthenticity, or as undifferentiated—i.e., characteristics of the self that were restricted to neither the authentic nor the inauthentic modes, but were applicable to each. To be sure, we learned *negatively* certain aspects of the authentic mode: we learned that it was *not* that mode which was characterized by the they-self in such inauthentic disclosures as curiosity, ambiguity, and idle talk. But before it is possible to analyze what it means to be, the interpretation of Dasein must also yield *positively* what it means to be authentic Dasein. Hence one major function that the interpretation of the phenomenon of death has for Heidegger is to reveal authentic Dasein. This is accomplished through the revelation of how Dasein is abandoned in his own dying by the they-self; the full import of the claim that each man dies his *own* death is fully developed.

Authentic existence is characterized by an explicit awareness of what it means to be. That is to say, someone who exists authentically must have ontological awareness. Inauthentic existence is that mode of existence in which one has hidden or forgotten what it means to be. In inauthentic existence, one's ontological awareness is dimmed and clouded by ambiguity, idle talk, and curiosity. If death-awareness somehow shakes off this veil or cloud, then there must be something in the phenomenon that focuses one's attention on the ontological question of what it means to be. Does the phenomenon of death actually focus one's attention on what it means to be?

The answer to this question is that it *can*. Even in death, however, the they-self tries to avoid the confrontation with the awareness of Being. Hence Heidegger includes in his description an account of how the they-self can so often muddy up even one's awareness of death.

Another major aspect of Heidegger's strategy is the demonstration that death provides us with a "complete" or "total" account of human existence. For very often one sees the human experience as beginning with birth and *ending* with death, so that death is seen as *that perspective from which one sees the whole or totality of human existence.*

There is a difficulty—one might even say dilemma—in this aspect, however. Death is something we cannot experience. There is an ancient Epicurean argument that attests to this: "If death is there, you aren't; if you are there, death isn't." The Epicureans used this argument to convince their followers not to fear death. But the argument can also be used to show that as a perspective with which to achieve a whole or total picture of human existence, it is not available to the inquiring mind. Not even the death of others can provide us with this perspective. Heidegger is acutely aware of this difficulty, and he spends a great deal of effort showing that the difficulty can indeed be overcome. Typical of his accounts, Heidegger gains a great deal in confronting this seeming barrier to a holistic or totalistic view of human existence; and it is with this difficulty that Heidegger begins his interpretation of death.

When Heidegger speaks of death, he is *not speaking of how one thinks at the time in which one is dying.* For the conditions of death are often not geared toward reflection at all. What is important in this analysis is not how one actually feels at the moment of death, but *what impending death can mean to one in the fullness of one's life.* The fact that I, as a healthy and secure individual with a good many years before me, can nevertheless realize that I will one day die provides me with sufficient speculative material to accomplish these insights. In fact, I do not even need to know with certainty that I *will* die; it is enough to know that I *can* die. Leibniz, for example, saw no contradiction in believing that man could one day conquer all diseases, even death, so that immortality would be a scientific project. Even if one accepted such a possibility, the reflection on the possibility of *not* being suffices to reveal one's terrible finitude as well as one's terrible *uniqueness* in thinking about one's death. It may well be that a sensitive and disciplined thinker in a period of great health and psychological love of life can achieve a profounder understanding of what it means to die than a somewhat less gifted individual, or even an equal, at the moment of death. One's personal experiences

of being "on the threshold of death," therefore, can have neither supportive nor detrimental effect on Heidegger's account.

THE PROBLEM: CAN DEATH BE GRASPED?

Epicurus had argued that death could never confront us, because as
long as we *are*, death isn't; and as soon as death *is*, we *aren't*. Unfortunately, for the fundamental ontologist, the same argument can be used
to show that *we* can never confront death. What is even worse: if death
is seen as that perspective from which the end or totality of human existence can be seen, then, *a fortiori*, as long as death is out of our grasp,
so too is our ability to see the end or totality of human existence. Heidegger does not see this as an empty threat: he spends a great number of
pages developing the problem. In fact, his style here is almost that of the
mystery-story writer—by making the mystery seem so insoluble, the success of the brilliant detective is all the more admired. This, by the way,
is a legitimate part of Heidegger's charm as a great teacher, and should
not be seen detrimentally. The dilemma, though, whether attractively
presented or not, is a real one. If only death can give us a total perspective, how can death, as an existential, be realized?

Heidegger puts it in these terms: As long as Dasein *is*, it is not-yet—
i.e., not all of its possibilities are fully realized. Yet as soon as Dasein
dies, it is no more (as Dasein anyway). Hence, it seems as if a total or
complete perspective of Dasein is impossible. The complete picture of
what it means for a human being to exist can be comprehended only
when all of the possibilities, all of the ways of existing, are tried out and
realized. This can be fully accomplished, however, only when one's life
is over. By that time, though, one can no longer reflect upon this complete
range.

One way out of this dilemma might be to analyze the death of others.
We see others die, and assuming that the others who have died were essentially like ourselves, we simply "put ourselves" in their shoes. Such
an attempt is refuted by Heidegger. According to his analyses, one cannot
discover the meaning of death by seeking to understand another's passing
away. All of section 47 of *Being and Time* is directed toward showing
that such an understanding of death through another's death is impossible. I see no need to comment on Heidegger's sensitive insights into the
phenomenon of another's death—the whole point is that this is not a successful way out of the dilemma.

According to Heidegger, the key to the solution lies in grasping the
proper nature of the not-yet element involved in Dasein's existence. How
is it that one must see the not-yet element? Part of the dilemma, as we
have described it, lies in the fact that there is something in Dasein's exis-

tence always "outstanding"—i.e., something that hasn't happened yet. Each of us has a future, which remains hidden and which is not as yet open to inquiry. Heidegger, however, argues that if this element of not-yet is seen "existentially," the dilemma will be solved, and Dasein as a whole will indeed be possible to grasp. The question then is this: How must the not-yet element of human existence be interpreted?

Heidegger first disposes of several possible but erroneous interpretations of the not-yet. In the first place, the not-yet of Dasein's existence cannot be of the character of ready-at-hand (as, for example, the unpaid portion of a debt is "outstanding"), nor as present-at-hand (as, for example, the last quarter of the moon is not-yet during the three-quarter phase), because Dasein is always more than presence-at-hand or readiness-at-hand, or even both combined. Rather, the not-yet element of human existence is something that is already there. Dasein is, in a very genuine sense, already its not-yet. Although we have already examined this characteristic in our analysis of the understanding as projection, Heidegger focuses his attention even more specifically here in the case of death.

Dasein is already its not-yet. The proper understanding of this characteristic as it applies to one's death must be distinguished from possible false interpretations. For example, Heidegger does not accept the metaphor of the ripening fruit. We say that a fruit's maturity or ripeness is contained in its unripeness; the maturity of the later Mozart symphonies were contained in the immature though delightful operas of his youth. There is a sense, of course, in which this is true enough, but it does not reflect the true "existential" meaning of how Dasein's "not-yet death" is already available for inquiry in a living and existing Dasein.

The perspective for which we are seeking necessarily includes the *end* of Dasein. We want to know existence in its totality—i.e., complete, at an end. The distinction that Heidegger makes to allow this completeness to be available for inquiry is this: One need not be *at an end* to realize that one is *going to end*. As Macquarrie and Robinson have translated it: the perspective is achieved, not through "Being-at-an-end (*Zu-Ende-sein*) but a *Being-towards-the-end (Sein zum Ende).* . . ." All that means is this: My awareness that I am going to die is sufficient to give me the perspective of totality; I do not have to actually die in order to see my "end." Is this distinction merely a clever juxtaposition of words, or does it contain a meaningful aid to our existential inquiry? How is it that the distinction between "to be at one's end" and "to be *going* to end" (which I take as preferable translations of *Zu-Ende-sein* and *Sein zum Ende*) solves the difficulty that I described as a "dilemma"?

For what reason would one want to argue that one must actually die in order to have the perspective necessary to grasp the "totality" or "completeness" of existing? Such would be the case only if what we were after was an account of the total range of actual experiences that one would have in a lifetime. In such a case we would indeed be frustrated in our attempts to render a complete picture. But we are not after the total range of actual experiences of any single Dasein, for at best that would give us only a particular account of *one* life. We are not interested in experiences—not even the death experiences—but in the universal awareness of Dasein *that it is possible not to be.* This provides the ultimate perspective, not because one's death puts an end to experiences and thereby limits what is actually lived by a single Dasein, but because the awareness that one is *going to die* means that one's existence is limited as such. In fact, even if one could, somehow, become aware of the experience of death, such knowledge would not limit one's ways of existence any more determinately than one's awareness that one is going to die. Hence the awareness *that one is going to end (Sein zum Ende)* provides the inquiry with the "total perspective" necessary to grasp Dasein as a whole. We do not need to look for some seance experience of actually *being at an end (Zu-Ende-sein)* in order to achieve this perspective. One might say that we have, through this distinction, been saved from having to become occultists.

This distinction, however, is not enough. As Heidegger puts it, we have achieved this perspective only negatively. We must now work out in positive detail what it means *to be going to end.*

Heidegger, however, does not immediately proceed to analyze the existential meaning of death. In section 49 he feels it necessary to determine again what it is he is *not* going to do in this analysis. Perhaps to a sympathetic reader such diversions are mildly annoying or overpedantic; but judging by the vast sea of literature from so many writers seeking a foothold in the Heideggerian analysis, it appears that Heidegger was well aware that there would be a tremendous tendency to misinterpret what he said, so he has tried to offset such misinterpretations by including sections like these. (One wonders how effective these sections are, however: in spite of his protests, many readers continue to misinterpret him. At least one cannot deny that Heidegger made an effort to avoid such misreadings.)

The whole point of section 49 is simply that the existential analysis of death does *not* take its sources and significance from other disciplines that have traditionally discussed the phenomenon of death. Heidegger's analysis of death has nothing to do with the *biological* account or its problems—it does not seek, for example, to give a more accurate description of "when life leaves and death begins." Nor is Heidegger's account concerned with the *psychological* disciplines—for such accounts are usually more interested in what happens during the last moments of life rather than with death itself. Far less is Heidegger's analysis concerned with *theological* questions—whether there is something after death is simply not even asked; nor does Heidegger's account give any preference for either the theistic or atheistic attitudes concerning this phenomenon. Heidegger is not even interested in what might be called the moral or *ethical* attitudes toward death—for the question as to whether death is an "evil" or the "wages of sin" simply does not fall within his analysis. That many theorists in these various disciplines have made *use* of Heidegger's analysis—above all theologians and psychologists—does not prove that Heidegger is wrong in separating his analysis from theirs. He did not deny that his analysis may be helpful to these other disciplines; what he does wish to deny, though, is that these various disciplines can present counterevidence taken solely from their own methodology to discredit Heidegger's account.

THE ONTOLOGICAL MEANING OF DEATH

Heidegger's account of the ontological view of death can be divided into four major stages: (1) the analysis of death in terms of the threefold method of Dasein's disclosure—existentiality, facticity, and fallenness; (2) an account of how the everyday they-self keeps one from properly grasping the significance of death; (3) an account of the "certainty" of death; and (4) the meaning of the authentic understanding of what it means to be going to die. This final element, coming as it does at the end of the chapter, provides an excellent point of transition to Chapter VII (Heidegger's Division Two), which deals with authentic existence as such.

Before we turn to the first of these four elements of Heidegger's interpretation of death, a word should be said about the key term used in this analysis. The existential that is to be analyzed in this section is called by Heidegger *Sein zum Tode*, which Macquarrie and Robinson translate as "Being-toward-death." It seems to me that in this case the more natural and idiomatic expression to-be-going-to-die not only allows for the translation of *Sein* in its more natural "to be" form, but also brings with it a more proper rendition of what Heidegger means by his German phrase. For what is contained in the existential is not the actual experience of dying, nor a morbid concentration on the fact that one day I shall die. What the term signifies is the existential awareness of the possibility of ceasing to be: a real awareness, then, that I am *going to die*.

1. How is this existential, that I am going to die, arrived at ontologically? Heidegger follows the structure of disclosure as laid down in the

preceding chapter. Dasein is disclosed through its existentiality, facticity, and fallenness.

A. What does Dasein's *existentiality* tell us about death? As we recall, existentiality is provided by understanding, which is the projection of possibilities. Death is certainly a possibility for Dasein; indeed, as we have seen, it is a possibility that focuses upon the very Being of Dasein. In so focusing on the Being of Dasein, it does so in three ways: (1) It shows us that my death is my own. I alone will die my death. As Heidegger puts it, it is *very much my own*—i.e., it is my "ownmost." If there is anything that is my own, it is my death. (2) Because it is my own, it cannot be shared by anyone. To be sure, certain lovers and martyrs have been known to "share" death in the sense that they have died for the same reasons for which another has died, sometimes even at the same time and in the same way. But such is not really sharing the same death: for only *I* can know what it means for *me* to be going to die. The term used to signify this inability to share my death is "nonrelational" (*unbezügliche*), a term that has absolutely nothing to do with the similar term in logic. (3) Finally, my projection of the possibility of death represents death to me as something that I cannot avoid. It is a possibility that is inevitable. The term Heidegger uses to represent this characteristic is "not to be outstripped" (*unüberholbare*). Taken all together, these three characteristics show that death "reveals itself as that possibility which is one's ownmost, which is non-relational, and which is not to be outstripped."[7] Experientially this means that when my consciousness becomes aware of death, it projects before me that I am really going to die, and that when I do I will die alone.

B. Dasein's disclosedness, as we have seen, is never restricted to what the understanding can project as possibilities. There is also always an element of what is due to state-of-mind or mood. What is it that state-of-mind tells us about our death? In the first place, since the chief characteristic of state-of-mind is to reveal what cannot be changed in our selves, we realize that death is something that is not *chosen* by us, but is forced upon us—or, to put it in more existential terms, we are thrown into it. The thrownness of Dasein reveals itself in the awareness that we are going to die. The mood that reveals this to us, however, is *not* the mood of terror or fear or even agonized frustration, but *dread*. We have already discussed this phenomenon; and if we recall that Heidegger's interpretation of it was so specialized, it

7. *Being and Time*, p. 294.

should be clear that just because everyone dies does not mean that everyone realizes what it means to be going to die. Nor does this mean that those who have experienced being near death necessarily have experienced dread—that state-of-mind which alone reflects the disclosure of what it means to be going to die.

As we recall from our previous examination, dread confronts us with ourselves. It was not, in the normal sense of the term, a *fear of death*. In fact, the description given to this mood suggested more of an alienation toward one's existence in the otherwise familiar world. To say, then, that dread is the state of mind that discloses to Dasein that he is going to die is to say something that may not be so obvious. For the claim here is that only in the somewhat rarefied awareness of dread does the full import of the *facticity* of death become disclosed. Again, this description strongly emphasizes that it is not one with many experiences of a harrowing nature who understands the meaning of death, but that man who has thought about death correctly— i.e., under the guiding influence of the ontological inquiry. This is made more explicit in the following section, which considers the evasion of death-awareness by the they-self.

C. Remaining true to the structure of disclosure, the final characteristic of the meaning of death must be its *fallenness*. According to Heidegger, Dasein tries to avoid the confrontation of the meaning of death. This does not mean that the they-self pretends that death doesn't exist, nor that one tries to avoid situations that may bring about accidental death. Fallenness, of course, refers to the tendency of Dasein to exist inauthentically in the they-self. Heidegger makes use of an entire section (51) to plot the various ways by which the they-self seeks to avoid a true understanding of what it means to die. Before we turn to that section, however, it may be well to reflect upon the fuller significance and strategy behind interpreting death according to the structure of Dasein's disclosedness.

The main point of the interpretation is quite simply this: The threefold structure of disclosure showed, in an earlier section, that the meaning of Dasein was to care. By following the same structural interpretation we show that the meaning of death is also grounded in care.

Heidegger has by no means abandoned his central existential claim that care is the Being of Dasein. His analysis of what it means to die has not weakened this claim; rather, by showing that a proper understanding of death can be reached only in terms of the nature of disclosure, he has shown that even in death the structure of care is still evident. On an intuitional level, of course, it comes as no surprise that someone might want to interpret the meaning of death as a form of caring, but it is nonetheless important for Heidegger's case that the relationship between death and care be constantly kept in mind.

2. We must now turn to the everydayness of Dasein, and how the inauthentic self interprets death. Specifically, the they-self interprets death in such a way as to convince us that death is *not* really our own (for the they-self seeks to avoid *any* kind of awareness or experience that cannot be shared by others and trivialized into commonness). The procedure or technique by which the they-self seduces the consciousness into believing that death is not one's own is to treat death always as an actuality and never as a possibility. If this seems somewhat odd, it must be remembered that for Heidegger possibility is more important than actuality—a claim that is most unorthodox and untraditional. If one considers the argument, however, there is a great deal of sense in it. If I treat death only as an actuality and never as a possibility, I can never consider my *own* death. As long as I am conscious, *actual* death belongs to someone else. Only others have *actually* died, hence for death to be properly meaningful to me, it must be seen as a possibility. The they-self, however, always tends to take more significance from what is actual than from what is possible. In the case of realizing what it means to be going to die (*Sein zum Tode*), the preference for possibility takes on a special meaning. For if death, in the inauthentic view, is always seen as something *actual*, then the feeling of discomfort that attends death-awareness is one of *fearing* something that is actually there. The inauthentic mood that discloses death is *fear*; whereas the authentic mood focuses not fearfully on an *actual event* but on a possibility in the mood of *dread*. If we recall the previous distinction between fear and dread, we can see that the account of these moods fits in quite nicely with this distinction between the authentic and inauthentic realization of death. Dread is never aware of some actual thing—it is rather that which forces our attention on possibilities. Fear, on the other hand, always has a definite object.

If we follow this argument, it naturally implies that I cannot fear my own death. (I must fear something actual; my own death is not actual, for if it were actual I could not fear. Hence when I fear death at all, I fear someone else's death.) This is why the *inauthentic* way to relate to death is to "fear" death. To *dread*, however, is to be uncannily aware of one's *own possible* dying. The strategy of our they-selves, then, in their effort to cover up an authentic understanding of death, is to treat death as an *event* or *object* that can be feared. Almost unawares, the self, in fearing death as an event, avoids ever fully realizing that *it*, the self, can cease to be. This is summed up by remarking that the fallenness of Dasein discloses that inauthentic existence *flees from* the face of death.

By describing the inauthentic mode of Dasein as fleeing from death, Heidegger does not intend to suggest that one's normal attempts to avoid dying are inauthentic. For again, we are not talking about the circumstances or conditions of the actual event of death, but what it means for one to know that death is a possibility. A casual reading of this section may lead one to the false assumption that Heidegger is urging everyone, hermit-like, moodily to contemplate that impending hour of doom. What is inauthentic is not avoiding the actual experience of dying, but avoiding the full significance of our ability not-to-be.

It may have struck the more acute reader that the inauthentic modes of the various existentials are never violently contradictory to the authentic modes. It is almost as if the they-self were far too "sly and clever." Our self-deceptions are not so crass and ineffectual as to try, for example, to convince us that there is no such thing as death. The they-self does not try to convince us of superhuman powers or immortality. It allows us to say: "Oh, yes, we will die someday." But it takes the stinging significance out of that awareness. The cleverest and deepest of lies, as we all know, are always those closest to the truth. There is an ontological significance to this insight. In Heidegger's interpretation of truth, we recall that untruth covers up or hides truth. *Hence the truth is still there,* but hidden. This is especially obvious in the case of the inauthentic view of death. That we are going to die—even that we are certain that we are going to die—is not denied by the inauthentic mode of existence. It is simply that the meanings of those claims are subtly emasculated. Thus in seeking for the truth, we do not have to look for different phenomena, but merely for more revealing interpretations. The locus of truth is the same as the locus of untruth. It is not the locus that differentiates them, but the perspective. The interpretation of the phenomenon of death is the key step in achieving that new perspective which will yield the "more ontological" understanding of what it means to be.

3. Before turning to the authentic account of death, a word should be said concerning Heidegger's interpretation of the certainty of death. Everydayness interprets the certainty of death in a merely "empirical" way. We are "empirically certain" of death. But what is empirically known is limited and determined by its "when." But the when of death is uncertain. Hence the harshness of the inevitability of death is softened by the uncertainty of its when. Once again, the subtle they-self buries the full significance of authentic comprehension. The they-self is too shrewd to attempt boldly to deny the inevitability and the certainty of death, but it buries the power of that awareness under the uncertainty of the time when we die. The everyday sentence "I shall die someday" can be made authentic only when that last word is cruelly torn away to

leave the stark: "I shall die!" or, to keep it in our translation: "I am going
to die."

We have seen how one avoids the full awareness of the meaning of
death by the everyday view. We can now turn to the *authentic* understanding of what it means to be going to die (*Sein zum Tode*).

4. The key to understanding Heidegger's interpretation of authentic
to-be-going-to-die is to recognize the peculiarity of the problem that Heidegger has developed for himself. Through the previous analyses of the
inauthentic view, we have found out several characteristics of the authentic view already: authentic awareness of death not only emphasizes that
it is we ourselves who are going to die and not the they-self; it also emphasizes that we must not see death as an *actual event* but always as a
possibility of our own Being. The difficulty in this, however, is obvious:
How can we be *toward* something (i.e., how can we be *going to do* something) unless what we are looking forward to is the *actualization* of that
event or experience? Heidegger has pressed the point that it is an *inauthentic* view of death to see it as future actuality. Yet he has described
the authentic view as a Being-toward-a-possibility! Can this phrase have
any meaning except as interpreted as looking forward to the actualization of something? To refrain from interpreting a possibility as something
becoming actual surely seems to reduce that possibility to a thin and in-
significant logical exercise of the mind. The question can be formulated,
then, in the following way: How can we interpret going-to-die as something not "wanting the actual" but yet keep it as a *meaningful* possibility?

The answer to this question lies in a proper understanding of what
is meant by to-be-toward-a-possibility or, in other terms, to-be-going-to-
be-possible. From the start we know that this going-to-be cannot be interpreted as "Being toward the actualization" of a thing. What, then, can
it be? Heidegger here makes a distinction that has significance not only
for his present discussion of death, but also for his subsequent development of time as the Being of Dasein. There are two modes, he claims,
of Being-toward something (i.e., there are two ways in which one can
be going-to-be something). To look forward to a thing as an actual, coming event is to be "expecting" it (*Erwarten*); but to look forward to a
thing as a possible way to be is to "anticipate" it (*Vorlaufen*). As in so
many cases, the translations cannot carry the full subtlety of the meaning.
Vorlaufen bears with it the etymological suggestion of "running before"
or "running into"; *Erwarten* means to await passively. One should not,
however, idly wish to be a native German in order to understand it, for
again there is no "word mystique" suggested. The point is that even for
a native German, the purely verbal distinction would not suddenly fill

his mind with great enlightenment; as with the English reader, the meaning of the term must be carefully extracted from its more detailed explanation and use.

What are the grounds for claiming that one looks toward the possibility of something quite differently in "anticipation" than in "expectation"? The distinction has come from an analysis of how one looks toward death. Surely Heidegger is correct in arguing that death is not meaningful to me purely in the sense of an event that will one day occur. For if that were the case, the Epicurean argument would indeed hold. It would be impossible to know death. But how is death meaningful to me? It has some significance, surely, in how I look at life. Look at it this way: On the purely speculative and logical level, there are two possibilities—to be or not to be. (This is not Hamlet's question, since we are on a purely logical level at the moment.) But if it is just as logically possible not to be, there must be some reason why one *is* rather than not. That is, there must be a meaning to Being *other* than the purely logical. If not-to-be were impossible, one would be God, a necessary Being in the old scholastic sense. Hence to know that it is possible not-to-be focuses one's attention on the possibility of being-able-to-be. To look forward to death as an *actuality* is to look forward to no longer being possible, and hence is to draw away from one's being-able-to-be. But to look forward to death, not as an actuality, but as a *possibility*, is to focus on one's being-able-to-be.

To a reader somewhat familiar with traditional philosophy, formulating the problem in this way suggests Leibniz's principle of sufficient reason. Although in *Being and Time* Heidegger does not make use of such references, in a subsequent work, *Vom Wesen des Grundes* (Of the Essence of Ground), he boldly argues that the ground of the principle of sufficient reason is freedom. The argument there is similar to the one suggested here: Not-to-be is as logically possible as to be. Hence there must be, in the confrontation of the possibility of not-being, an awareness of the ground for being rather than not-being. We are not speaking here of substantial efficient *causes*, but of meaning. We can ask two questions: What does it mean to be? and What does it mean *not* to be? If by these questions we mean *in actuality*, they are both meaningless. Why? Take the second question first. If by this question I mean: What does it mean actually not to be? then I can surely say that the question has no meaning at all, for if I don't exist, there is no meaning to me at all. This seems clear enough in the second of the two questions—the one about not-being. But since the two questions have the same logical status, the same must be said for the first. If my question what does it mean to be? is a question about my *actuality*, it is as meaningless as the question about my not-being-actual. If, however, the two questions have meaning at all, they must have meaning as *possibilities*. In this way, both questions are very meaningful. The two questions then present us with an understanding of our finitude. To know that I am capable of not-being also reveals that I am capable of being. I am free to be or not to be. Again, this "freedom" does not suggest that I am free to create myself or destroy myself; rather, it means to be free to grasp fully that I *am* capable of being and not-being, or *not* to grasp it. Authentic existence is to be fully aware of one's ability-to-be (which must include, of course, the possibility, though not the actuality, of being-able-not-to-be). This is why Heidegger claims that anticipation is the possibility of authentic existence. By looking forward, not to *actual* existence and nonexistence, but to *possible* existence and nonexistence, I am aware of the *ontological* question—even though I might not have all the explicit details of its significance. By shifting the focus of attention, then, from the traditional philosophical view of inquiring into what man is, to the question of man's possibilities, Heidegger has shown that the authentic view of death is far from being morbid and fatalistic, and is rather an exciting and courageous awareness of one's finitude.

What is it that we learn from Heidegger's analysis of death? Two claims strike me as being the most important characteristics of one's awareness of death. The first is that death focuses *specifically* on the question of what it means to be—i.e., the so-called Being question (*Seinsfrage*). Since the existential to-be-going-to-die means the awareness of the ability of man not-to-be, this existential deals directly with the awareness of Being. The second characteristic, however, is even more revealing. The awareness of death points out one of the most persistent doctrines of Heidegger's philosophy: that possibility means more than merely a future actuality. As a human being I live in the realm of possibilities—and it is in the realm of possibilities that authentic existence is realized. Heidegger has shown that possibilities cannot be defined in terms of the simply not-actual. The moral responsibility involved in a serious decision, for example, has far greater existential significance than the subsequent facts resulting from the actual choice made. To suggest that the simple chronicling of actual events can reflect what it means to be is to overlook the most important characteristic of existing—responsibility. We have seen that Heidegger considers it *inauthentic* to evaluate the coming of death merely as a future event which will be factually noted in the obituary columns. It is, however, an almost outrageous claim to suggest that death can be viewed not as an actual, future event but nevertheless as a meaningful possibility. For that claim implies that there is a meaning to possibility that is not exhausted by its future realization or nonrealization. How can possibility be meaningful outside of its becoming actual? The existential answer is freedom—an answer that obviously cannot belong to the study of the simple logic of possibilities, and that has thus heretofore been relegated to the study of psychology or emotions. But to locate freedom in the study of emotions is to deny it any ontological and universal status. By showing that death, as an existential awareness of possible not-being, is meaningful authentically only as a possibility, Heidegger has laid the foundation for treating freedom and authenticity as ontologically significant terms. The next chapter, which deals with the meaning of authenticity, carries out this inquiry more specifically, but for the moment it is enough to realize that reflection upon the possibility of not-being (to-be-able-not-to-be) reveals the possibility of being (to-be-able-to-be) in a way in which "possibility" is no longer seen merely as an abstract logical function of not-yet-actual, but is seen rather as an essential manner in which a human being exists; and that essential manner is given the name "freedom." Heidegger's analysis of death, then, is not the basis for morbidity and despair; it is rather the source of freedom and authentic existence.

VII.

AUTHENTIC
EXISTENCE

In Dostoevski's *The Brothers Karamazov* there is a chapter entitled "The Grand Inquisitor," in which the great struggle between freedom and security is powerfully portrayed. Although Dostoevski formulated the problem in terms of the nature of Christianity, the insight into human existence revealed in this remarkable chapter is far more universal than any one religious view. The thesis of "The Grand Inquisitor" is this: If Christ were to return to Christian Europe today, he would be rejected by his own church; for the official Church affords a security sponsored by an almost mechanistic institution of religion in which the people know exactly what to expect and what to do in order to achieve salvation; whereas Christ himself offers no such security, but only freedom. The cardinal of the Church, the Grand Inquisitor, condemns the reincarnated Christ for not showing as much love for the people as he, the cardinal, manifests. The cardinal maintains that he gives the people what they *want* and, hence keeps them happy. Christ, on the other hand, would want to deprive them of what they want—security—and instead burden them with the terrible weight of freedom.

The remarkable sensitivity and insight of the great Russian author has almost unlimited application, and it is not my purpose here to render a definitive interpretation of such a great literary masterpiece. There is, nevertheless, a great deal to be learned from "The Grand Inquisitor" that is directly applicable to the claim being made by Heidegger in Chapter II of Division Two of *Being and Time*. For both authors focus their remarkable acumen on the twofold characteristic of freedom: first, that it places a terrible burden on the free man, often forcing him to seek almost any means to avoid its full significance; and second, that it *isolates* the free man from the comfort and security of an ordered existence. Furthermore, both authors recognize that a loss of freedom is coincident with a loss of one's authentic character: the cardinal really thought that he was a Christian even at that moment when he was denying the true essence of Christianity; the inauthentic self is most confident of having solved all its problems when it covers up that which it really is, something capable of choice. For the they-self and the cardinal both, the choices have already been made. There are no more choices. All that is left is to live out the implications.

Heidegger begins this second chapter of Division Two with a very brief reference to the ultimate locus of authenticity: freedom. He points out that by avoiding choices one becomes snared in inauthenticity, and that the problem is to find the basis from which such choices can be made. But as in the case of the cardinal in "The Grand Inquisitor," the basis from which choosing and freedom occur—namely, the authentic self— has been lost sight of. Hence the task of Chapter II is to *locate* the authentic self. In "The Grand Inquisitor" it is made clear that the reason the cardinal felt he must put the reincarnated Christ to death was not because of any evil hatred, but because the cardinal did not know what it meant to be a true Christian. The authentic Christian, in Dostoevski's eyes, was *free*; it was the *in*authentic Christian who did not value freedom, but the safe and sure way to salvation.

If we grant for a moment the validity of the claim that freedom is the determining factor in authentic existence, and if we further grant that the authentic self must be located before we can even begin to know what this "freedom" means, the question that then must be asked is this: How is it that we can reveal the authentic self? How can we expose the nerve of freedom, so to speak?

One point must be made in advance. From whatever source or manner of existence the chief insight into authentic selfhood will be won, *it must be available to everyday Dasein*. It must be reemphasized that Heidegger's philosophy is not based on some "special kind of experience" or mysticism. The source of authenticity must lie in the range of that which is already (if vaguely) understood. From the very beginning we have insisted that Dasein has a basic understanding-of-Being (*Seinsverständnis*: "to understand what it means to be"), and that the task of the existential analytic is to make specific (thematic), through interpretation, that which is vaguely understood. The nerve of freedom which we seek to expose, then, is within the everyday mode: it is the exposure itself that excites the nerve and awakens the reaction, which is authentic.

The source from which one can focus directly upon one's authentic self is, according to Heidegger, the voice of conscience. To some this may seem an extraordinary claim. In the light of certain tendencies of modern Freudian psychology to deemphasize guilt, to try to *remove* guilt, it may even sound like downright heresy to certain orthodox psychologists. But conscience and guilt are, according to Heidegger, the great human existentials that expose authentic self-hood and the basis of freedom. Before we turn to an examination of Heidegger's own presentation, it may be worthwhile to consider on a common-sense or intuitional level some aspects of this central Heideggerian claim.

There are various kinds of self-awareness. In addition to the purely empirically verified evidence of a self (such as one's personal tools, one's dirty dishes, and one's image in a mirror), there are those modes of self-awareness that center upon the subjective *agency* of the self—e.g., the self that results in the famous *rational* discovery of Descartes's *Cogito ergo sum.* All of these modes of awareness do indeed reveal something of a "self"; but the question is, do these modes reveal my own unique self *as* a self? Is there another kind of experience that reveals the self in the full poignancy of its "mineness"? Here we must recall that the term "authentic" is a translation of the German *eigentlich*, which contains the root *eigen*: "own," as in "*my own.*" So that when we seek after "authentic" selfhood, we are seeking after that disclosure which reveals the unique "mineness" of a self.

One of the experiences within the range of most human existents that focus upon the self is that of guilt. Surely the *ego* which is understood in a situation of moral significance has a kind of personal reference which is not the same as the merely logical demand that all acts of knowing must have a subject. When I think about the "who" or the "self" that caused a friend needless pain, for example, I am terribly aware of who it is that's responsible—me. The reader may wish to engage in a little thought experiment to try this out. Try, if you are willing, to recall to your mind something in your past that you have done, about which you are not particularly proud; something, in fact, of which you are ashamed. It may well be something that is "objectively" trivial, but it should be something about which you would honestly say: I ought not to have done that. Now suppose I were to ask you: Who did that act? Who is responsible, who bears the guilt for that particular act? Compare the meaning of the "I" in the answer "I did that act" with the "I" in the sentence "I think, therefore I am." What is it about the first "I" that does not seem necessarily contained in the second? Heidegger's claim is that guilt or conscience (and I shall deliberately keep the meanings of these two terms vague and indistinct for the moment), which allows the first "I" (the "I" contained in the admission of guilt), has *existential* significance, which in *some* sense is lacking in the second.

There seems to be, at least on this uncritical intuitional level, an awareness of the "guilty self" which is not contained in the purely subjective agency of the *cogito*. Even certain analytic philosophers, such as H. L. A. Hart, argue that there are *ascriptive* meanings to sentences, which are not exhausted by either the descriptive or the prescriptive meanings. It is to the *reference* of such ascription that we are directing the present inquiry.

Let us follow this particular line of inquiry a bit further. We have said that there is something "authentic" about the awareness of the self who is guilty. Suppose you do something morally wrong. If you reflect upon the fact that you committed such an action, you become *aware of yourself as someone capable of being held responsible. You* are guilty. At this moment of awareness, however, there is a new decision to be made. You can, of course, seek to deny your guilt to yourself. You do this, however, not by denying that such-and-such an act *occurred*, but that there were external causes that determined your action. You may even go so far as to deny that any action is free, that no one person is ever guilty at all. At least it is a familiar trick to search for external circumstances that will help alleviate your guilt. On the other hand, you can decide to admit your guilt, to recognize that you are responsible for the action and are deserving of the censure that goes with it. Now this is all common enough. But what does it mean? Heidegger claims that if you decide to *avoid* the significance of your guilt, you are also avoiding an awareness of your self. By avoiding guilt you become a non-self (inauthentic) self; whereas if you confront the guilt you are a true (authentic) self.

The inquiry thus far seems to lead to the dubious conclusion that one must actually be guilty of some unsavory act in order to be authentic. This is of course not the meaning of Heidegger's interpretation, but it must be made clear why this meaning does not apply. Obviously we do not wish to maintain that only those who have really committed evil acts are authentic, nor do we wish to suggest that authenticity is dependent upon the circumstances of a particular act. For it is the whole persuasion of this inquiry that there are no *circumstances as such* that have ontological or existential significance. Hence Heidegger argues that it is not the actual experience of guilt for a particular act that is authentic, but rather *wanting to have* a conscience, wanting to feel guilty if there were grounds to do so. Here too we can notice certain elements of support from an "intuitional" level. An authentic self is surely one willing to be open to the calls of conscience. If a man is totally deaf to any conscience at all, if he feels no guilt at all, we might well say that he is "lacking" in an awareness of what it means to be a man. But the point made by Heidegger is not quite so simple. He claims that to *want to have* a conscience is the basis for authenticity—this implies that to want *not* to have a conscience is inauthentic. Hence one who seeks to live in such a way as to be without any possibility of ever being guilty—one who seeks to deny the very possibility of guilt—is one who is hiding behind the they-self and hence inauthentic.

The obvious humanitarian advantages of the last century in the fields of psychology and penal law through which many unfortunate people were treated as pathologically incapable of guilt are not here being denied. There are, to be sure, many cases in which morally reprehensible acts were performed by people totally incapable of recognizing what they were doing. In such cases there should be no urging of guilt. Furthermore, there are those unfortunates for whom guilt has taken on pathological dimensions and for whom an awareness of guilt has no redeeming value at all. Nevertheless, there is among many intelligent people a vague feeling of uneasiness in the carefree abandonment of any and all forms of guilt. One senses a kind of loss of human respect and dignity among those who so quickly seek to alleviate guilt from the consciousness. One senses that it is perhaps a good thing to want to have a conscience. Heidegger's claim goes far beyond this rather vague sense I have just described. I have sought, however, to awaken a kind of general sympathy for the more severe interpretation of guilt and conscience that Heidegger uses to disclose authentic existence.

The tendency that the reader might have at this moment to interpret *Being and Time* as a kind of "existential ethics" must be resisted. But since the possibility of falsely interpreting the present section as a study in ethics seems likely, I shall use this opportunity to sketch out more fully what Heidegger means by calling his work "fundamental ontology," and how it is that this interpretation of human existence lays the ground (fundament) for the rest of the philosophical enterprise.

The study of the existential-ontological structure of guilt does not belong to the discipline of ethics—indeed, Heidegger claims that ethics and morals emerge from an understanding of guilt rather than the other way around. Guilt, then, as an existential is the foundation of morals. This is somewhat in opposition to the traditional view, which usually interprets guilt as dependent upon an already established moral code. Normally one conceives of guilt as a psychological reaction which occurs because of a violation of a certain established mode of behavior. The implication of such a theory is that without such established codes or mores there would be no guilt at all. Hence, the traditionalist would argue, guilt is *dependent upon* an ethical structure or a moral code.

Heidegger's view is that ethics and morals *presuppose* guilt, making guilt prior to morals. For what reasons would one want to claim that guilt is prior? Suppose we consider the claim of an ethicist that reason can tell us what it is we ought to do. A Kantian, for example, would maintain that reason instructs us to treat all human beings as ends and not merely as means, or that all actions must be universalizable. Now is it the case that only after such a principle has been accepted that the feeling of guilt, on violation of this maxim, can occur? Or is it the case that *prior* to the formulation of such a maxim one has an attitude that compels one to search for such a guidance as reason dictates? To put it more primitively, Is it that I first find out or learn what I ought to do, and then feel guilty if I violate that maxim or commandment; or is it that I first feel a call to be good or authentic, and then establish an ethical or moral order to satisfy this desire? If the second is the case, then guilt (conscience) is the foundation of ethics; if the first is the case, then ethics is the foundation of guilt. Heidegger argues that guilt is the foundation of morals and ethics. For the question that Heidegger asks is this: Granted that there are such things as morals, and that there is such a thing as ethical understanding, *what must be presupposed about the human consciousness in order that there be any inclination or desire to do what is right or to know what one ought to do in the first place?*

Suppose I were to ask: What ought I to do? And suppose reason (either independently or with the help of other "faculties") can tell me what it is I ought to do. Why should I do what I ought to do? Or, what is perhaps more significant, why did I ask myself what it was I ought to do unless there is *already*, in the very structure of my consciousness, a kind of persuasion that it *indeed matters* that I do what I ought to do? Isn't it the case that the question "Why should I do what I ought to do?" is in fact a pseudo question? Does not the "ought" carry with it a necessary presupposition that exposes a *prior* commitment to some form of genuine existence? Presupposed in all questions of moral commands or ethical understanding is the realization that one is capable of being responsible, guilty, or justified. Unless there were such a presupposition, there would be no reason for morals at all. "Why be good?" is a profounder question than, "What is it that I ought to do in order to be good?" The important point to remember in Heideggerian thought, however, is that the first question is answered existentially rather than teleologically. This means that the question "Why be good?" is not answered in terms of a future hope (if you are good you will be happy) but in terms of an already existing existential awareness of authenticity.

The priority of guilt over morals is an excellent insight into the primordial nature of fundamental ontology. Although in later years Heidegger abandoned the term "ontology" as descriptive of his thought, he never abandoned the basic claim that the study of what it means to be is the ground of all other disciplines. He dropped the *term* "fundamental ontology" merely because it was continually misinterpreted as a type of metaphysics. In the case of his interpretation of guilt, the nature of this claim for the primacy of ontology is clear. Such *metaphysical* questions as the nature of moral imperatives *are based on* such ontological characteristics of existence as guilt and conscience. In *Kant and the Problem of Metaphysics*, Heidegger points out that such disciplines as ethics and morals belonged, in the traditional view of Leibniz-Wolff, to what was called *metaphysica specialis* ("special metaphysics"), which even the traditionalists tried to ground in the more primordial *metaphysica generalis* ("general metaphysics": the old "ontology"). The error of such traditionalists was to interpret ontology as a kind of extension of substance cosmology, another "special" metaphysics. For Heidegger, the fundamental discipline is indeed an ontology, but not an ontology of substances; rather, it is ontology of existence. If one accepts the Kantian view of morals as a question of metaphysics, then "general metaphysics" (ontology) must be the foundation of that discipline. By showing that the existential-ontological characteristic of *guilt* comes *before* ethics, Heidegger has again shown that fundamental ontology is the primordial discipline.

It is perhaps difficult to assess the validity of this claim without further examination of what Heidegger *means* by guilt and conscience, and why it is that guilt and conscience expose the nerve of freedom, which is authentic existence. As we turn, however, to the actual analysis of the text, it should be emphasized that it is essential to know *why* Heidegger has chosen to analyze conscience and guilt, and that it is not, then, enough merely to know *what* his theory of guilt entails. I have sketched out a brief statement of *why* guilt is important; we can now turn to *what* is meant by the Heideggerian analysis of these terms.

INTERPRETATION OF CONSCIENCE

Heidegger's interpretation of conscience is fairly straightforward as a phenomenological description. As long as it is kept in mind that his whole purpose in interpreting conscience is to focus on his final analysis of authentic existence as *resoluteness*, there is little need to comment except to point out a few of the major characteristics.

In earlier sections, Heidegger has already established the structure of Dasein's disclosure as based on existentiality, state-of-mind, and fallenness; the disclosure of conscience for the most part follows this general pattern. The only deviation from this pattern is that "fallenness" cannot be a characteristic of *authentic* Dasein; hence Heidegger uses discourse (*Rede*) as the third element of disclosure. This is especially fitting since Heidegger's interpretation of conscience as a kind of *calling* adapts itself quite well to the disclosure of discourse. The essential character of conscience is that of calling—and the corresponding mode of authentic existence is keeping silence: reticence. The point being that, unless we are quiet and listen to the call of conscience, we will never *hear* it.

What is the import of describing conscience as a call? Basically it is this: To treat conscience as a kind of calling exposes four dimensions to the character of conscience, which are too easily overlooked in describing conscience as a "feeling" or as the psychological fear of an induced moral code. These four dimensions of conscience are true of *any* form of calling: when there is a calling, there must be (1) someone who does the calling, the "caller"; (2) someone who is called; (3) something that is called *about*; and (4) that *to* which someone is called. It is this last point that distinguishes calling from other forms of discourse. (When one *calls* another rather than merely *speaks* to him, an *action* or direction of attention is expected: thus one might *call* on another to be careful or wary.)

In Heidegger's analysis of conscience, all four of these dimensions are the self. (1) It is the self that does the calling; (2) it is the self that is called; (3) it is the self that is called *about*; and finally (4) it is the self to which the self is called—i.e., to its own unique and authentic self. All of these dimensions, of course, reflect different aspects of the self. The self that *does the calling* is in dread (*Angst*) and is "uncanny" (*unheimlich*: "not at home"). Hence the self that does the calling is a self that has lost the comfortable feeling of belonging with the crowd. This is surely a sensitive insight into the occasions of conscience, for there is often a feeling of loneliness and terrible isolation when we are forced to concern ourselves with "matters of conscience." The self that is *called*, on the other hand, is precisely the self that has been lost in the they-self—and the calling is an attempt to bring that self to *leave* the company of the they-self. The calling is *about* the self in the sense that conscience awakens an awareness of the mode of existence in which the self finds itself—authentic or inauthentic. The call is *to* the self in that it is an appeal to the self to be authentic.

The advantages of interpreting conscience in this way should be obvious. In the first place, it avoids having to search outside the self for some "God" or mystical entity. Furthermore, it makes it possible to describe the phenomenon of conscience independently of any particular moral code. The call to authenticity is hence primary to any code that merely sets guideposts and aids toward achieving authenticity. (In this sense, then, Heidegger would accept the inquiry of Socrates in the *Euthyphro*.) Most important for Heidegger's purposes, the focus is irrevocably on the existence of the self that has hitherto been hiding behind the inauthentic or the modally undetermined existentials.

Unless it was genuinely possible for someone to be *guilty*, conscience would have no meaning. This seems terribly obvious when stated abstractly, but its truth is often overlooked, for many seem to strive to achieve a conscience without guilt, as if one could maintain a meaningful code of moral conduct without any awareness of lack or deficiency of conduct if that code were violated. In fact, it is precisely the reverence for one's moral code that finds its basis in guilt. The role of guilt, then, is an important one in Heidegger's analysis of conscience.

The existential interpretation of guilt *cannot* be seen as arising from a state of affairs in which debts and laws are owed or enforced; nor can it even be seen simply as a form of responsibility for action. Above all, it cannot be seen as a fear of reprisals. Rather, it must be seen in terms of the question, What does it mean *to be* guilty? (*Not*: "What are the circumstances of guilt?" or "How does one *feel* when one is guilty?") Heidegger interprets "*to be* guilty" as a form of *negative* existence. That is, guilt contains a "not." What does this mean? Certainly it does not refer to "not possessing something." Heidegger warns against interpreting the "not" of Being-guilty as any kind of presence-at-hand. Rather, the "not" contained in being guilty is the "not" of Dasein's finitude. To be guilty, Heidegger says, is for Dasein to be the basis of a nullity. "To be a basis of . . ." is the existential meaning behind the normal view of guilt as "being responsible for." Hence "to be the basis of a nullity" suggests that Dasein is the *ground* (*Grund*: "basis") of a nullity. And what does "nullity" (*Nichtigkeit*) mean? With a certain degree of reluctance, I might suggest that a better translation would be "notness." This means that, just as all of Dasein's possibilities are what can be, so too are they what can *not* be. The ability *to be* is also, in Dasein, an ability *to be not*. (I do not say not-to-be, for that implies the concept of death, as was discussed in the previous chapter.) As a possibility, to be honest is countered with the ability to be dishonest (*not* honest). Ontologically speaking, since guilt focuses upon the unique self, it does so in terms of the self's ability to exclude possibilities as well as to accept them.

Two things seem to result from this. One is that Dasein is always guilty. This does not mean, of course, that Dasein has always done something for which it is ashamed, but rather that as long as Dasein is, it *is* in such a way as to be the ground for not being in such a way. The second point is that *to be* guilty is more primordial than any knowledge about it. This again reflects Heidegger's break with the traditional version, which usually insists that one cannot be guilty without first knowing about it. But, ontologically speaking, one is capable of notness before one need be explicitly aware of deviation from what one ought to be.

The whole point of this is that, since conscience has been interpreted as a call from the self to the self, there must be a meaningful choice for Dasein, either to be or not to be the self. The latter possibility is grounded in Dasein's being the basis of a notness—guilt.

It is not enough to describe conscience simply as a call. It must be disclosed in terms of its being an existential of Dasein—in terms, that is, of existentiality, state-of-mind, and discourse. Let us consider existentiality first.

Existentiality, as we recall, is the projection of possibilities. Its function is that of understanding. To understand, ontologically speaking, is to project possibilities. What is projected in conscience? Being-guilty. Experientially, this means that among my possible ways of being is to be guilty—and I know that I am the ground of my notness, that I am responsible for what I am because I am that kind of being who is free to accept or reject the possibilities I have. I also realize that my guilt is uniquely my own (it is my "ownmost"); in guilt I am no longer protected by the loudness of the "they."

The state-of-mind that discloses conscience is dread. We have already described this phenomenon in detail, so that all that is needed here is to emphasize that dread *individualizes* by making Dasein feel not-at-home (uncanny) with the "they," and focuses terribly upon the possibilities of being and not-being.

The form of discourse that discloses conscience is keeping silent—reticence. Obviously if we are to hear the call to authentic existence, we must be quiet enough to listen to it. This particular characteristic emphasizes that one of the chief modes of inauthentic discourse is loudness, for when one is "loud" one cannot listen.

If we add all of these characteristics together we get the following description of Dasein's disclosure in conscience: a "reticent self-projection upon one's ownmost Being-guilty, in which one is ready for anxiety [dread]."[1] A careful contemplation of this can be very helpful. Heidegger uses the term "resoluteness" (*Entschlossenheit*—etymologically connected with *Erschlossenheit*: "disclosedness") to refer to this disclosure of conscience. We can see, then, that the analysis of conscience and guilt focuses upon this description of authentic existence.

---

1. *Being and Time*, p. 343.

RESOLUTENESS

Heidegger's choice of "resoluteness" as the term most suited to describe authentic existence is in keeping with his general development. "Resoluteness" is a translation of *Entschlossenheit*, which also means "decision", "resolve," "having made up one's mind," etc. Its close connection to freedom and choice must not be forgotten. Intuitively it is easy to grasp this claim: surely to be authentic means to be resolute, to be free to choose one's own manner of existence, and so forth. The term focuses upon an individual's unique assertion of his own existence, freely grounded in responsibility and guilt. In spite of this insistence upon the authentic character—i.e., upon its "my-own-ness"— Heidegger insists that resoluteness, as "to be authentically one's self," does *not* imply a detachment or isolation from others in the world, or from Being-in-the-world. For the self, after all, even the authentic self, is by nature *with* others and *in* the world. Authenticity, then, never implies hermit-like loneliness or stoic detachment from world events. It does suggest a clear awareness of the self as a self, and a realization that one alone is responsible for the way one exists, and it avoids the slavery of the they-self.

As the reader accustoms himself to the use of "resoluteness" as authentic existence, it must be kept in mind that conscience and guilt remain essential grounds for this manner of existence. Hence resoluteness is never an arrogant self-assertion which tends to shuffle off guilt and conscience, nor is it an impervious and ruthless assertion of one's rights. The resolute man is guilty, he knows that he is guilty, and he wants to have a conscience. In fact, it is in realizing the nature of his conscience and his guilt that he becomes resolute.

It may seem that one might object that one is never simply "resolute," but is always resolute *about* something. Resoluteness, then, requires a *situation*. Heidegger analyzes this concept of "situation," and a few remarks should perhaps be made here about it. In the first place, a "situation" of resoluteness is not even possible for the they-self. The existential meaning of what constitutes a situation is not that there is first a set of circumstances into which Dasein establishes his resoluteness; rather, as resolute Dasein (and *only* as resolute Dasein) a situation is already present. It is authentic Dasein that constitutes situations—situations do not provide a background for authentic existence. This might sound somewhat strange, but its meaning is, I think, clear and ultimately defensible. The ground for this claim is the essential teaching that possibility is more important than actuality. Situations are not actual events that are somehow "sanctified" by an "attitude" in which possibilities are important. Rather, it is the case that situations exist only in terms of Dasein's projection of possibilities.

What do we call a "situation" anyway? We say that a situation is "fraught with emotion" or that there is a "very dangerous situation." For there *to be* a human situation, there must be possibilities—i.e., the *meaning* of the situation is not represented by a simple listing of the facts or circumstances that actually occur, but rather, it is the amount and intensity of human caring and concern that establish what we call a "situation." (I do not mean to suggest that one can analyze the use of the word "situation" as it is used in English to find that Heidegger's meaning always prevails; I only intend to suggest that there is a peculiarly human aspect to some instances of the word "situation" which do indeed correspond to Heidegger's highly specialized usage.) There is a sense, anyway, in which the meaning of "situation" can be truly reflected only by a focusing upon the projection of possibilities by a human being, and it is to this special use of the term that Heidegger wishes to restrict its meaning as an existential of Dasein.

What does this interpretation of authentic existence amount to in terms of the structure of *Being and Time*? In the attempt to find a single grasp of authentic existence, Heidegger first had to isolate the self. The attempt to ground this "whole" ontologically in time is the task of the next chapter. But this present section must be seen above all as the clarification of what it means to be a self. Heidegger's choice of guilt and conscience as the existentials most suited to reveal the authentic self has been established. One final consideration may prove helpful in seeing the strategy of his argument.

Traditional philosophy as well as simple reflective common sense provide us with two immediate and obvious pictures of the self. The first is the self of the *cogito*: the self is that which thinks. The other is by empirical evidence. I can look at my experience and my own body (at least part of it) and discover the "actual" empirical self. But both of these interpretations of the self, valid though they may be, have certain drawbacks. One might oversimplify it by saying that the self of the *cogito* is "too universal," whereas the self of the empiricist is too arbitrary, too dependent upon particularities, "too particular." The self of the *cogito* is forced upon us by the irresistible logic of the argument. It is a "subject," not a self. The self of the empiricist is, strictly speaking, an "object," and not a self. However, the self as the free and authentic existent, whose possibilities as well as its actualities are meaningful, is neither arbitrary nor abstract. Guilt focuses on the *particular* Dasein, but it does so in a way that is not arbitrary, and is not limited by actualities and accidental circumstances. It is, in a sense, that which unifies the abstract and idealistic formulations of pure reason with the immediate and limited world of actual experience.

Guilt and conscience focus, then, upon authentic existence, which has been phenomenologically interpreted as "anticipatory resoluteness"—and which, of course, is discussed in greater detail in both *Being and Time* and this commentary. The formal ontological description of authentic existence remains, however, as that form of existence which is aware of what it means to be. Hence to exist in anticipatory resoluteness is to be aware of what it means to be.

VIII.

TIME

sections 61–71

The title of this work makes it clear that time plays a central role in Heidegger's thought. Throughout the entire preparatory analysis of Division One, and even in the first two chapters of Division Two, time was seen as that focal point to which all of the existential analyses were directed. In the chapter directly preceding this one, there were even strong hints of how the analysis of time would be carried out.

In spite of hints and suggestions, the major import of the analysis of time has been held in suspense. It may even seem strange to introduce the time analysis in connection with a discussion of "potentiality for being a whole." Indeed, time does not even occur as a major theme until late in the chapter. Of the six sections that divide this chapter, the first four have nothing to do with the analysis of time. A full two-thirds of the chapter, then, continues to postpone the time analysis: and when time is finally discussed, it seems almost anticlimactic or at least secondary. Time seems to be stuck on as a kind of afterthought to the discussion of authentic selfhood.

In spite of the seeming evidence to the contrary, the central issue of this chapter and indeed of the entire *Being and Time* is to show that, for a human being *as* Dasein, "to be" is always "to be temporal"—that the ontological meaning of Being is time. Such a claim needs not only explanation but support. What does Heidegger *mean* when he says that Being is time? What evidence does he bring to bear in *support* of this claim?

These are, of course, the most important questions to be asked of this section, and it is to their consideration that I direct most of my commentary on this chapter, in spite of the fact that Heidegger devotes only one-third of it to the discussion of temporality. The first four sections, however, are not to be completely passed over—especially section 63, which deals with the circular structure of the analysis. Accordingly, I treat the first four sections of this chapter somewhat briefly.

PRELIMINARY SKETCH (section 61)

In previous sections, two crucial concepts—resoluteness and anticipation—were existentially analyzed. Resoluteness was seen as a free consciousness, aware of its responsibility and guilt, with emphasis placed upon possibilities; anticipation was the view of the not-yet (possibility) of death. Each of these analyses was necessary to provide the total picture of human existence. But it is not enough merely to know these two aspects of existence independently, as it were.

How are resoluteness and anticipation to be joined together? This, then, is the task of this chapter: to achieve an ontological ground, a source of unity, from which these two aspects of authentic existence can be joined together. In so doing, the question, What does it really mean to *exist*? becomes, What does it really mean *to be*? The first is answerable in terms of reflection upon the ways in which one actually goes about the business of existing. The second, however, must seek for a deeper *ground* which gives support for these ways of existing. The first question—What does it mean to *exist*?—is resolved into the rich and varied understanding of one's own self in anticipatory resoluteness. The second question—What does it mean to be?—is resolved by going beyond the simple modes of existence to the ultimate reference by which these modes have meaning. This is temporality. The ultimate ground in which the two aspects of authentic existence (anticipation and resoluteness) can be understood cannot remain on a simple *existential* level—for that has already been exhausted. On the other hand, the comprehension of the ontological ground cannot be any mere arbitrary solution. It must be founded and be discoverable in the existential analysis. Hence it is that the solution, so to speak, of the existential question What does it mean to exist authentically? opens the door for the first time to the ontological structure. Section 61 simply focuses the procedure onto this precise problem: How is it that we proceed from the existential to the ontological?

Making no attempt to answer that problem, it merely sketches out the solution as it will occur in the subsequent sections.

ANTICIPATORY RESOLUTENESS (section 62)

The key to understanding this section lies in keeping clear that Heidegger is talking about an existentiell (not an existential) joining of anticipation and resoluteness. According to Heidegger, the union of anticipation and resoluteness must be accomplished first on the level of an existentiell analysis. It must be accomplished on this level as well as on the ontological level, which comes in subsequent sections, because Dasein is never a wholly "ontological" being. This means that any ontological insight will have its effect, and indeed its source as a problem, in the mode of existentiell awareness.

Early in the Introduction (E-33/G-12) Heidegger distinguished between two kinds of awareness of existence. Existentiell awareness he defines as merely "leading along the way" of deciding its own existence. He seems to equate existentiell awareness with ontic awareness. On the other hand, existential awareness is a comprehension of the *structure* of existence, and as such approaches ontological awareness—though, as we have seen, it is not to be completely equated with it.

The exact definition of "existentiell" seems difficult to pin down, but by its usage it is clear what Heidegger means by it. To be aware of existence *as an entity* is an existentiell awareness. To be aware of existence *as existing* (i.e., not as a thing or substance) is existential awareness.

Heidegger, then, wants to establish the relationship between anticipation and resoluteness on the level of an existentiell awareness of the self. If this can be accomplished, then the character of that relationship can be examined to expose the ontological aspects. This method of always beginning on the *lower* ontological level (and existentiell awareness is ontologically lower than existential awareness) is in keeping with his entire analysis; for even from the very beginning of the analytic, the perspectives of all the existentials were established first from the point of view of everydayness and inauthenticity. How, though, does Heidegger show the relationship between resoluteness and anticipation to exist on an existentiell level?

The method is quite simply this: If one examines the characteristics of authentic anticipation, even on the existentiell level, it becomes obvious that resoluteness is an essential ingredient of anticipation. Likewise, if anticipation is carefully examined, it is seen to possess resoluteness. The so-called relationship between anticipation and resoluteness lies in that they are both already contained in each other. Resoluteness reveals to Dasein that it is guilty *all the time*, and hence already contained in the idea of resoluteness is the concept of "as long as it is" or "until it ends." To be guilty means to be responsible and free for responsibility as long as one lives. But "as long as one lives" implies awareness of death. But since Being-guilty is an authentic mode of existence, the awareness of being-able-not-to-be, which is contained in it, must also be authentic, and authentic Being-toward-death is anticipation. In a similar way, the investigation of anticipation will reveal that resoluteness is always existentially implied by it.

Heidegger's analysis of anticipatory resoluteness as the meaning of authenticity has provided some fairly ridiculous misinterpretations. Does Heidegger mean that I am somehow "more authentic" if I stick out my jaw like a wind-in-the-hair romantic and boldly go forth into the world, anticipating events like some dedicated religious or political fanatic? The suggestion is absurd, for it confuses the entire *level* of the analysis. First, Heidegger does not believe that any particular conduct or way of living is "more authentic" simply because in such a program the term "authentic" does not belong. We recall that to be authentic simply means to be able to receive or to grasp what it means to exist. To be inauthentic is to be unaware of what it means to exist. Why then does Heidegger interpret authenticity as the conjunction of anticipation and resoluteness? This question reveals the need to begin with an existentiell analysis: i.e., to begin with what *kind of being Dasein is* in order to understand how Dasein *can* raise the higher kind of question about what it means to exist.

First, Dasein must be in the world in such a way as *to expect*; that is, it is precisely because we are the kinds of beings for whom being in time matters that we can be said to "anticipate." To exist in such a way so that one is only *in* time, and not alert to what it *means to be in time*, is not to expect but to *wait for*. Secondly, if I am the kind of being who is capable of being resolute—and this means to exist so that who I am matters (it does NOT mean to be aggressive or pushy or eager or excitable or romantic)—then, if I can exist so that both my being in time is meaningful and my being who I am is meaningful, I can be *able to be as* authentic. A quiet, reflective person is just as able to be authentic as a bold and assertive one; indeed a morally weak person can be as authentic as a morally upright person.

But this entire discussion has taken place in terms of what kind of being I am in order to be authentic. This is, then, a mere existentiell account. But by making this analysis we now comprehend the fundamental ontological meaning of authenticity: to exist in such a way as to have the meaning of existence possible.

Once again Heidegger's analyses must be seen as *philosophical* and not psychological or ideological. It is carried out to reveal the *truth* about our existence. Yet the language seems to stir us to some sort of dedicated devotion to bold and assertive action—which a close and critical reading of the text will not allow. The very richness of his analysis becomes a stumbling block to the extent that it permits a seeming hortative interpretation. Heidegger as philosopher is seeking the truth, but some of his readers interpret him as trying to persuade us to live a certain kind of life. This interpretation must be resisted.

CIRCULARITY OF THE BEING QUESTION (section 63)

I have already mentioned Heidegger's view of the circular nature of interpretation in general. Now it is fitting to apply this general structure to the specific question of what it means to be. The reader may recall that Heidegger presents the circularity of interpretation along the lines of a process by which that which is vaguely "had," seen, and grasped in advance becomes more specific and more thematically clear. In other words, hermeneutic analysis does not set out to discover something brand new, but focuses upon what is *already* "known" or "felt." The hermeneutic process is a circle in that it proceeds from a whole to a part, and then back to the whole, as in the case of language, words, and language again. What are these steps, and how is the process applicable, in the case of questioning what it means to be?

The existential analytic is based upon the fact that, already and in advance, I have a vague understanding of what it means to be. But if I already know what it means to be, then why analyze the *ways* of Being (the existentials) in order to discover what it means to be? The answer is because my first understanding of what it means to be is not very profound, it is unthematic, distorted, and, because of its lack of certainty and clarity, *covered up* (untrue). In saying this, however, we do not say that an awareness of what it means to be is totally *absent*. The task is to make this awareness meaningful. (Perhaps it might even be better to say that our task is to make it *more* meaningful, since there is a sense in which one already is aware of what it means to be.)

What, then, is "meaning" in terms of the existential analytic? As we have already seen in Chapter IV, meaning is structured upon the fore-having (what is had in advance), the fore-sight (what is seen in advance), and the fore-conception (what is grasped or conceived in advance). All we have to do is to fill in, as it were, these general terms with the specific forms of the fore-structure that are characteristic of the Being question.

The fore-having of the Being question is: authentic potentiality-for-being-a-whole (*Ganzseinkönnen*). The fore-sight of the Being question is, one's *own* ability-to-be (*Seinkönnen*). The fore-conception of the Being question is, the existentiality of Dasein.

What do these terms mean? The fore-having of any interpretation is Dasein's totality of involvement in the primordial relationship to the subject in question. Hence in this case it is Dasein's whole or total relationship or involvement to what it means to be. The fore-having of the Being question is, for Dasein, the fact that it *can be as a whole*. (The real significance of the last two chapters here comes into play.) To put it negatively, unless Dasein were able to grasp its existence from a total or holistic perspective, the existential analytic would not be possible. It is only because Dasein *has in advance* an awareness of its existence *as a whole* through the awareness of the *possibility* of death that Dasein can inquire as to what it means to be. The fore-having that constitutes the interpretation of the Being question is, then, Dasein's ability-to-be-as-a-whole.

The fore-sight of the interpretation of the Being question is one's own ability-to-be. This means that that perspective from which the inquiring Dasein can view the problem of Being is its own existence. Unlike ontical inquiry, which always seeks its object in another's existence (and in ontical self-inquiry, even the "self" is treated as if it were another), ontological inquiry takes its point-of-view (fore-sight) from one's *own* freedom to be. Notice too that it is not simply one's *own* existence, but one's ability-to-be—i.e., one's own freedom of existence is that reference point from which one can investigate the problem of what it means to be.

The fore-conception of the Being question is existentiality. This means that that concept or leading theme by which one interprets the various phenomena of existing is the question of Being. Rather than investigating human existence along the lines of a scientific object or even as a metaphysical substance, the theme or concept of the ontological inquiry is simply what it means *to be*.

One manner of making this clear is to reflect upon what has actually occurred in *Being and Time* thus far. For the sake of eliciting the methodology, let us suppose that everything that Heidegger has said is true and accurate. Where did he get his information? How did he arrive at the truths contained thus far in his analysis? He reflected upon his own existence, and in so doing he achieved a basis for his inquiry that was genuinely open to his investigation. In the first place, he was aware that there was such a thing as his existence, and that there was a way of thinking about his existence that unified the myriad experiences and attitudes of that existence. This unification was due to his ability to see himself as possibly not-being. A life span has a unity or wholeness about it because it begins and ends. Hence there is a meaning to a single concept—namely existence. This, by which a totality of involvements is made into a conceptual whole, is the fore-having.

In addition to the conceptual wholeness of existence, he was able to continue his analysis by means of his understanding that he himself had certain possibilities. This meant that his own existence was not a mere actual fact, but also was meaningful in terms of possibilities that were uniquely his own. This awareness provided the perspective or fore-sight necessary for all interpretations.

Finally, the method or clue by which the various events and experiences of human existence could be formalized into a coherent structure was the idea of existentiality. If Heidegger could describe the variety of human experiences and awarenesses *in terms of* a single theme—in this case, the question of what it means to be—then there would be a basis for making a genuine philosophical analysis, and not merely a random sampling of acute insights into the nature of his own personal existence structure. The fact that the *problem of* existence presupposes the *fact* of existence is not a drawback, since every form of inquiry possesses this elemental kind of circularity. To point out that the question of what it means to be is circular is not to say that the inquiry simply repeats itself. One's familiar acquaintance with the Beethoven sonatas does not take away the delight in listening to them. In fact, one listens to the sonatas of Beethoven far more profoundly after having heard them quite often. As we learn the sonatas, they become more familiar and hence more meaningful to us. In like manner, even though we "already know" our existence, as we become more familiar with its structure through the existential analysis, like the oft-heard sonatas it becomes more meaningful to us. However, just as it is easy to miss the full beauty of the sonatas by merely hearing them and not listening to them, so too is it a danger that the full meaning of existence can escape our grasp. One must listen creatively to the sonatas of Beethoven, and this kind of listening does violence to a mere hearing of them in the background. Likewise, the awareness of existence requires violence done to the everyday perspective of existence. Unless "violence" were done to the circle of interpretation, there would indeed be a meaningless return to it.

We exist. Furthermore, to some extent we understand our existence. This understanding, however, must be perfected, enriched, and thematized. To give meaning to our existence, however, we do not need to go to any source *other* than our own existence (to a substance-God, for example, or a teleological humanism). This is the whole point of the "circle." The meaning of our existence lies within our existence, not outside of it. If this is true, then to *find* the meaning of existence one must analyze what one is.

Heidegger insists that violence be done to the everyday interpretation of existence; but this by no means suggests any kind of *arbitrary* rejection of the everyday perspective. The everyday perspective is never *abandoned*; it is transcended.

CARE AND SELFHOOD   (section 64)

The discussion of the circular nature of the Being inquiry has focused upon the final consideration before turning to the analysis of temporality and time: the self. That this should provide the focal point is not obscure: we are speaking of existence, and it is the self that exists. But what is it that can be said in addition to all that has been discussed up to this point?

Heidegger's purpose in this section is to emphasize two points, one negative, the other positive. The first point is that traditional theories of the self, based upon epistemology, are essentially incorrect because they interpret the self either as an object or as a subject. Even Kant, according to Heidegger, sees the self as a subject. The second point is that the self must be seen existentially, and that means to see the self as grounded in the phenomenon of care. A few remarks will suffice to elucidate these two points.

Heidegger spends some time on Kant's analysis of the self as the purely logical "I" of the "I think." He agrees with Kant that the Cartesian analysis of the self as substantive is wrong. On the other hand, he disagrees with Kant in interpreting the self merely as a subject. The main point of Heidegger's dispute with Kant is that Kant continued to interpret the "I" as something present-at-hand, that he did not go on to an *ontological* description of the self. Kant saw the self as another thing in the universe that one encounters in one's affairs. Although Kant is right in denying that the self has substantial objectivity—that it is a "thing"—this denial loses all of its force. For it is not enough to accomplish—as Kant did—the destruction of the paralogisms committed by the rationalists. One must go further and characterize the ontological structure of the self. Kant left the self "in the logical air," so to speak. By failing to see the *existential* and ontological importance of Being-in-the-world, Kant left the self an isolated subject. The only avenue open to any inquiry about the self as an isolated subject is an ontical inquiry, which treats the self, in spite of Kant's objections, as a kind of entity or substance.

What, then, is the proper ontological characterization of the self? It must be analyzed in terms of Dasein's Being-in-the-world. The self is not an isolated subject; it is not an entity within the world as other entities or substances. Rather, the self is an "I who cares." Hence the path of inquiry that is properly open to expose the self as it is, is not ontical but ontological. The self is structured within the phenomenon of caring. This means that one does not proceed from the analysis of "I think," which yields an isolated and independent subject, but rather from "I care," which necessarily describes the self as already in the world. What, then, is the self, the "I"? It is that which is exposed through *authentic* existence and is covered up in inauthentic existence. The self then becomes that *quality* which distinguishes the authentic from the inauthentic. It is that which is aware of what it means to be. The self appears to be more of a condition or a characteristic of existence rather than a thing. For in inauthentic existence, we *lose* the self, cover it up (which could hardly be the case if it were a substance). The "what" here is not the self, but Dasein. Whenever Dasein is aware of its Being, it is authentically its self. "Self," then, is not an entity. It is a characteristic of Being, which is also not an entity. Dasein alone is the entity. One must never ask, then, What *is* a self? but rather, What does it mean to be who one is? When asked in this way, the ontological answer can make sense.

With this characterization, the purely existential meaning of Dasein is complete. It is now time to ask, not for the existential meaning of Dasein, but for the *ontological* meaning. Since we have already seen that Dasein's Being is care, the question then becomes, What is the ontological meaning of care? The answer is: temporality.

THE ANALYSIS OF TIME

Heidegger's interpretation of Dasein's Being as time may seem, at first consideration, to be a sharp departure from his Kantian heritage. Kant's interpretation of time as the form of the inner sense restricts its use and locus to the realm of phenomena. The thing-in-itself and noumena are, according to Kant, not of the temporal order. For Heidegger to assert that the Being of Dasein is time certainly seems to be a bold denial of Kant's view. As a matter of fact, however, Heidegger's existential interpretation is not as much at variance with Kant's as might at first seem. There are two teachings of Kant that give great support to Heidegger's interpretation: (1) The first is that, for Kant, time is the form of the inner sense, and that time characterizes the empirical self. It does not, to be sure, characterize the logical subject; but the *logical subject* is a purely formal subject, devoid of any content or basis of investigation. (2) More important for Heidegger, however, is the role in Kant's philosophy of the imagination, which has characteristics of both time and rationality. In his *Kant and the Problem of Metaphysics*, Heidegger takes Kant to severe task for failing to develop fully the spectacular truths that he glimpsed in his doctrine of the imagination.

Before any considerations of the ultimate effect of Heidegger's interpretation of time can be made, the first task, that of understanding just what Heidegger says, must first be accomplished. It is important to remember that Heidegger derives the temporal analysis of Dasein from the characterization of authentic existence as anticipatory resoluteness. The form of the question that is used to extricate the temporal interpretation from the existential account is this: How is it possible for there to be anticipatory resoluteness? The answer: Because there *is* a future. (Not: there *will be* a future.)

The thematic development of Heidegger's analysis should be kept clearly in mind. In section 65 the temporal basis of authentic existence is exposed, and the three ekstases of time—past, present, and future—are analyzed ontologically. Time is revealed as the Being of Dasein—i.e., what it means for Dasein to be is always to be in time. Hence the title *Sein and Zeit*: "To Be and Time." In section 66, however, it becomes clear that if time is the Being of Dasein, then the entire analysis of Dasein's structure of existence must be *repeated* in terms of this temporal structure. All that we have learned about the existence of Dasein has been merely an existential discovery; to make it an ontological discovery, it must be reinterpreted along the lines of time. Above all, the existential understanding must be reanalyzed. Hence, in Chapter IV, Heidegger re-evaluates all of the existentials in terms of the temporal perspective. After the series of existentials are reanalyzed on the higher ontological basis of time, there remain two tasks to be accomplished. Time, presented as phenomenon, is history. Thus Chapter V evaluates the ontological basis of history. Chapter VI contrasts Heidegger's view of time with the traditional views and with that the published version of *Being and Time* comes to an end.

Heidegger's analysis of time and temporality begins with an account of the ontological ground of care.

TEMPORALITY AND CARE   (section 65)

On an uncritical and intuitive level, the claim that the ground of human existence is time is not too difficult to accept. Certainly everything we do is in time; and, more particularly, when we do reflect upon existence, we often think of it in terms of a passage of events, or of hope, expectation, fear, and wonder at what is yet to come in the future. But this uncritical acceptance of time as the ground of existence fails to locate and emphasize just *how* one should conceive of time *as* a ground of existence. To say that all human events happen in time is not to say that time is the ground of existence, for among other things it is unclear just what "ground" means. At first reading, a tolerant reader may be willing to accept on vague feeling the claim that time is the ground of existence; but until that claim is clarified and solidified in analysis it cannot be maintained as philosophically significant.

When one asks for a "deeper meaning" or even an "ontological meaning," what is being asked is the question, How is such-and-such a thing possible? This is what Heidegger means by defining meaning as the "upon-which of primary projection of possibility." Leaving the difficult language aside, one can translate Heidegger's definition in this way: When I ask for the meaning of something, I ask for that which makes something possible. Kant's question as to what is the meaning of science was answered by a consideration of how science is possible—the categories. To ask what the meaning of liberty is, one might well answer in terms of what makes liberty possible—the individual wills of free men and the respect and dignity of men. Such is what is meant by Heidegger in asking for an ontological meaning.

The question that is asked, then, is this: What is the meaning of care? And this question now takes the formulation: How is it possible for there *to be* such a thing as care? The last two chapters have explicated the *existential* meaning of Dasein as caring. Now we must ask, How is care (and anticipatory resoluteness, which is authentic caring) possible? What makes possible the Being of Dasein?

We have seen that anticipatory resoluteness is the authentic mode of Dasein's Being-possible. Hence when we ask for the ground or the possibility of Dasein's existence, we must formulate the inquiry in terms of anticipatory resoluteness. Anticipatory resoluteness has been exposed as Being-toward one's possibilities. But how is it possible to be "toward" anything at all? Only because there is a future. What, though, does it mean to have a future? The future is not something that is simply a not-yet now waiting for our arrival on the "path of time," as if time were a street on which the objects of our future occurrence already lay in waiting. Rather, the future is meaningful to one because one *goes toward* the future. To have a future means to expect, to anticipate, to look forward to. Hence the future is meaningful. If the future were merely a not-yet now, it could have no meaning for us at all.

We all know that there is going to be a future. Before one begins to spin elaborate theories of time, however, suppose one simply reflects upon how it is possible for the future to exist as a meaningful concept or awareness in our lives. I look forward to the completion of this chapter. I anticipate a certain amount of satisfaction from the work having been accomplished. The future is not meaningful to me in any abstract way of not-yet nows. The future is meaningful to me because it is one of the ways in which I exist. In fact, the future, *as a way of existing*, turns out to be the ultimate presupposition of authentic existence. The varied and multifarious forms of awareness and consciousness, of thought and calculation, all presuppose, to some extent or another, the basic attitudes of Being *toward* a future and *from* a past.

What Heidegger is doing here in this section is quite profound; and many of his severest critics recognize his brilliance here. He is rendering a phenomenological account of what it means to be in time. Notice that the question Heidegger asks himself is: What does it mean *to be* in time? rather than: What *is* time. This is in keeping with the general phenomenological spirit, in avoiding any elaborate metaphysical prejudgment and focusing instead upon that which is more available to our *inquiry* than to our speculation. We are all in time. Surely we can reflect upon what it means *to be* in time. Heidegger has described the future as "coming toward"; and by this term, which in German is simply the normal word for "future" with a hyphen inserted—*Zu-kunft*—is meant our existence as anticipating, expecting, looking forward toward, as feeling oneself *going toward*, etc. The most elaborate and compelling form of this awareness is the comprehension that one is *going to not-be* (is going to die), which has already been analyzed in our discussion of Being-toward-death.

Of the three ekstases of time, the future is by far the most important for Heidegger's analysis. It is not the *present* that bears the locus of existence but the future. This should be especially emphasized in terms of the priority of *possibility*, which is of course a central teaching of Heidegger's. Second in importance to the future is the past. The present is the least significant of the three ekstases. We have seen Heidegger's characterization of the future as a "coming toward": we must now turn to the past.

As an interpretation of how the past is meaningful to Dasein, Heidegger has chosen the term *ich bin gewesen*, which is often translated simply as "I was." Heidegger, however, emphasizes the fact that in German, the past tense of *sein* uses a form of the verb to be (*sein*) as the auxiliary. Translated literally, then, instead of "I *have* been," the Germans say, "I *am* been." Macquarrie and Robinson have translated it: "I am as having been" in order to emphasize the sense that Heidegger places on the term; namely, that the past is significant in a present sense.

The point can perhaps be made most clearly by presenting the problem in terms of exaggerated naïveté. Suppose I were to argue that the past, since it is no more, cannot ever have any meaning at all, since to be meaningful something must be actually existing, and what is past is not existing any longer. My promise of yesterday, then, has absolutely no meaning or significance at all, because yesterday *isn't*. Now such a claim would be met with general disapproval. And yet, in refuting such a naïve position, there is exposed something that remains only presupposed— namely, that the past *is* meaningful. We do not even use the past tense in asserting this. We do not say, The past *was* meaningful.

That is not all. In addition, if we consider what it is we are right now, it is almost impossible to understand what we are without conceiving of ourselves as having already been. By themselves, these observations hardly seem revolutionary; they appear so obvious on the surface that one who articulates them stands in danger of stating the obvious. On the other hand, their articulation exposes a very important point: Neither the past nor the future can be theoretically described as no-longer or not-yet. The past and the future are significant, they *do* have meaning, and as such they must be seen as *essentially* tied to human existing. To argue that the phenomenon of *memory* can account for the past's significance is inadequate; for such an argument merely locates the *function* by which the past is presented to consciousness. To make an appeal to memory does not elucidate how the past must be conceived in order that it be remembered at another time.

From these considerations we are now in a position to present the question somewhat more clearly: What must be presupposed about the past in order to account for the past's being significant to us? Similarly, we may pose the earlier question along these lines: What must be presupposed about the future in order to make it meaningful to us? The answer to both of these questions lies in the realization that both ekstases of time, the past and the future, must be interpreted in terms of human existing. The future is meaningful in the sense of "I *am* as coming toward"; the past is meaningful in the sense of "I *am* as having been."

What, then, of the present? In traditional theories of time, the present has usually been seen as the only meaningful focal point in which reality and existing took their significance. But even in such traditional theories there is a great difficulty about this priority of the present ekstasis. *When is* the present? Is there such a thing as the knife-edged present? If the present is the locus of reality, how broadly must the present be conceived? Does the split second after a moment of consciousness fade into the no-longer of the traditional past, or does the forthcoming split second not-yet avoid any ontological status because it has not as yet been realized? Or is the present merely to be seen as that nexus between the arriving future and the departing past?

Such questions inevitably plague those who would make the present the focal point of significance. Heidegger, however, has made the future the focal point of significance, and has thereby avoided these difficulties. But the present is still a genuine ekstasis of time, and must be existentially described. The same method of presenting the difficulty will here be followed. We have asked how the past and the future *are meaningful* to Dasein. We now ask the same question of the present.

Heidegger's answer to the question of how the present is meaningful shifts the inquiry from seeing the present as that *in which* something occurs, to the actual carrying out of an action. Ontologically conceived, the present is *making present*. Thus it is the actual carrying out of an action that makes the present significant. Surely it is what we are actually doing at any moment that makes that moment *as the present moment* meaningful. The *primordial* significance of any given "present moment" lies in the fact that one is directly aware of one's own activity as an action. Hence to conceive of time as a string or series of isolated moments or "nows" is completely foreign to one's existential experience. It is for this reason, then, that the present, as the last of the three ekstases and not the first, is interpreted as a making-present.

To sum up these interpretetions of the temporal analysis, it may be helpful to oversimplify: As a human being, I have a future. This means that the future is significant to me. It is because of my possibilities that the future is significant; in fact, ultimately, my ability to have possible ways of Being is what the future *means*.

On the other hand, I perform actions and find myself creating situations. In this way the present is significant to me. The present is not significant as a knife-edged instant, nor as an abstration from the measure of change. What it means for me to be in the present is to perform actions and be in situations.

Finally, the basis from which the past is significant to me is my forgetting and remembering. Unless I existed in such a way that I was capable of remembering and forgetting, the past would not be meaningful.

Throughout the discussion of the ontological meaning to the past, present, and future, I have made use of the generic term "ekstasis." By simple contextual reading, of course, the meaning is already somewhat defined. The term comes from the Greek ἔκστασις, which literally means "standing out." To focus upon the present, the past, or the future is to "stand out from" the general flow of time and existence. The English word "ecstasy" comes from the same Greek stem.

It is only when one interprets temporality in terms of *ekstases* that a proper ontological view of time is possible. Heidegger derives these ekstases from the structure of authentic existence, which has already been discovered in the previous chapters. We should recall that the earlier sections contained a discussion of authentic existence as care, in which the structure of care involved a projection of possibilities, along with being already in a world alongside those entities encountered in a world. Care, then, has three characteristics: (1) it is ahead of itself in terms of its awareness of possibilities; (2) it is already in the world; and (3) it is alongside the entities it discovers, whether in the mode of solicitude for other Daseins or in that of circumspective concern for entities other than Dasein. From these three characteristics, which are *existential*, Heidegger asks for their ultimate possibility or ground, which is *ontological*. It is possible for Dasein *to be ahead of itself* because of its ontological *future*; it is possible for Dasein *to already be* in a world because of its ontological *past*; and it is possible for Dasein *to be alongside* entities because of its ontological *present*.

The basic structure of Heidegger's analysis is this: Given the authenticity of his account about the structure of care, what must be presupposed in order for such a structure to be possible? The answer: a form of temporal existing whose structure corresponds to the structure of care. The three characteristics of authentic existence are grounded, then, in the three ekstases of time. It may seem extraordinary to some readers that one would want to describe the future as that ground from which guilt, responsibility, and the awareness of possibilities all spring; or to define the past as that ground from which one's significance as already thrown into a world is revealed; or the present as that ground by which actions and situations are made possible. One might want to argue that although Heidegger may have a point in showing that time is indeed required in order for such existential awareness to exist, it is surely not enough to describe time in terms of those existential awarenesses. Surely one conceives of time in a broader sense than simply the ground of existence! Or does one? To be sure, it is all too common that one will devise a conceptual structure of time (as, for example, an endless chain of "now" moments), but we must question whether such constructions genuinely support or even reflect the existential meaning of what it means to be in time. What Heidegger has scrupulously avoided is precisely such a formulation of "metaphysical time" as would treat time as some sort of entity or substance. He avoids the ontical description of time, in order for the ontological to emerge.

One objection that might be brought against Heidegger's interpretation is answered by Heidegger himself. If time is to be conceived in terms of the ekstases of temporality, then it seems that time is limited to one's own finite existence. Surely, though, I can imagine a time before my own existence, as well as a time that will extend beyond my existence. Does the fact that such extensions of time are indeed meaningful to me in any way discredit Heidegger's account? Heidegger argues that such possibilities in no way refute the finitude and temporality of time. Even though I might imagine events occurring without end beyond my death, it is still the case that time temporalizes and limits, so that time is finite.

Since authentic time is finite, *in*authentic time is *in*finite. The genuine ekstases of temporality have been shown to be the foundation of one's existential understanding of oneself as finite. To describe time in any other way is to describe time as based in something other than the self— i.e., the non-self, the inauthentic. If such a thing as infinite time were metaphysically possible, it would not be available to us in any existential way. At most it would be a highly abstract and speculative mental creation, which could be the ground of no human activity whatsoever. In order for time to be meaningful, it must be the time established from our own finite ekstases of temporality.

To conceive of time, then, as either subjective or objective is to over-look the essentially *existential* character of how to view time. Time and temporality are not objective, in the sense that they can be conceptualized as independent entities, or that they have significance independent of human existence; nor are they subjective in the sense that they are the pure forms of intuition or the mere faculty by which change is measured. Time and temporality *are* insofar as a human being *is*; but this is not to suggest a subjectivism, because it has nothing to do with the problem of knowledge or the subject of any other kind of activity. Temporality is exposed as the necessary ontological condition for the ways in which we exist.

In section 65, Heidegger merely describes in the boldest of outlines the existential characteristic of temporality. He emphasizes four points that constitute the major doctrines of his analysis:

1. Temporality makes possible the structure of care. We have already seen that it was from the three characteristics of care that the three ekstases of time were derived.

2. Temporality is ecstatical in character. This means, as we have seen, that temporality takes its ultimate meaning from the ecstatical way of exist-ing that is peculiar to Dasein, so that temporality is the basis of time, rather than time being the basis for temporality.

3. The future is the most determinate and significant of the three ekstases, and Dasein's basic focus of meaning is future.

4. Finally, primordial time is finite. This last point does not rule out the possibility of an infinite; it merely shows that the primordial *meaning* of time is its limiting finitude.

This brief survey of the existential character of how temporality is meaningful to Dasein by no means exhausts the full analysis of time. It is only the beginning. In section 66 Heidegger explains that if the onto-logical ground of human authentic existence is temporality, then the en-tire edifice of the existential analytic must be repeated and reexamined under the guiding influence of the temporal character of Dasein. This does not mean that every single argument must be repeated, nor does it imply that the same order of presentation must be followed. It does mean, though, that the major existentials must be more deeply examined to reveal the underlying ontological structure of time. It is in the actual carrying out of the repetition that the full significance of Heidegger's claim will be made clear. Up to now we have merely seen the general theory that the basis of human existence was finite time. He proceeds to work out in detail the major existentials, already exposed in our earlier analysis, to show that their underlying structure is indeed a temporal one. Heidegger spends the whole of his next chapter, Chapter IV, in carrying out this "repetition."

THE REPETITION (section 67)

It has already been shown, in brief outline, that the structure of care is temporality. This "repetition," then, must show that the various characteristics of care—i.e., understanding, state-of-mind, and fallenness—all are grounded in the ontological base of temporality. Since the hermeneutical nature of self-reflective inquiry is circular, it is not surprising that these important elements of Dasein's existentiality must now be reevaluated on a more ontological level.

Heidegger interprets each of these elements of the care structure in terms of the ekstases of time. For the most part these detailed discussions are not difficult to understand, and I merely sketch out the general aspects of each. It is important to keep constantly in mind that Heidegger is seeking merely to expose the *temporal* nature of the ontological ground of each of these elements of care. Hence as interpretations their purpose is quite simple: to show that temporality is the base of all the elements of care. One who wished to quarrel with Heidegger's accounts would have to argue that temporality is *not* the ontological ground of care, and to argue in this manner one must show that Heidegger's interpretations are incorrect. But underlying his interpretation, of course, is his presupposition that *to be is to be in time*, and it is the consistency of his program (despite any quarrels over details) that is impressive.

UNDERSTANDING AS TEMPORAL   (section 68)

Since the existential meaning of understanding is the projection of possibilities, the central ekstasis for this existential is the future. In the case of state-of-mind, as we shall see, the central ekstasis is the past; and for fallenness, the chief ekstasis is the present. It must be stressed, however, that all three ekstases have significance, and that to say that the future is the most representative ekstasis of understanding is not to say that the past and present are not likewise involved in understanding. The same is true for state-of-mind and fallenness.

Understanding in its existential sense as a projection of possibilities is not primarily a species of cognition. The cognitive aspects of understanding are *derived* from its existential aspects. This has already been noted in a previous section. The question, then, that must now be considered is this: How can understanding as a projection of possibilities be interpreted so as to reveal the temporal basis of its existential significance?

Understanding is significant not only in terms of each of the three ekstases, but also in terms of the distinction between authentic and inauthentic. We should remember that understanding plays an important role in the authentic-inauthentic distinction, for it is in the projection of the possibility of not-being that Dasein becomes aware of itself for the first time as a Being capable of authentically going-to-die. Together with the three ekstases of time, the authentic-inauthentic distinction, which occurs in each of the ekstases, constitutes six different modes of understanding. This means: Dasein projects its own possibilities either authentically or inauthentically in each of the three ekstases of time. Heidegger refers to these six modes of projection in the following way:

Authentic	*Inauthentic*
Future: Anticipation (*Vorlaufen*)	Waiting (*Erwarten*) [M & R: Expecting]
Present: Moment-of-vision (*Augenblick*)	Making-present (*Gegenwärtigen*)
Past: Repetition (*Wiederholen*)	Forgetting (*Vergessenheit*) ·

Since the future is the most important ekstasis of understanding, the distinction between the authentic and inauthentic modes of futural projection should be made clear. Anticipation is understanding as authentic future, in which Dasein, "existing authentically, lets itself come toward itself as its *own* being-able-to-be."[1] This means that, in anticipation, Dasein sees the future as consisting of its *own* possibilities; that the future *has meaning* insofar as one is aware of and is capable of possible ways to be. The inauthentic future, on the other hand, does not see possibilities in terms of Dasein, but merely in terms of circumstances and events that surround the activity of daily business. The inauthentic future, which is characterized as waiting, projects possibilities only in terms of that which, in everydayness, Dasein is concerned with.

It must be stressed that inauthentic understanding is *not* an account of error. What is inauthentic about waiting for the future as opposed to authentic anticipation of it is the manner in which the projections of the future are made significant. The inauthentic mode projects merely those possibilities about the objects of our concern; the authentic mode, on the

---

1. Cf. *Being and Time*, p. 386.

other hand, projects to Dasein not only the possibilities of our concern, but also our own decision and resoluteness in the matter—i.e., it projects *our* possibilities. Authentic projection of the future, aware of its finitude and the power of responsibility, makes possible not only awareness of possibilities, but also the role that Dasein, as agent, plays in such possibilities. Speaking somewhat loosely, one might say that authentic understanding (anticipation) lies in Dasein *going toward* the future, whereas inauthentic understanding (waiting) lies in the future *coming toward* Dasein.

A similar distinction can be applied to the ekstasis of the present. Authentic present, which is called moment-of-vision, makes specific use of the moment and the situation by an action that reflects Dasein's freedom; the inauthentic present, called making-present, merely sees the situations and actions as a part of a natural kind of activity. The inauthentic present is more carefully analyzed in the section concerning inauthentic everydayness, and need not be considered here. The present, by the way, is the least significant ekstasis of the three, and it is important here merely to show that all three ekstases do belong to the projection of Dasein's possibilities.

The past, however, like the future, holds an important place for the projection of Dasein. According to Heidegger, that which constitutes inauthentic having-been is the existential characteristic of forgetting, whereas the authentic past is repetition. This description of the authentic and inauthentic past is of great importance for Heidegger's theory of history (cf. Chapter IX, below) as well as his general theory of the history of philosophy. It is only because forgetting and repeating are genuine modes of human existence that temporality can provide the ontological ground of projection through the understanding. Since much of the significance of the past ekstasis is described in terms of history, further comment on these terms in the present context is not necessary. All that is really important for the reader here is to remember that all three ekstases, in both their authentic and their inauthentic modes, play the ontological role of ultimately justifying understanding as projection.

Heidegger, then, has accomplished an interpretation of understanding that exposes its temporal roots. Understanding, however, is merely one-third of the "here" of Dasein. He must still interpret both state-of-mind and fallenness in terms of temporality, before he can claim with assurance that the ontological meaning of care is time.

STATE-OF-MIND AS TEMPORAL   (section 68)

It would be a herculean task of thankless detail to examine all possible moods to show their respective temporal bases. Such a task would not only be all but impossible, it would also be unnecessary. Instead Heidegger chooses those two forms of state-of-mind that have been analyzed in the existential analytic: the inauthentic mood of fear; and that essential characteristic of authentic existence, dread. If it can be shown that the model states-of-mind that reflect authentic and inauthentic existence, dread and fear respectively, do indeed have temporal bases, the task of showing the temporality of state-of-mind in general will have been accomplished. The question, then, in this section is, How can both fear and dread be interpreted as temporal?

Heidegger maintains that the central ekstasis of state-of-mind is not the future, but the past. In light of the fact that fear always seems to be a fear of something in the future, this seems at first to be a dubious effort to maintain the architecture of his interpretation. But a closer look at what it means to be afraid and to dread shows Heidegger's insight to be grounded more deeply than in a mere attempt to achieve symmetry. Moods, which make up the structure of state-of-mind, reveal how Dasein *turns away* from its Being. The fact of having-been (*Gewesenheit*) is the ground of one's moods and hence one's state-of-mind. Heidegger explains this by saying that moods *bring* one *back* to something. That is, a mood recalls one to a perspective or status that is essentially one of having-been. It should be emphasized again that both the future and the present also belong essentially to state-of-mind. It is merely meant here that the past is the distinctive ekstasis peculiar to moods, even though moods also have futuristic and present-directed characteristics.

Why is it that fear, then, is not futural but is significant in terms of the having-been (the past)? Because, simply speaking, when one is afraid it is the future that one *retreats from*. Fear *holds back*. Existentially speaking, when I am afraid I am taking my locus from my existence *as I was*. It is because the future *threatens me* that I establish as my focus of values and center of attention the kind of Being that I am as having-been. The security of the past, so to speak, is that against which the threat of the future makes its mark. To be sure, fear sees the threat in the future, but *that which is threatened* is that which *is* as *having-been*. Fear is a kind of "forgetting of one-self"; it is a bewilderment. Forgetting, as we have seen, is that characteristic of the past which is inauthentic. In fact, the reason why fear is seen as a mode of *inauthentic* existence is precisely that fear, through a *forgetting* of one's Being, directs one's attention away from the question of Being. Forgetting, the inauthentic mode of past projection, is an essential ingredient of fear.

If inauthentic fear is temporalized by forgetting, which is the inauthentic mode of the past, then authentic dread must be temporalized by the authentic mode of the past, repetition. This is indeed precisely what Heidegger argues. Repetition, the authentic mode of having-been, is the ontological ground of dread. Dread, as we recall, is the awareness of nothingness, a feeling of alienation from an otherwise familiar world. One's thrownness and involvement in the world reveal a kind of *repetition* of possibilities. The reader may find the interpretation of dread as being based in the temporal ekstasis of having-been somewhat hard to grasp; the main point, however, to keep in mind is the similarity of fear and dread, and that both must reside in the past ekstasis of having-been. Dread, which is the authentic mode, must be seen in terms of the authentic ekstases: repetition, moment-of-vision, and anticipation. Fear, the inauthentic mode, must be seen in terms of the inauthentic ekstases: forgetting, making-present, and waiting.

TEMPORALITY OF FALLING   (section 68)

Unlike understanding and state-of-mind, falling can have no authentic ekstasis at all. It is the very nature of falling that it be inauthentic. Not only that, the characteristic ekstasis of falling is the present, which, as we have seen, is the least significant in terms of ontological value. Such assignment is, only to be expected, of course, since falling is by its essence that which turns us away from ontological significance.

The everyday view of time is usually that in which the present is seen as the locus of significance and reality. Such a view of the present makes the happening and occurrence of events a series of actual facts which can be indifferently observed. It is the view of time presupposed by substance metaphysicians and scientists. Unfortunately, from the ontological viewpoint it is inauthentic. Any view of time that stresses the *actual* must necessarily see the present as the chief mode of time, and indeed a kind of present that is merely making-present—i.e., a background for actual events. The temporality of falling is quite easy to elucidate: Those interpretations of time that center upon the actual rather than the possible provide the ontological ground for falling. Thus the ontological ground of the *present* is, in terms of falling, that present which is made up of actual entities; the authentic present (moment of vision) sees the present in terms of *possibilities* freely chosen and determined. The ontological ground of the *past* in terms of falling is, similarly, a view of the past that sees it in terms of a series of no-longer-actual events (forgetting) rather than authentically as still significant possibilities (repetition). The ontological ground of futuristic falling is likewise restricted to actual not-yet events (waiting) rather than possible projections of one's ability-to-be (anticipation).

In the description of the temporality of falling, only the phenomenon of curiosity is used. If we recall that curiosity is the inauthentic mode of seeing, and that its essence lies in seeing things from the indifferent and "objective" point-of-view of one who looks at actual entities or facts, the assignment of the temporal ekstases in their inauthentic modes is quite easy to follow. We have already seen that the inauthentic modes view the world from the point of view of *actualities*. That the temporal ekstases would have a similar structure is inevitable if, indeed, time is the ontological ground of existence.

TEMPORALITY OF DISCOURSE   (section 68)

This section needs merely a single remark to show its significance. The *tenses* of grammar in most modern sophisticated languages make it impossible to speak a meaningful sentence unless that sentence is formulated in some form of temporal significance. If language itself is structured on "tenses" like past, present, future, past perfect, present perfect, etc., then the very structure of language reveals the ultimate *temporal* nature of our consciousness and the manner in which we are aware of ourselves and the world.

Heidegger himself sums up his temporal analysis of the care structure beautifully (E-401/G-350, second paragraph) and no commentary is needed.

TEMPORALITY OF BEING-IN-THE-WORLD   (section 69)

At the very beginning of the existential analysis it was pointed out that the first characteristic of existing was that one existed in the world. To-be-in-the-world, then, provided the starting point for the preparatory analysis. All of the other existentials—fear, understanding, dread, etc.—were predicated upon this first and most extensive existential. The point has now come, however, when Heidegger maintains his central doctrine, that to be is to be temporal. Heidegger's claim is that the ontological ground of all the existentials is ecstatical temporality. This means that Dasein's temporal characteristics are what *make possible* the modes of existence that we know as existentials.

In what way, then, can the ontological ground of the temporal ekstases make possible Being-in-the-world. Is it really the case that to-be-in-the-world means to be temporal? And if so, what is the *specific* formulation of the ontological ground by which Being-in-the-world is made possible?

TEMPORALITY OF CONCERN   (section 69)

"Circumspection" is that term which refers to the kind of "seeing" one does in one's involvement with daily matters, such as to relate things in their use (ready-at-hand). The question, then, that is being asked is this: In what way do our daily dealings with the world as equipment involve our *temporal* character? The question can also be formulated with greater ontological significance: How does our ecstatical temporality *make possible* our involvement with the world of equipment (ready-at-hand)? Heidegger's answer, roughly speaking, is this:

One's *involvement* with equipment consists of awaiting and retaining. Both awaiting and retaining, though, are characteristics of making-present. We have already seen that to-be-in-the-present has existential significance in terms of performing actions and responding to situations. The inauthentic mode of the present is to treat such activity merely in its *actual* form, overlooking the unique projection of the self. Hence, derivatively, involvement with equipment also relates to the inauthentic past, forgetting; since the self, involved with the ready-at-hand, forgets the self.

The very rough sketch of how the ready-at-hand is grounded in temporality needs further consideration. The key to seeing Heidegger's argument lies in his use of the two terms "awaiting" and "retaining." It is easy enough to see how, in the busy involvement of working with equipment, one responds to the learned expectation of certain occurrences. A skilled driver, by *retaining* from his experience, knows how his automobile will respond to certain throttle manipulation; he *awaits* or *expects* the same kind of response as he now manipulates the throttle. These are *not* elements of the future and past; rather, they make up the *actual activity of the present*. The driver, in pushing in the throttle, does not say to himself: "I will speed up"; rather, as he pushes the throttle, he feels: "I *am* speeding up." The present, after all, is significant existentially only in terms of action and situations. It is only because there is such a thing as a *meaningful existential present* that such a thing as "involvement" in equipment is possible. That is what we mean, after all, when we say that the temporality of Dasein *grounds* the existential phenomenon—by "grounding" is meant, "making possible." Hence involvement in the world as ready-at-hand, which is to be involved with the world as equipment, is *made possible* because of the existentially significant present— i.e., the awaiting and retaining of responses, purposes, and functions of an activated process.

Heidegger makes a great deal out of a tool that fails to operate in its normal manner. By emphasizing this negative readiness-at-hand, he pinpoints even more explicitly how it is that we do indeed relate to objects of equipment. Basically, the in-order-to of every item of equipment is revealed as we use it. The purpose of a piece of equipment, however, becomes sharply underlined when that piece of equipment suddenly fails to function. The stark in-order-to of something that does *not* operate is more real to us than a smoothly running item of equipment.

The language used to describe this manner of relating to the world lends itself to a machine-like model, but it must be remembered that we are speaking of a *general way in which one relates to the world*. It is not only complex machinery, but doorknobs, forest paths, knives and forks, et al. to which we relate in this most primordial of ways of Being-in-the-world. Even as innocent an act as wrenching a doorknob consists of awaiting and retaining, and it is made meaningful by the temporal ekstasis of inauthentic present—making-present.

FROM READY-AT-HAND TO PRESENT-AT-HAND   (section 69)

The foregoing analysis has shown how the world of circumspective concern (i.e., the world which is seen as objects ready for use) has its ontological foundation in time. But there is another way of seeing the world, in which entities are no longer viewed in terms of their equipmentality, but are seen merely "as things"—i.e., present-at-hand. Heidegger's task is incomplete until he accounts for how the present-at-hand also has temporal foundations.

The solution to this problem directs attention to a very thorny problem that lies at the base of all epistemological theories: What is the relation between praxis and theory? For if, in loose and general terms, we identify the world of the ready-at-hand as a kind of *praxis* (i.e., the world of use and involvement with equipment), and the present-at-hand as a kind of *theory*, then the problem as to how a human person shifts his activity from merely using an object to reflecting on its properties becomes ontologically significant. This is as close as Heidegger comes to formulating what might be called a philosophy of science.

The rather simple task, then, of showing the temporal structure of the present-at-hand presupposes a more difficult task: An explanation of the "changing over" is satisfactorily interpreted if the temporal basis of the present-at-hand has already been explicated; for the present-at-hand *comes from* the ready-at-hand, whose temporal structure has already been shown.

A man can relate to a hammer in two ways. He can *involve* himself with it as a tool by using it to drive nails into a wooden shelf. On the other hand, he can also reflect upon the hammer as an object and consider its physical and even metaphysical properties. Heidegger calls the first mode of relationship ready-at-hand; and he is strongly persuaded that this mode is indeed the primordial and most immediate manner in which Dasein relates to the world. The second mode of relationship is called present-at-hand; it is a *derived* mode, and hence can only occur because of what takes place in the first mode. The question, though, to which we now must direct our inquiry is this: How is the second mode *derived* from the first? How is it that a man changes from his *use* of the hammer to the *reflection* about it?

In the first place, Heidegger insists that the two modes, praxis and theory, must not be seen as totally independent of each other. Praxis always involves some sort of theory, and theory always has its praxis. The model of purely intellectual comprehension is as impossible as total untheoretical immersion in practical activity. A very important aspect of this is the process of *deliberating*, which is *not* theoretical in nature, but belongs to the activity of praxis. The structure of deliberation is if . . . then . . . (*If* I pull this lever, *then* this wheel will spin.) Thus deliberation does not change one's view of the world from involvement in the ready-at-hand to present-at-hand. This process of deliberation is also temporal in character, since it is based upon retention and awaiting. But when I *theorize*, I no longer concern myself with the if . . . then . . . functions of the entity as a piece of equipment; in fact, it is precisely from this kind of dealing with the thing that I turn away when I change over from praxis to theory. What constitutes the change, then, from praxis to theory is how my manner or mode of Being changes. I *look at* the object in a totally different way, and, for me, the object *is* something different.

An example may make this difference somewhat clearer. Suppose we consider the difference between a heart surgeon (whose realm is that of praxis) and a theoretical biologist in working out a new theory of the role the heart plays in the life process. Both men are directly concerned with the human heart. In fact, one can picture these two men with an actual human heart directly in front of them. For the surgeon, what the heart is as an entity present-at-hand is not even considered. The various muscular elements, valves, arteries, etc., are *tools* to be utilized for the sake of his ultimate task—saving the life. As the surgeon works over his patient, he is certainly *deliberating: If* he pinches this muscular element or closes this valve, *then* such-and-such an action will occur (which he has *retained* from experience and *expects* in this case likewise to occur). This deliberation may well be complex and to some extent even speculative, for in the midst of his surgery he may confront a sudden reaction that would necessitate a rapid calculation of various possibilities: If the heart momentarily stops beating, the surgeon must rapidly consider whether to massage the heart, introduce Adrenalin, bring about a shock, or wait for a natural return to the pumping. But these deliberations are meaningful *only in terms of the ready-at-hand*: i.e., they belong to the realm of praxis.

If we turn now to the theorist, who is looking at a model of a heart, or even a real heart, we shift from seeing the elements of the heart as tools and equipment for the sake of a task or service, to seeing them simply in their presence-at-hand. The theorist sees an entity with properties. His calculations are not made in terms of the functions of the various elements; rather, they are directed toward speculative ways of seeing them *as* entities. Ought he to see the valve as a property of the heart or as the property of the bodily process as a whole? The choice between such alternatives might ultimately affect the construction of a theory that may produce a superior interpretation of the life process, but it does not directly affect the heart as a living organ, the way the surgeon's decision would. The point is that for the two men, the heart *is* differently—i.e., its Being is different. Not only that, the Being of the theorist and of the surgeon are different, since what they *are*, at the moment of their professional activity, is quite distinct each from the other. The theorist does not involve himself with the if . . . then . . . deliberations of the ready-at-hand. He views the heart, and indeed the whole world at that moment, as nature—i.e., an aggregate of entities present-at-hand. The particularity of *this* heart at *this* time in *this* place ceases to be significant. The locus of significance is the general world; place and time are indifferent, for they are seen merely as *properties* of the entity. To see the world as made up of entities present-at-hand is a way of understanding Being; and the more precisely this view of the world relates to and takes its guidance from an understanding of Being, the more successful will that way of "seeing" the world be. Mathematical physics, for example, is successful not because of its rigid adherence to "facts" (since there are no such things as plain facts), but because of its development along the lines of mathematical projection. To a reader acquainted with Kantian epistemology, this may not seem too terribly revolutionary; but taken in the context of the entire relationship between ready-at-hand and present-at-hand, it is impressive.

If the proper understanding of the scientific activity is to see science as a projection along the lines of the understanding of Being, then the roots of science stem from authentic existence. Heidegger, then, by no means wishes to lower the status of science, as some might feel, for science belongs to the general range of authentic understanding. What Heidegger does wish to lower, however, are mistaken views as to what constitutes the methodology of science (the positivists), and those who take *technique* as a mode of life—i.e., those for whom the projection of possibilities beyond the actual event is not significant.

The scientific projection of nature as present-at-hand is a form of *thematizing*. Thematizing is the total projection of a subject matter in terms of one's understanding of Being. *Being and Time* is a *thematic* inquiry. Science also is *thematic* in character. But in order for thematizing to occur, Dasein must *transcend* the entities thematized. This is again a strongly Kantian doctrine, the point of which is quite simple: In order for something like thematizing to occur at all, that which does the thematizing (or those presuppositions which make thematizing possible) cannot be a part of that which is thematized. What is not so simple, however, is how one must view the whole problem of transcendence.

TEMPORALITY OF TRANSCENDENCE   (section 69)

The problem of transcendence is an ancient one in the history of Western thought—though the term "transcendence" has not always been used to refer to what it means today. The term should above all be kept clearly distinct from the similar-sounding term "transcendent," which is a theological term, referring to the status of God in the universe. "Transcendence" refers to that state or locus by which or from which one can reflect upon the totality of human experience. Kant refers to his kind of philosophizing as "transcendental," and by that he meant that his philosophy takes its point of departure from asking how such-and-such a thing (experience, for example) is possible. The *problem* of transcendence is indigenous to philosophizing itself: one can always ask how an *account* of any human activity is *itself* possible. For example, even if we grant that the Kantian account of science is correct, it can always be asked how Kant himself was capable of coming to know the elements of his account. Unless one's account of any kind of experience, or even experience in general, also contains within it an account of how the transcendental perspective employed by such an account is possible, the philosophical position is always open to serious question. It seems, in fact, that every philosopher must talk as if he were God, or at least as if he enjoys some sort of God-perspective. There are some intriguing paradoxes involved in such a problem. Consider an empiricist, who might want to say that only sense experience can reveal true judgments. Is the sentence "All true judgments are based on experience" itself based on experience? If it is *not* based on experience (which surely seems to be the case), then the very meaning of the sentence refutes itself. This objection is not, of course, totally insurmountable, but it does show the terrible importance of what is known as the "transcendence problem."

Heidegger has said that Dasein must transcend the world of entities. This is clear enough, for unless Dasein were capable of transcending the world of entities, such an account of these entities as is given in *Being and Time* would itself be impossible. But how is it that Dasein transcends these entities? Heidegger speaks of the "transcendence of the World," which is a subjective genitive (i.e., the world is not that which is transcended, but rather that which does the transcending); on the other hand, if the world transcends, what does it transcend? The world? Does the world transcend itself?

For Heidegger, to say that the world transcends itself sounds confusing only because the word "world" is here used in two different senses. The world as the aggregate of all objects present-at-hand and all relations ready-at-hand is indeed transcended by Dasein's Being-in-the-world. To-be-in-the-world ontologically is what makes "world," in the sense of Nature, possible. Hence the existential to-be-in-the-world transcends the world as made up of objects present and ready-at-hand. This transcendence itself, though, is made possible by the ontological ground of temporality. It is temporality, then, that makes transcendence possible. How does Heidegger accomplish this reduction?

When I relate to the world as a user of tools, when the world is equipment to me, then the world is *significant* to me in three ways: (1) The piece of equipment with which I am directly involved is significant in that it exists *for my sake*. It is *for Dasein's sake* that Dasein projects before itself the various items of equipment within the world. (2) The world is also significant as equipment in the sense that the world exists as a background of many inevitable characteristics which I cannot control and which determine my moods. There is, then, in the significance of the world that *in the face of which* I, as Dasein, have been thrown. (3) There is also, in my use of the items of equipment that constitute the world, an understanding of actions taken *in order to* accomplish something else. The various items of equipment take their independent significance in terms of what they are meant to accomplish, or in what they do *in order to* accomplish their purpose. (A hammer *means* in-order-to drive nails.) These three aspects of significance that make up what it means to-be-in-the-world are called "horizons," and each of these horizons corresponds to an ekstasis of time. For-the-sake-of is the horizon of the future. All this means is that whenever I involve myself directly with the world, I use the world as made up of items of equipment for-the-sake-of my existing, and when the world is significant to me in this way, it is significant because I am futural—i.e., I have a future. The *horizon* of the future ekstasis is, then, the for-the-sake-of. The term "horizon" as used by Heidegger seems to mean: the total range of possible modes of significance for a particular ekstasis. The present's horizon is the in-order-to. This means that whenever I involve myself with the world as ready-at-hand (equipment) and perform actions and declare situations (which is what the present *means* existentially), I do so in terms of a kind of purpose (Why was the action done? In-order-to accomplish such-and-such). The horizon of the present, then, is the in-order-to. The horizon of the past is the in-face-of-which, which declares and establishes moods and state-of-mind.

It has already been shown that the *significance* of what it means to be in the world lies in the threefold unity of the in-order-to, the for-the-sake-of, and the in-face-of-which. It has now been shown that this threefold signification provides the horizon of the ekstases of temporality. But in what way does this accomplish transcendence?

In order for a subject to relate to an object, there must already exist a basis for relationship between Dasein and the "world" of present-at-hand objects and ready-at-hand relationships in the fact that Dasein is *already in the world.* Hence that which makes the subject-object relationship *possible* is Being-in-the-world. In order to *transcend* the entities that make up "Nature" there must *already be* a way of Being (Being-in-the-world) to which the transcendental stepping-out can step. We must bear in mind that "ekstasis" means "to step out."

The argument formally is this:

To transcend means to "go beyond."
But there must be some "place" to go.
Transcendence, then, is possible only because there are ekstases.
But ekstases do not "step out" to nowhere; they must have horizons.
The horizons, though, are temporal in character.
Hence to transcend is possible only because we are temporal.

The strict formality of the argument, and the rigidity with which Heidegger's use of his own language is used to support the argument, have a tendency to remove the argument from the arena of common understanding. We must look, though, a bit more deeply at this new doctrine. What does it *mean* in terms not so closely tied to Heidegger's jargon?

Quite simply, the claim is this: Some form of "transcendence" is necessary if philosophy is to be possible at all. Heidegger's claim is that it is only because we are *finite* that we are capable of transcending the entities of the world and our use of them. Our finitude provides us with transcendence.

The various ways in which I deal with the world all come down to my having a *significant* past, present, and future. How can the past, present, and future *be* significant to me? They are significant because of my existence-structure. That is, the way in which I exist is such that I have temporal ekstases. These ekstases are so structured that it is possible, in each of them, to do a kind of stepping-out, by which I am capable of reflecting upon my existence-structure. Unless I were temporal, unless I were finite, then, I could not transcend. Transcendence is based upon temporality.

The problem of transcendence has a very interesting history since the time of Kant. It was a theme of great significance for Hegel and the other idealists. But it was Nietzsche who argued that the real meaning of transcendence was in existence. In *Thus Spoke Zarathustra*, Nietzsche argues that man himself must "go beyond" to the transvaluation of all things, even value itself, because "God is dead." It is no longer the *infinite* perspective that allows philosophy, but rather the *finite* perspective: the overman. Heidegger was much influenced by Nietzsche, and although he did not follow the latter's exorbitant use of language, nor his focus on value, he *did* follow Nietzsche in establishing the basis of transcendence in finite man. Indeed, Heidegger goes further than Nietzsche by arguing that the very ontological ground of transcendence is man's finitude. The argument is simple: There can be no transcendence without temporal ekstases with horizons.

REMARK ON SECTIONS 70–71

Heidegger ends his chapter on temporality with two brief considerations. In section 70 he argues that Dasein's spatiality is also based in temporality, and in section 71 he notes that the ultimate meaning of Dasein's everydayness as temporal must await the next chapter, in which Dasein's history is made significant. Both of these sections are self-explanatory and are meant to finish out the analysis rather than to provide new dimensions to his philosophy.

REMARKS ON THE TEMPORAL ANALYSIS

Before we turn to the study of how history is possible, a few remarks concerning this chapter should perhaps be made. It is, to some extent, a tortuous chapter, in which the detailed analyses of temporality have a tendency to emasculate the full import of Heidegger's message. At times, to be sure, Heidegger seems to be stretching the point. Although his arguments for the temporal structure of the general character of human existence seem strong enough, to make every single existential discovered in the first division now suddenly be based on temporality seems straining for the sake of symmetry and balance. In spite of these shortcomings—and indeed, they may not be shortcomings if the analyses can be made to hold water—the overpowering persuasion of his analysis is immense.

Heidegger is arguing that the meaning of human existence is based upon the temporality of man. The amazing thing about Heidegger's claim is that he does not leave the insight to a kind of intuition or mystical grasp. He painstakingly ferrets a temporal basis out of every single way in which man reflects upon himself or functions within the world. Even more remarkable, he accomplishes an analysis of the very ability to philosophize at all—transcendence—along the lines of his temporal interpretation. In addition to this, even for those unwilling to accept his final ontological doctrine, he has accomplished a truly remarkable phenomenological account of how time is significant to man as an existing being. His accounts of the future as expectation or anticipation, the present as making-present by actions and situations, and the past as remembering and forgetting, are examples of interpretive philosophy at its best. To speculate upon the far-reaching effects of the doctrine of time is a great temptation, but it must be resisted in the present context.

IX.

HISTORY

sections 72–83

The youth, slender and gaunt, his dark eyes burning as brightly as the June sun overhead, waited with inner turmoil but outward calm for the man he despised. Though his lungs were already corrupted by tuberculosis, the fever in his brain was that of a fanatic nationalist. In his pocket was a loaded Belgian pistol. Alienated, idealistic, dedicated, intense, but sadly misled, the boy waited in the unlikely Francis Joseph Street until suddenly and unexpectedly the open car with its famous passenger made a false turn, presenting him with the opportunity to alter forever the course of history. His name was Gavrilo Princip; and, through an almost farcical series of events and opportunities in this Bosnian town of Sarajevo on June 28, 1914, he managed to shoot and kill the Hapsburg Archduke, Francis Ferdinand of Austria-Hungary. As a result of this bold and pitiful act of misplaced courage, Princip ignited the fuse that was to detonate the explosive end to all the old systems of Christian princes in Europe, and set the world on a Herculean journey of savagery, blood, and unmeasured suffering.

It is possible, of course, that had Princip been unsuccessful, the war, known as the Great War, or World War I, may not have happened. It is also possible that, given the developing and conflicting spirits of the age and the unusual personalities of the various leaders, the war was inevitable. But both of these suggestions are mere speculation. What is surely true is that Princip's single act was not the only cause of the war; the fates, the heritage, and destinies not only of Gavrilo Princip but of all those even remotely responsible for the actions that led up to August 1, 1914, tell a story in which the grim events became a part of history. For history is a story, and the story gives meaning to the events—even the event of Princip's assassinating the Archduke—and not the other way around.

It is necessary to point out that the German term for "history" (*Geschichte*) is also the term for "story," as is the French "*L'histoire.*" To understand the ontological meaning of Dasein is to understand that the telling of a story is the fundamental way in which the meaning of existence is illuminated. Long ago Aristotle had recognized that the structure of a story consists of a beginning, a middle, and an end. The similarity between the seemingly mere aesthetic analysis in the *Poetics* and the three-fold analysis of time into past, present, and future is profoundly revealing. Unless we were able to tell stories, whether fact or fiction, the meaning of our existence would not be available to us. And here it is the formal character of the story and not its accuracy or factual correspondence that matters. When Heidegger speaks of "the stretch between birth and death," he means the *story* of an existence; and a story is just *how* the meaning of existence is made manifest (i.e., made "true").

But here we must be careful. The story of Gavrilo Princip does not really begin with his birth. For he was born into a culture and a tradition—indeed a heritage—that preceded him and yet was surely as much a part of him as his own limbs. Nor did his death end the meaning of his act on that grim day in June of 1914. (Oh, that it only had!) The story of Princip is what makes his existence meaningful, but his heritage (which came before his birth) and his destiny (which outlives him even today) are also a part of his story.

This too must be emphasized: it is not the events that make a story; it is a story that makes the events possible and meaningful. Contemporary epistemologists remarkably spend almost none of their time and energy on the examination of how stories function to illuminate our understanding. Yet, from a children's fairy tales to epics and histories, the very structure of a story, which is *a priori*, is used constantly to illuminate how we exist in the world. Heidegger's term "*Geschichte*" therefore should always be interpreted not merely as history in the narrow sense of what is written in textbooks but as a *story*.

Such events in the current of human history can surely be significantly described in terms of fate and destiny—in fact, in some sense the event so described is meaningless without such concepts. But terms like "fate" and "destiny" are almost embarrassing to sophisticated philosophers, and at best they are often described in terms of general social consciousness or psychological attitudes that have nothing to do with truth or validity.

And yet Heidegger argues that fate, heritage, and destiny are what make historicality possible. "Historicality" means, to Heidegger, that existential awareness through which one understands Being in history, and as such it is the ultimate ground and cause of historical awareness and historical research. For Heidegger, the existential view of having a fate or a destiny, along with the power of a story to reveal meaning, is what makes human history possible.

The question as to how history is possible, and the ensuing general interest in such historico-philosophical questions as the nature, methodology, and presupposition of historical knowledge, became the focus of special inquiry in the nineteenth century, above all with Hegel and the idealists, but also very much so in the works of people like Karl Marx and Wilhelm Dilthey. Few if any of these thinkers, however, would have set the discipline of history upon such uncertain foundations as fate and destiny. Yet even as Heidegger makes this unorthodox claim, one senses a kind of intuitional sympathy with the idea; for if nothing else, such an interpretation of history brings the philosophy of history to a remarkably immediate level. The tremendous advantage of such a view of history is the *availability* of the focal entity, Dasein. In other words, the methodological problem of trying to build a science on a series of events or entities that no longer exist, and hence in an important sense *are not*, ceases to be such a major stumbling block. For the *foundation* of history is not, according to this interpretation, people, artifacts, situations, and events that *no longer exist*; rather, the foundation of history is the existing human Dasein—a Dasein that has a fate and a destiny.

That Heidegger should concern himself at all with the question of history seems in accordance with his interpretation of time as the ontological ground of human existence. Surely a concern for history, which is the significant past, belongs to the temporal structure of human existence. In fact, however, Heidegger's concern for history goes beyond the natural interest within his theory of time. History essentially affects the nature of the reflecting self, and as such, an account of history must be completed before the ontological ground of human existing can be properly understood. For this reason, the understanding of the destined self (which in the case of the young Serbian nationalist changed all of us) alone can provide an existentially meaningful basis to history. For surely the poignant reality for Princip in understanding himself at the moment of his personal boldness was the historical significance of the event—and that significance is rooted in the personal fate and national destiny of Gavrilo Princip.

Heidegger's claim that fate and destiny are the ground of human historicality must be examined thoroughly; and again, the section-by-section commentary on this penultimate chapter of *Being and Time* seems the best way to present his view. For the most part, the chapter is not overly burdened with difficulties and, with a certain degree of creative tolerance on the part of the reader, may even become acceptable.

EXISTENTIAL EXPOSITION OF HISTORY   (section 72)

Heidegger introduces the problem of history in terms of the completeness of the existential analytic of Dasein. Up to now the central focal point from which the view of Dasein was taken lay in the awareness of Dasein's ability-not-to-be—i.e., its death. But the death of Dasein can be seen as the end of a series that begins with birth. What about "birth"? And what about the period between birth and death, that stretch of human experiences and modes of existence that constitutes the life span or history of an individual Dasein? The introduction to the problem of history, then, becomes the basis on which Heidegger addresses himself to one of the most persistent and perennial of all philosophical questions: How does one account for the unification of that which "has" the diverse experiences of life?

One form of the traditional account of such a problem is to posit some kind of soul substance, which persists as unchanging through the course of changing events. This account had been seriously discredited by Kant's paralogisms; furthermore, for Heidegger to accept a theory of the substantial soul at this stage of his development would be totally inconsistent with his thought.

The problem, though, remains. If we grant that life provides us with a great variety of experiences and events, and we wish nonetheless to maintain a unity of the self that has these experiences, some explanation must be given. To shift subtly the emphasis from a substantial soul to a formal subject would also be unacceptable to the Heideggerian view, since he has so consistently argued that there is no such thing as an isolated "I" or subject, but rather a self that is already in the world and already characterized by its concerns and involvements.

Dasein's existence structure is such that part of its Being (i.e., part of the way in which it can be said to be) is to be between birth and death. One need not posit the *substantiality* of that entity in order to account for its unity, nor need one posit its *subjectivity* in order to render an explanation of the events as objects of experience. One need only take

account of *how* the entity (Dasein) *is* such that it is conscious of itself as persisting through the time series of events. One of the ways in
which Dasein exists is to stretch along between birth and death, and
this stretching-along is Dasein's historicizing.

Historicizing, then, emerges from the Heideggerian discussion as an
answer to a problem. It must be posited if Dasein is to have sameness
throughout the manifold variety of its experience. The structure of this
historicizing is Dasein's historicality.

Right away there are some intriguing consequences of such an interpretation. The locus of history shifts from past objects, artifacts, or even
events to the existing Dasein. It is only because a human being can exist
in such a way as to stretch along between birth and death that he is capable of having an historical sense by which the "facts" of history are made
relevant and significant. For Heidegger, then, the "problem" of history
is not the peculiarity of its methodology, nor even its metaphysical presuppositions, nor its epistemological aspects, but quite simply the possibility of historicizing at all. What must be known about the way in which
human beings exist in order for these human beings to concern themselves with and take significance from the past? The answer is that if indeed there is such a thing as history, then there must be some existential-
ontological ground that makes it possible. The existential term used
for that which makes history possible is "historicality." A phenomenological interpretation of this existential—historicality—now becomes
necessary.

Before we turn to this phenomenological description of historicality,
however, a brief investigation into how Dasein regards that which is "historical" is in order.

DASEIN'S HISTORICIZING   (section 73)

After giving a brief but revealing account of various uses of the term
"history," Heidegger turns his attention to a peculiar yet intriguing problem of how the term is applied. If we consider a certain item of equipment
that was used in the past but exists in the present merely as an item of
historical significance, there is a problem. Let us take as an example
Lincoln's pipe. We call it "historical" in the sense that its meaning for
us is its significance as an item of equipment (ready-at-hand) in the past.
Yet in its simple thinghood (presence-at-hand) it is present, lying there
before us in the museum display case. And even though it *could* be used
in the present as ready-at-hand (someone could smoke it today), in such
usage it loses its peculiar historical significance.

The fact that the pipe still exists today does not make us forgo our
consideration of it as historical. Why not? Because the *use* of the pipe

(its readiness-at-hand) is restricted to the past, even though its existence as present-at-hand has location in the present and probably in the future. What does this tell us about the meaning of the term "historical" as it applies to Lincoln's pipe, and perhaps to all its uses? It tells us that what is historical is not the simple presence-at-hand existence but the existential involvement with the *world*. We recall that the primary meaning of the term "world" for Heidegger is one's involvement in it as a user of tools (circumspective concern). Hence it is the *use* of the tools of the world's equipment that describes a world that is historically significant. It is Lincoln's Being-in-the-world in terms of his circumspective concern for the pipe (that is, his *using* the pipe as an instrument of relaxation) that *is no more*—that "world" no longer exists. The pipe *itself*, though, still exists. Hence it is not entities as such that are "historical," but the "worlds" to which these entities are existentially related. "Worlds," in this sense, however, are existentials of Dasein, and hence only Dasein is historical. It is *Dasein's* Being-in-the-world that is historical.

This analysis of the piece of historically significant equipment is remarkable in that it focuses so tellingly on Heidegger's general theory of existential meaning. It certainly does no violence to ordinary ways of speaking to say that Lincoln's pipe is considered to have "historical value" because it was Abraham Lincoln who used it. Yet in saying such a thing we expose our attitude toward the meaning of "historical," in that it refers to Dasein's Being-in-the-world. It was Lincoln's own stretching-along from his birth to his death that made him historically significant, and it was his use of his pipe during the stretching-along that gives historical significance to his still existing pipe. It is not the simple brute existence of the pyramids that sends the mind reeling along its corridors of historical feeling but the fact that the pyramids were part of the "world" of the ancient Egyptians in their everyday Being there.

What is history *about*? It is about the *worlds* of those Daseins whose stretching-along between their respective births and deaths constitute a significance of the past. In short, it is the historicality of the various Daseins in terms of their Being-in-the-world that is not only what history is about, but also what constitutes the ground of history.

CONSTITUTION OF HISTORICALITY (section 74)

We have said above that it is a Dasein's Being-in-the-world that provides its historicality. But surely not every form of Being-in-the-world is historically significant. The basic constitution of that peculiarly *historical* way of Being-in-the-world must be exposed. What is it that makes *Lincoln's* pipe an item of historical interest, rather than, say, the pipe belonging to Lincoln's barber? What is it that makes the aged paper on which the Gettysburg Address was written more historically significant than Lincoln's laundry bill? Surely not every and any mode of Being-in-the-world, then, is a basis for historicality. According to Heidegger, that which makes authentic historicality possible is fate, heritage, and destiny. The intrusion of the adjective "authentic" here is not an innocent accident. If, indeed, the essence of history is Dasein's existence, then *authenticity* must come into the picture. We must not concern ourselves with inauthentic Dasein's historicality, for that would be an historicality that is not uniquely one's *own*, and hence would not be historically significant at all. Rather, the description or interpretation of how one *authentically* exists as an historically significant Dasein must be elicited.

The three terms that Heidegger uses to ground historicality are "heritage," "fate," and "destiny." Unfortunately, Heidegger does not define these terms specifically. His *use* of them, however, makes it possible for us to approximate his meaning. One's *heritage* seems to be that existential awareness of one's tradition as significantly determining, to some extent, the makeup of the "world" that one is "in" as Being-in-the-world. Heidegger speaks of one's heritage as that to which one "comes back" in thrownness. Since it is an authentic coming-back, it must be characterized by resoluteness and guilt. What appears to be implied here is something like this: One's heritage seems to consist in one's understanding of the various stories and interpretations of past events that directly affect one's comprehension of oneself. A member, for example, of an early American family may well see as part of his own personal significance the battles of the American Revolution and the spirit and values that were exhibited there. But it is not merely the knowledge that one's forefathers had in fact engaged in certain activities that constitutes heritage: rather, it is the bold *acceptance* of both the guilt and the honor that go with that history. Dasein is *resolute* in that it does not merely *know* the history of one's tradition and family, but indeed freely commits itself to the full significance of the values, judgments, weaknesses, strengths, and pride of the human decisions that went into the making of that history. Heidegger's point seems to be that unless one's heritage is existentially realized in such a resolute manner, authentic historicality is impossible. The fact that one's acceptance of one's place in one's heritage may be highly uncertain or vague does not lessen its authenticity: hence a member of the DAR may not have as much "heritage" in the existential sense as an orphan boy who simply accepts his role as a "son" of American history in an authentic way.

"Fate," on the other hand, seems to be used by Heidegger in the sense of one's awareness of one's finitude. Of the three characteristics of Dasein's historicality, fate seems to be the most important, since it is fate that is exposed as being temporal. What do we mean by one's fate, in the sense of being aware of finitude? The reader must be warned *not* to consider this use of the term "fate" in any "Greek" sense—i.e., in the sense of a predetermined way in which one's existence is confronted by events plotted by the gods. Rather, fate is awareness of one's *limited possibilities* and the ensuing *significance* of one's choices and decisions made in the flux of these possibilities. Thus one is *fateful* because of one's resoluteness in the midst of one's possibilities, and this resoluteness is historically significant. Caesar's resoluteness in crossing the Rubicon is what made that action fateful, and hence historically significant. The decision to so act on Caesar's part is significant to us only because we ourselves are capable of authentic—i.e., *resolute*—historicality. From this it follows that an irresolute man (an inauthentic man) can have no fate and hence no historicality.

The final term, "destiny," is applied only to peoples or to nations. It is a kind of fate on the level of a whole people, as one might speak of the "fate of a nation." Heidegger would prefer to speak of the "destiny of a nation." Like "heritage" and "fate," though, "destiny" is a characteristic of authentic historical existence, and without it historicality could not occur. It is grounded in Dasein's Being-with of others. One must be aware of the destiny that one's group, nation, people, or religion can manifest in the course of history. Heidegger, unfortunately, does not expand the possible application of this term, so that how broadly or how narrowly one must apply it is not clear. Whether or not one can speak of the "destiny" of the whole of mankind is an open question.

In speaking about the existential ground of historicality, Heidegger seems to use the single term "fate" to refer to all three of the terms we have discussed above. In this broader sense, fate is described as a "powerless superior power." It is "powerless" in the sense that the finitude of man is unalterable: It is also "powerless" in the sense that it cannot explain any event that occurs. But it is a "superior power" in that it asserts itself as resolute, and hence as free, toward the possibility of death and guilt. It is only from the perspective of one's fate-heritage-destiny that the full significance of one's Being-in-the-world can be realized, and it is from this realization that one achieves authentic historicality.

Having described fate existentially as the ground of historicality, the next task for Heidegger is to show that fate itself is grounded in Dasein's temporality. From the manner in which fate was treated, such a task is not too difficult. Dasein's fate, and hence its historicality, is possible because of the ecstatical ground of its existence. Because Dasein is free for its own possibilities, it is essentially futural. In authentic future, however, Dasein is aware of the possibility of death; and, as such, it is also aware of one of the terminal perspectives that describe its "life," that stretching-along between birth and death. As having-been, Dasein is also aware of its heritage, an awareness that makes having a past significant. The future and the past are also significant for the acts and situations that make up the authentic present (moment-of-vision), so that one's fate is essentially tied up with one's decisions and actions in the present. In this way, fate makes one "timely." Man's historicality, grounded in fate, makes him both a "child of his time" and a "child *beyond* his time" as well.

What is significant about Heidegger's analysis of fate is not so much that he should attempt to show that fate is grounded in temporality; that is true of all existentials. Rather, what is crucial is that the most meaningful ekstasis for history is the *future* (which, if historicality is to be authentic, must be the case). Authentic historicality is significant in terms of Dasein's future, because, as Dasein projects into its possibilities, it does so in terms of its heritage and its fate. Its actions (which make up its authentic present) and its projections into possibilities (which make up its authentic future) are both *historically* significant. This means that history is a characteristic of the living Dasein rather than the dead past.

In an earlier section it was noted that the mode of the authentic understanding in the past ekstasis was *repetition*. Historicality is the authentic repetition of possibilities, not as a mere enslavement of what has gone before, but as a sharing in the decisiveness and guilt that made the situations of the past significant. To speak, then, of "living the past" is not to deny the future; rather, it is to take hold of the future in such a way that the future is indeed one's *own*. "Authentic," as we have seen, means "to be one's own self." It is only fatefully, and from a heritage, that one can grasp genuinely significant possibilities. Without a heritage, the possibilities that would be grasped would not be one's own.

HISTORICALITY AND WORLD HISTORY   (section 75)

The question to which Heidegger directs his inquiry in this section is this: Why is it not possible to build history merely upon the sequence of actual events? Why is it necessary to ground history upon such existential ideas as heritage, fate, and destiny? Heidegger's answer is that history is not about *facts*, no matter how they are bound together in any kind of sequence, but rather it is about "worlds" in which resolute Daseins *are*. By the term "world history" Heidegger does not mean the study of the history of all human peoples, as opposed, let us say, to "German history" or the "history of the Russian revolutions." In Heidegger's sense of the term, the history of the Russian revolutions may well be a much finer example of "world history" than a rather amorphous account of the major events in the history of mankind, since the latter might well overlook the "destinies" and "fates" of individual nations or peoples.

The question that Heidegger asks here suggests further commentary. Why is it that history cannot be explained as a series of facts? Suppose we consider such a view of history. How is it possible to account for the unification of these disparate facts? In the midst of one's many diverse experiences, what is it that provides one with a principle of unity? Can we say that the *subject* (the ego) provides this unity, and that the subject is hence historical? Heidegger says that subjects are not historical, but worlds are. What are his reasons for saying this?

If we are to try to establish a unity of a series of experiences by positing a subject, soul, or ego, we must first establish an account of how the subject relates to the objects. As we have seen, a subject-object relationship *presupposes* a world in which the subject and the object take reference to one another. There is no such thing as an isolated and denuded subject, just as there is no such thing as a plain, bare "fact." Both the "knowing subject" and the "fact" that is known occur in a world of *already existing significance*. Hence what is historical in the primordial sense is neither the subject nor the object, but that background of significance which makes the subject-object relationship possible. This "background" is called the "world." What history historicizes about is Being-in-the-world.

If what is historicized is Being-in-the-world, then the connection between a presently existing Dasein and no-longer existing events and other Daseins can become significant. For what it *means* to-be-in-the-world has been analyzed and described in great detail in *Being and Time* in terms of resolute possibility. The freedom, resoluteness, and even the anxiety of what belongs to our heritage and our fates and destinies are existentially significant to us in terms of our *present* understanding of ourselves. My own present resoluteness can be significant in terms of my heritage only if I do not limit resoluteness to what "would be actual as 'Experience' only as long as the 'act' of 'resolving' lasts."[1] Resoluteness is rather significant in terms of possibilities, and insofar as I am historical, this resoluteness can be applied to my heritage and my fate.

It is due to my fallenness and my inauthenticity that I look upon history as made up of facts. It is the chief characteristic of the "they" to avoid and overlook possibilities, and search out only the safety of the facts. The inauthentic view of history, the view of the "they," which sees history as a series of no-longer "facts," *cannot in principle be significant.* To be sure, facts can be learned. Indeed, facts about a no-longer past can be analyzed scientifically. But that is not *history*, for history must be *significant.*

---

1. Cf. *Being and Time*, p. 443.

HOW HISTORY IS DONE   (section 76)

"Historiology" refers to the actual thematizing of historical research—i.e., science. Heidegger's argument here is that the very activity
of doing historical research is possible only because man has historicality.
To students of history or of the philosophy of history, the question as
to how history is possible is a familiar one. What is asked by this question
is this: Granted that there is such a thing as historical research and
thematizing, what are the *a priori* presuppositions of how a science
of history is possible and what are its categories? The problem of
historicizing, however, is plagued with a special difficulty. The "facts"
are in the past. They are no longer. Hence we must ask questions like
this: From historical evidence can one discover universal laws applicable
to all forms of human activity? Can we, from an analysis of what man
has done in the past, predict the future? Does history consist of a series
of unique events—that is, events that only happen once: *einmalige* (which
Macquarrie and Robinson translate as "once-for-all")? Heidegger's answer to these questions is to show that they are indeed misguided questions. For these questions would be significant only if history investigated
actual facts. Then and only then would the questions about whether there
are "hidden laws" behind these facts be meaningful. Heidegger argues,
however, that history studies "the silent power of the *possible*." The only
sense in which history studies fact is that it studies the "facts" of fate,
destiny, and heritage. In other words, to historicize is to be aware of existence. That which makes historicizing different from other forms of existential inquiry is simply that history concerns itself with human existence
as having-been—but that is *not* to say that it concerns itself with past
(no-longer) events, but with possibilities (whose significance is both present and futural) contained in one's existing as fateful.

The criteria of history, then, are not the criteria of technology (in fact,
the criteria of no science is identical with the criteria of technique). History is interested in neither the "universal laws" extracted through statistical abstraction, nor a mere chronicle of unique (i.e., once-for-all) events.
On the other hand, Heidegger is not an historicist, though he is often
interpreted as being one. To some extent, the fallacy of interpreting Heidegger in this way is due to his own vocabulary; hence it is important
to clarify this persistent and annoying issue.

"Historicism" has come to mean that each epoch or period has certain
presuppositions that are fundamental to that period only; therefore no
real communication between periods is possible. Furthermore, since these
presuppositions are usually implicit and rarely identified within the time-
span of the epoch, it is impossible to escape their influence or even recognize them without enormous effort. As a consequence one can only

vaguely appreciate the philosophers or poets of a past age. This makes our own present presuppositions merely some among many possible others; so there is an inevitable relativism of historical values and moral judgments, including that of truth itself. Nothing could be further from Heidegger's understanding. He is not an historicist and certainly not a relativist, as historicism implies.

Yet it is perhaps easy enough to see why interpreters such as Karl Löwith and the followers of Leo Strauss have read a kind of historicism into Heidegger's thought. Primarily the reason can be found in Heidegger's use of the plural form of the term "world." He speaks for example of the different "worlds" that certain figures in history shared with their contemporaries, and this seems to support a kind of multiplicity of worlds, which in turn implies a multiplicity of possible truths and values. But such a reading of Heidegger is highly ungenerous. There can be only one world. However, we do use the term "world" in two totally different senses. First, we use the term as equivalent of "realm"; so that we speak of the the "world of opera" or the "world of finance." In this sense, of course, there are many "worlds" for there are many realms in which certain activities and actions are meaningful only because of the assumed relevance of the particular interest or task that the realm identifies. This way of speaking can indeed be applied to historical eras, as when we speak of the "world of the Elizabethans." By this we mean there are certain ways of doing things, certain shared beliefs and attitudes that were dominant during the time of the reign of Elizabeth Tudor, Queen of England. Many of the values held by the men and women of Elizabeth's time are certainly different from our own today, and so it seems legitimate to contrast their world with our world. However, no matter how bold the differences are, it does not mean that *all* principles are distinct and separate, nor does it mean the absolute judgments of logic, mathematics, or morality are different. After all, lovers in the twentieth century do identify with *Romeo and Juliet*; and, though we do not all have kingdoms to divide, we know how sharper than a serpent's tooth it is to have a thankless child.

As legitimate as these uses of the term are, however, there is another more fundamental and indeed more philosophical sense to the term "world" that means the entire universe, including the worlds of opera and the Elizabethans. It is this broader sense that Heidegger means by "world" when he uses it in such phrases as "Being-in-the-world" (not: Being-in-a-world). The wisdom of Plato, the dramatic poetry of Sophocles, the savagery of the thirteenth century, and the optimism of the eighteenth are all a part of this one world, and because of it we are capable of reading these past authors and not only understanding them but also becoming a part of them because they are a part of our history.

The strict adherence to historicism in the relativist sense is not only antithetical to Heidegger, it is also self-contradictory. If I seriously maintain that a prior epoch *cannot* be understood *because* it is so different, I would have to *know* what the prior epoch believed and maintained, which is precisely denied by the argument itself. In other words, if I assume I can understand Romeo's love for Juliet, the historicist must deny it just because the Elizabethans had a different view of love. But they can maintain this only if, in fact, *they* know enough about the Elizabethans to assure me that I am mistaken. How they could know this is difficult to comprehend if the very fact that the view is in a prior epoch makes it unknowable. Surely the one thing that cannot be different is the world, for differences themselves presuppose the sameness of the world. The very word "difference" is meaningful only if it is in the world. Heidegger has argued that the world cannot be my representation, since both "my" and "representation" both presuppose a single world. The world is therefore not dependent on the variant system of values; rather the variant values presuppose the sameness of the world. Of course, the Elizabethans did have many values we do not have; but the very fact that I *know* they had different values shows that the historicist must be wrong.

Furthermore, historicism is a metaphysical view, or an ontical view, to use the terminology of *Being and Time*. Heidegger is seeking to realize an ontological view in which there can only be one world, and that is the world in which Dasein already finds itself. This one world is, granted, an historical one, but not an historicistic one. Historicism, however, is only one of many relativistic and nihilistic attitudes that critics have tried to foist upon the reading of Heidegger. But a careful analysis of the text and a truly ontological understanding of what it means to be (the Being-question) reveals that such grim interpretations are exactly the opposite of what Heidegger reveals in his analysis. One can appreciate the vast differences between epochs only because we all belong to the same world. Unless this were so, a study of history in any philosophically revealing and authentic way would be impossible.

Suppose we consider this question: What would one conceive to be the "perfect history"? Let us imagine a technologically "advanced" situation where spy satellites are capable of recording every event that transpires on earth, and do so accurately and impartially. If such a recording were to be put on film, and a future generation were to be able to watch this film, would this constitute the "perfect" historical methodology? If so, then what history means is a simple chronicling of unique events, available for independent and disinterested observation. But it seems obvious that one would not recognize such a methodology as necessarily "historical." For again, it is not the mere fact of something actually occurring that makes it historical, but its *significance* as part of human existing.

In like manner, a compilation of all causes and statistical patterns, no matter how accurately achieved and refined, and no matter how amenable to codification into "historical laws," would not constitute a "perfect" methodology of history. If a series of accurately tested laws (such as: "Whenever the social conditions of a community reach a point of intolerance, there will always ensue a revolution of social norms") *were* possible—and there seems to be no *a priori* reason why they would not be possible in a general sort of way—even under such conditions one would hesitate to admit that the study of such laws exhausted the meaning of history, or even constituted what was most important in history.

History must be *existentially* significant, otherwise one would not concern oneself with it. Heidegger's account of existential historicality, based on authentic fate, heritage, and destiny, provides an ontological ground as to why and how historiology is possible. Again, as is usual in Heidegger's analyses, the key lies in emphasizing the *possible* rather than the *actual*. The *actual* is *knowable*, but the *possible* is *significant*. Hence, since the past is no longer actual, in order for it to be available to us at all it must be seen as significantly possible, and this means, if it is to be authentic, our *own* possibility. But the past can be our *own* possibility only if it is rooted in our heritage, our fate, and our destinies.

DILTHEY AND YORCK   (section 77)

Heidegger ends his consideration of historicality by showing that much of his own insight into the nature of history had been seen in embryonic form in the philosophies of Wilhelm Dilthey and Count Yorck. Dilthey, for English-reading people, is somewhat more familiar than Yorck, but neither has achieved much response in this country. Most of the major works of Dilthey have not been translated. He is recognized in a general sort of way as a kind of Kantian philosopher of history, whose perspective of *Lebensphilosophie* ("Philosophy of Life") is an attempt to show how history is possible. Count Yorck was his friend and correspondent, with whom he frequently discussed his theory of history. In any event, the section does not seriously alter or add anything to Heidegger's view of history.

This chapter of my commentary began with an account of Gavrilo Princip symbolizing the destiny and fate of 1914 Europe. We have seen how such an account is genuinely historical in a way that a mere chronicling of events is not. More importantly, however, it has also been made clear how one's historical self is an essential part of authentic selfhood and existence. In this way, then, an account of Dasein's historicality is not a mere interesting "addition" to the existential analytic but is a necessary and essential step in the working out of the ontological ground of existence. An interesting consequence of Heidegger's theory of history is something that Heidegger himself does not comment about but that merits consideration. If history is indeed grounded in one's fate and destiny, then history must constantly be *reinterpreted*; not only because of each generation, but indeed each individual adds his own unique perspective to the understanding of his fate and his people's destiny, and hence the historical perspective must be changed to fit that aspect of human existence which asserts itself as most important in a particular era or group, or even in a single great man.

TEMPORALITY AND TIME   (section 78–83)

The final chapter of *Being and Time* has an unusual theme: to show that time is temporal. If at first reading this task seems like bringing coal to Newcastle, it must be kept in mind that the two terms, "time" and "temporality," are quite distinct, though up to now we have not explicitly focused upon their differences. Indeed, in a vague sort of way we have even treated the terms as belonging to at least a family of meanings. In this present section, however, Heidegger draws sharp focus on the difference of meaning between the two terms, and he does so for what he considers to be very important ontological considerations. It might seem immediately obvious that time is temporal, but such "obviousness" is deceptive.

In the first place, as Heidegger uses the terms, "time" refers to the world, or to objects within the world, or even to the relationship between subject-knower and object-known. "Temporality," on the other hand, refers to Dasein's existence. Dasein, as temporal, "creates" time or "sees" time. Time, then, is grounded in temporality, *and not the other way around*. For Heidegger it is essential to insist that the existential or ontological perspective take precedence over the metaphysical or even anthropological view. But in the case of time, the ordinary way of interpreting it is so seductive in its error that Heidegger's accomplishment in showing that time does indeed come from Dasein's temporality is one of the major themes of his work. This chapter is essentially self-explanatory; therefore the section-by-section comments serve as an outline.

The Problem Stated   (section 78)

The account of temporality as both the ground of human existence and as the ultimate explanation of history does not, upon reflection, seem to have any support whatsoever for what is ordinarily understood as "time." One speaks of "taking time" (from where does one "take" time?), or of "having or not having time" (is it then a "substance" that can be possessed?), or even of things being "in time." How do these meanings arise from the basic constitution of human existence as temporal? Is "time," as distinct from temporality, "subjective" or "objective"? What, in short, is the nature and structure of time? For Heidegger, this problem takes its focus from another form of the same question: What is the relationship between existential temporality and that which we call "time" but which we don't seem to know very much about? In the sections that follow, Heidegger answers these questions in terms of the existential analytic.

Temporality and Concern with Time   (section 79)

The ways in which one normally "deals" with time are grounded in one's temporality. The world, as we recall from earlier analyses, is presented to us not as an isolated "object" but as a reference for our own existence as Being-in-the-world. In the first order of our relationship to our world—i.e., the circumspective concern of the ready-at-hand—we make use of the equipmental structure of the world in terms of awaiting, retaining, and acting.

Awaiting, as an existential mode of Being-in-the-world, gives us a perspective which is represented by the simple temporal term "then." (If I *await* the reply to my letter, I do so by imagining a not-yet then—"at that time" when the return letter actually comes.) Retaining, as an existential mode of Being-in-the-world, gives us a perspective represented by the simple temporal phrase "on that former occasion" or even "ago" (e.g., three days *ago*). (If I *retain* my awareness of the taste of *escargots*, I do so by imagining that occasion several weeks *ago* when I actually dined at a French restaurant.) *Acting*, as an existential mode of Being-in-the-world, gives us a perspective which is represented by the temporal term "now." (If I am aware of what I am doing in an *action*, this awareness is realized as something happening *now*-at-this-moment.)

Hence, from retaining, awaiting, and acting, one can discover the primordial time references: then, ago (or "on that former occasion"), and now. These temporal differences are not merely incidental characteristics added on at random. They belong to the essential way in which one deals directly with one's world in the mode of ready-at-hand. The structure of this existential is called *datability*. Such primitive temporal terms as "now," "then," and "ago" are part of the essential meaning of circumspective concern. But where do they come from? Are thens, nows, and agos substantive objects, present-at-hand? Surely not. How, then, are we to conceive of them?

By showing that these temporal concepts by which one dates (and hence structures meaningfully one's actions) come from the modes of awaiting, retaining, and acting, Heidegger has shown the simple answer: The temporal terms come from the ways in which we exist. To ask, Where do the elements of datability come from? requires a simple answer: ourselves. "The making-present which awaits and retains, interprets *itself*."[2] Thus Dasein does not get its nows, thens, and agos from some external source, but from its own structure of existence. *Dasein's temporality is the basis for time.* It is only because I can await, retain, and act that I have understanding of now, then, and ago.

Heidegger interprets phenomenologically a great number of such temporal terms as "meanwhile," "during," "throughout," "lasting," etc., pointing out that all of these elementary temporal terms are grounded in Dasein's temporality. There is no need to discuss or comment on these terms, as long as the reader bears in mind that Heidegger's intent in this section is merely to show completeness of his account. The key to the understanding of this section lies in the original grounding of the three modes of concernful time in Dasein's Being-in-the-world.

Within Time—Time as the Object of Concern   (section 80)

Time, however, is not understood merely as the datability of our existence. There is also what Heidegger calls *public time*. Public time is that measured and counted time which is available for everyman. The question to which Heidegger now directs his attention is this: What *is* it that is counted or measured? How is such counting and measuring possible?

In the very beginnings of philosophical speculation, the nature of "public time" was variously interpreted. Zeno, the subtle Eleatic, showed through his paradoxes that there was an inherent contradiction in thinking of time as made up of small units of "time stuff." To be sure, the full significance of Zeno's paradoxes has been variously interpreted, but at least he has accomplished sufficient grounds for doubting the substantial nature of time. But if time is not made up of tiny time units present-at-hand, what is its nature? Heidegger's point is that one cannot ask the "nature" of public time until one has first examined the prior question: What does it mean to have such a thing as public time? Where does "public time" come from?

Even in the most primitive forms of self-awareness in terms of one's daily activity, the fact that much of one's activity requires *light* has made the rising and the setting of the sun especially meaningful. Daytime and

2. Cf. *Being and Time*, p. 460.

nighttime are *not* first and foremost foundations for a simple time structure. Rather, they are the chief characteristics for being-able-to-work and not-being-able-to-work. Sunrise, then, in a primitive kind of understanding, means: "Now I can go to work—now I can *see*." On the other hand, sunset means: "Now I can no longer work or see. It is time to rest." In other words, the most elemental and primitive time referents, the rising and the setting of the sun, are conceived *as part of* one's circumspective concern. The way in which I make use of the universe as equipment is the background from which time determinants, such as sunrise and sunset, take their meaning. By extension, modern man, though he no longer relies on the rising and the setting of the sun as his chief elements of time, nevertheless still understands his time determinants in terms of his circumspective concern. Five o'clock *means* getting off work; eight o'clock *means* meeting one's girl friend at the corner; etc. Heidegger discusses the public sundial. Why is it the case that the shadow's falling on a certain measured line has significance? Time is not that shadow, nor that line, nor even the combination of the two. The shadow on the line represents a kind of activity that occurs whenever that shadow falls on that line. (When it falls on XII, it's time to eat.)

Such is the existential meaning of public time. But as public time becomes more and more accurate and as man begins to reflect on the nature of things, he sees that "time" always accompanies him, and so he begins to wonder what time is "of itself." Here the fallenness of man asserts itself, and the ensuing interpretation of time is to use *that which measures* as the key to understanding it. However, that which measures is present-at-hand, and its ability to measure is due to its ability to be broken down into parts. A sundial is gross, an Accutron timepiece is refined; but both function by breaking down certain movements into measured divisions. That the delicate timepiece is supposed to correspond ultimately to the movement of the stars merely reflects the dependence on the conception of the timepiece to the primitive understanding of time measurement— the rising and the setting of the sun.

Such an interpretation of time, based upon *that which measures*, inevitably leads to the view that time is made up of a series of now-moments. Just as the sweep-second hand of a fine quartz watch jerks along in sporadic movements, so too time is seen as "jerking" along actually existing seconds. This is, of course, an erroneous view, as Zeno, among others, had well demonstrated. Time does not lie at the basis of a measuring device; rather, a measuring device lies at the basis of public time. It is when I shift from the *significance* of 8:00 (I will meet my friend at the restaurant) to the substantial *existence* of 8:00 (there is actually a moment that bears the title 8:00, followed by another moment called 8:01) that the essential inauthenticity of self-understanding enters into the picture.

In one sense, however, Zeno's objections against public time are not well founded. The ability to treat time as that which can be measured, and even finely measured, is a genuine capability of human consciousness. Public time, seen as something *used* (ready-at-hand within the world), is indeed made up of moments. I can and do speak of split seconds or "the piling up of hours." This is not serious, for public time is as ready-at-hand, something for-the-sake-of existing Dasein. It is only when I lose sight of the temporal ground of this view, or when I begin to attribute metaphysical characteristics to public time, that I am making serious errors. Public time belongs *in the world*; and this means that the significance of the world is to some extent determined by nows, agos, and thens. If this is true, however, then the ontological ground of public time is not some metaphysical characteristic, but *Dasein's temporality*, since Dasein alone has Being-in-the-world.

Public time, then, is neither subjective nor objective. It is not subjective, because it is not a characteristic of the subject, but rather a mode or way in which the subject *is in the world*. It is not objective, because it is not the characteristic of that which is known, since it comes before knowing (in this sense, Kant is right). On the other hand, it cannot come *before* subjectivity or objectivity, since "to be before" presupposes time. Public time can be properly explained only as an existential characteristic of Being-in-the-world, which itself is the background for any subject-object distinction.

The task for Heidegger in this section was to show that time was temporal. Strange as the task may seem, it has amounted to an interpretation of time that saves it from the ridiculousness of objective metaphysical reality, and the meaninglessness of a simple *a priori* epistemological form of intuition. The basis for time is Dasein's temporality.

Ordinary Time   (section 81)

Heidegger now describes the essential inauthenticity of the ordinary conception of time. According to his analysis, there are three things that make the "ordinary" view of time inauthentic: (1) it lacks datability; (2) it lacks significance; and (3) it is seen as infinite—i.e., an endless series of now-points.

Ordinary time—i.e., the time "by the clock"—is seen as made up of a series of "nows," in which each instant or moment is conceived of as an independent, actually existing point along the line of duration. Heidegger does not intend to use an existing metaphysical view of what time actually is; rather, he is referring to the way in which time is ordinarily understood. Such ordinary understanding of time-as-made-up-of-nows not only is an inaccurate account of time, but, far more importantly, constitutes an inauthentic way to exist.

Ordinary time, according to Heidegger, can have no significance or datability. As we have seen, datability refers to that temporal understanding of agos, thens, and nows which make up our understanding of Being-in-the-world. But to conceive of time as clock time is to make these three modes of Being-in-the-world without any real justification, since the *moments* of ordinary time are not existential. In the same way, ordinary time is not significant, since significance is to participate in the as-structure, which a mere counted moment cannot do. Significance must, in the case of ordinary time, always be *added on* to an event that occurs in time.

One of the ways I am in the world is to conceive of my existence in terms of agos, nows, and thens. From this, I build up an understanding of time so that one of its functions is represented by the datability of my actions. If, however, I conceive of this time (which was originally conceived in order to account for datability) as made up of independent moments that do not render an existentially adequate account of datability, then I have conceived of time in such a way as to undermine its very ontological beginning point. Significance must now be added on to temporal events rather than constituting their very nature. Time is treated as something present-at-hand rather than as a mode of the ready-at-hand within the mode of Being-in-the-world.

The serious objection that Heidegger has against the conception of ordinary time, however, is that ordinary time is seen as infinite. If time is seen as pinpoint nows, there is no reason for the mind not to conceive of their being an endless series or chain of nows. (One of the main reasons for there being no objection to such an endless chain of nows is that such a chain, independent of meaning, would make no difference. If time were *built up from existential meaning*, however, it could not be infinite.) But if time is infinite, then the understanding of the world is such that the world is also seen as infinite (this does not follow logically, but it does psychologically, on an inauthentic level). The voice of the "they" is infinite—as long as there is time. But time is infinite, so the "they" does not die. I, however, as that entity which has significance, *can* die. And hence an infinite time is not at all applicable to me.

To be sure, inauthentic existence does not make any overt claims to being infinite; as such, it would be exposed as false. Rather, it conceives of time in such a way that time has *no meaning*, and hence no end. A time without end does not relate to Dasein as a significant concept. As long as ordinary time is treated *as if it were* infinite, Dasein is forever kept from fully realizing its finitude, and hence its own self as able-not-to-be. Rather than *sub specie aeternitatis* being the proper manner in which to reflect upon the nature of the self and the world, it is "under the aspect of finitude." The perspective of the infinite is not available for man; any attempt to employ it destroys the true understanding of the self: the full meaning of one's death and one's essential finitude.

Heidegger's interpretation of ordinary time, then, comes back to support the doctrines exhibited in the very first sections of the existential analytic. Consistently with the entire argument, the whole view of authentic and inauthentic existence comes down to a proper or improper understanding of time. A misunderstanding of the *finitude* of time characterizes inauthenticity. What is authentic must be finite. Authentic existence means to be aware of the possibility of not-being, to be aware of one's finitude. To be is to be in time (*Sein* is to be in *Zeit*).

On Hegel on Time   (section 82)

Heidegger's interpretation of time as existentially significant may seem to have a kind of parallel to Hegel's interpretation of the spirit as temporal. The similarity is not extensive, however, and Heidegger takes pains in section 82 to show that his own views of time do not correspond with Hegel's, though he does admit certain significant similarities which represent a deeper sharing between these two thinkers than is usually admitted.

In Heidegger's view, Hegel is the boldest and most advanced theorist of "ordinary time." Hegel metaphysically grounds time as the "negation of a negation" (punctuality) to make it a meaningful part of his dialectical scheme. As such, time has the same formal structure as that of the spirit, which is also negation of negation, the self grasping—and hence overcoming—the non-self into a unity. In this way, Hegel argues that history is the progress of the spirit, since time and spirit are formally similar.

Heidegger is impressed by Hegel's understanding of the kinship between spirit and time, and he seems to accept Hegel's arguments as to some extent supporting his own. Heidegger does not identify his theory of time with Hegel's, however, for he insists that the existential analytic is superior to Hegel's dialectical analysis. The existential analytic begins with the given "fallenness of the spirit" *in* time, maintaining—against Hegel—that the spirit (Dasein) does not fall into time, but in fact exists as a being already in time.

The import of this section is not so much that Heidegger has shown Hegel to be lacking, but that there are philosophical and historical precedents for identifying temporality with human existence. As in the case of Kant, Heidegger's use of the history of philosophy is twofold: he accepts creatively what support he can find for his own thought and rejects as unacceptable those views that are not ontological.

Fundamental Ontology *(section 83)*

In an excessively brief section, Heidegger ends the published version of *Being and Time*. It is, in spite of its brevity, a rich section in which Heidegger puts into focus just what has been accomplished. And it is, fortunately, very clearly written. Heidegger obviously meant the published form of *Being and Time* to be seen as a preparation for further work to be done. As we all know, the projected work was never published. What Heidegger has accomplished in the published version is not without value, however, even if it is cut off from its originally conceived completeness. His emphasis upon temporality as the basis of existence, his emphasis upon possibility as opposed to actuality, etc., all provide an intriguing and sometimes brilliant treatment of human existence.

There is no need to comment on this last section, which takes less than two pages in the original. To do it justice, one would have to review Heidegger's entire inquiry, and I hope that what I have attempted in these pages is at least an approximation of that. The reader may well feel, however, that Heidegger has ended his book rather abruptly (as indeed he has), and the expected final resolution of so many loose ends is not forthcoming. One might still want to ask the question, What is it all about? After one has read *Being and Time*, what then?

POSTSCRIPT

After *Being and Time*

Heidegger's publication of his major work in an incomplete and unfinished form does not mean merely that there were sections and chapters he had not yet written and could later be added. No thinker conceives an entire philosophical vision at one time and then simply writes it down over the following years. Ideas grow, and the fecundity of the original insight develops into richly complex ideas that may reach their full fruition only after years of husbandry. Heidegger did not stop thinking in 1927, not even about the very ideas over which he labored so mightily and creatively at Marburg and Freiburg. It is not surprising that many of the central doctrines of this original work expanded and developed over the maturing years. To be sure, *Being and Time* is a work that deserves continual re-examination and study just as it is. Had Heidegger died or ceased writing after publishing the first edition it would still be worthy of great speculation and comment. But, as one of the richest and productive works on the literature, it provides an endless source of ideas that could not help but develop and grow. Luckily for us, Heidegger himself continued to work on some of the key concepts he unearthed in *Being and Time* and added new ones that help us understand that early, seminal work. In commenting on the text, it would have been unfair and indulgent to discuss these ideas except as Heidegger originally presented them. But in this postscript it may be beneficial to take the opportunity to look briefly at some of Heidegger's subsequent analyses to see what light the later works, with their fuller development, throw on the published text of *Being and Time*. I consider three such issues: poetry, language, and truth.

POETRY

In 1935 Heidegger gave a series of lectures entitled "On the Origin of the Art-Work," which he later published in *Holzwege* ("Forest Paths") in 1950. In spite of its title, the essay in no way can be understood as a work in aesthetics. Rather, Heidegger adopts the rather bold position that art, particularly poetry, is not primarily a mere source of refined pleasure but a profound way in which truth happens.

We are, of course, familiar with the claims of some poets that artistic beauty and truth are akin in some way. Keats, Auden, Dickinson, Tolstoi, and Murdoch have all argued that truth and art are either one or at least intimately connected. But how are we to understand this? Perhaps we merely mean that good poets sometimes have revealing insights about human nature which they then incorporate into their plays, poems, and novels. Shakespeare, then, would be an astute observer of the human condition, and his insights make his plays more realistic because of his psychological acumen. Such an understanding would, of course, dismiss the importance of the poetry itself. A nonpoetic observer could just as well have the same insights and reveal them at a dinner conversation or a board meeting. Or perhaps it is a device by the poets to make the deep sensitivity of their work somehow more elevated by calling it, falsely, "truth." Disappointed with the pale accolades that acknowledge poetry as satisfying our intellectual gratification, the poet reaches into his verbal resevoir of lofty terms and extracts a somewhat metaphoric usage of the term "truth." Stirred by the nobility of the suggestion, the reader then feels good about this entertainment of his mind. This interpretation is mere disdain, however. But if we reject both of these candidates, the question becomes all the more pressing: in what way could art, which seeks to please, have anything to do with truth, which seeks to inform?

Heidegger rejects both of these accounts and replaces them with a philosophical analysis. "Art," he says "is the becoming and happening of truth. . . . [Poetic] language brings what is, as it is, into the Open for the first time." To show this, he first analyzes various art-works, such as a painting by Van Gogh of peasant shoes, a Greek temple, and a poem, arguing that there exists in all these works a fundamental tension between what he calls the "earth" and the "world," terms obviously used in a metaphoric sense. He uses these terms without defining them, letting their meaning be revealed as he uses them to account for the dynamic character in art, and likewise the dynamic character of truth itself. In each work, whether painting, music, architecture, or poetry, there are elements that represent the familiar, the protected, the immediate (earth); these are coupled with countering elements that lift, project, reach beyond, and provide the broader understanding of horizons and realms (world). At times it seems almost as if "earth" can be understood as the warmth of the glowing pigment, the sonority of the rich vibrations of the cello, the heaviness of the stones that makes up the temple. "World" on the other hand seems to indicate the insights or meaning that draw out from these earth-elements their resistance to disclosure. But neither "earth" nor "world" can exist independently; rather it is the tension between them that reveals truth.

Many aestheticians have pointed out that art-works occur in the conflict or at least the mingling tension between opposites. For Plato, beauty is both mental and physical; Kant characterizes beautiful art as partaking of both the conceptual and the perceptual; so there are precedents. But neither Plato nor Kant would dare go so far as to suggest that in partaking of these two realms, mind and sense, art produces truth. Heidegger speaks only of art, not of beauty, and for him all art is essentially poetry, because it *speaks* the truth. The key lies in the connection between the term "open" and Heidegger's fundamental understanding of truth as unconcealing or revealing. This is never meant simplistically. He insists, for example, that truth is both concealment and unconcealment, that we often reveal ourselves most clearly when we try to hide or disguise ourselves. But the fundamental image remains: to bring about truth one must somehow bring whatever is concealed out into the open, even if this is accomplished by an attempt to conceal. This "open" is achieved in art, especially poetry, by the conflict between earth and world. Truth in art therefore becomes a rather rarified, perhaps even unusual event. In this, there seems to be a change from *Being and Time*, but it is a minor change that is essentially consistent with, and perhaps an advance on, his original analysis.

We have seen in the Commentary that truth as unconcealedness emphasizes the need to account for how the meaning of a thing reveals itself to us and that truth just is this revelation. Now, in this later work, he seems to be suggesting that the revelation of meaning occurs only in the rather special circumstances of which poetic art is perhaps the most outstanding. Poetry is interpreted as the highest form of language because poetry reveals the very nature of language itself. A poem about love, for example, is not merely a resource for understanding love, it is also an instance in which language is uncovered as a resource of truth. He points out that in ordinary prose the words are "used up," whereas in poetry the words remain as things to be enjoyed, appreciated, and understood solely on their own. When someone speaks to us in everyday language we attend to what is communicated; the words are simply there as vehicles of thought. But this is to do violence to language by making it disappear as soon as the service to the communication is over. Since thought itself, however, is dependent on language to be, prose is not as true as poetry. The actual sounds of the words, their stunning ability to disclose not only the world about us but the very meaning of speech, make them precious. To hear the conveyed meaning (world?) as an intimate part of the actual word (earth?) provides a tension that forces out into the open the actual happening of truth.

We are all familiar with this. As a great poet speaks, we not only hear what he is speaking about but we hear the words and care about them as a part of the disclosure of language. We not only discover the information conveyed *by* the word but we actually notice the words themselves. Thus the word as a conveyor of truth is recognized or disclosed. We do not merely receive the information, but we hear the words as words, and this double awareness creates a tension that is truth rather than mere information.

Heidegger remarkably asserts that the actual phenomenon of truth, the happening of truth, occurs only in rare and spectacular events, such as in the essential sacrifice, the founding of a state, the contemplation of the Being that is most of all (God?), in the act of philosophizing, and in poetry. On the other hand, science is not a happening of truth. This is because science merely tells us what happens, or how we should think about what happens in terms of mathematical projection. For the scientist, the information, the facts, is all that matters, and hence the revealing of these facts is outside the field of science itself. There is in science no tension, no dynamic occurrence that uncovers or reveals as in a poetic utterance or a philosophical argument. (Of course, the great insights of the revolutionary scientists like Galileo, Newton, and Einstein are considered a part of philosophy, not science itself.)

According to this later refinement, then, truth is now a fairly rare event, restricted to those kinds of events that Heidegger includes in his provocative list, like founding a state and making the essential sacrifice. What is it that is shared by the items in this curious list? In all the events on the list what seems to be happening and what qualifies them *as* truth is that they all establish fundamental meanings. The founding of a state gives meaning to the acts and lives of its citizens; the sacrifice gives meaning to the relationship with the loved one; and so forth. This activist notion of truth, which in poetry is dynamic because of the tension between earth and world, tells us that truth is a phenomenon that is restricted only to those occasions in which the meaning of Being is spectacularly revealed. This makes "spectacle" important in understanding truth. As before, truth is not a mere static relation between a knower and a known nor is it a mere correspondence between a sentence and its referent. Rather, truth is an event, an event as a spectacle. And one of the few ways in which this event can occur is in poetic art.

LANGUAGE

The analysis found in "The Origin of the Art-Work" demands that we think more profoundly on the very nature of language. In a series of essays called *On the Way to Language,* Heidegger continues his revolutionary reappraisal of this peculiar philosophical phenomenon. The most revealing, if not the most readily accessible of these essays is "A Dialogue on Language," which Heidegger holds with a Japanese visitor. In the course of the dialogue, language is characterized as "the House of Being"—a rather charming phrase that indicates the growing tendency of Heidegger to abandon the formal analysis of Dasein and substitute a more rigorous but more ephemeral style. By calling language the house of Being we are at least made aware of the enormous range of language as well as of its elusive character. A house is what gives location and significance to all the other items essential for dwelling (the furniture), but it also shelters and establishes a foundation of human meaning. If language is the house of Being, then all the different ways of Being, all the multifarious ways of existence, are made intelligible and even recognizable only under the curious roof of language. Does this mean anything more than the obvious point that if I am going to consider the meaning of anything I must have a sufficient vocabulary to be able to identify and label concepts? The image of the "house of Being" suggests more than this. It also suggests that language as the very protective enclosure that gives a place for existence and Being to occur cannot be isolated as merely another event or as an entity alongside other entities. Thus the study of language cannot be made from a scientific or even metaphysical viewpoint because language is always presupposed by any linguistic account.

In the dialogue, Heidegger describes language as the bridge between beings and what it means to be; i.e., it bridges the ontological difference. Heidegger calls this linkage between Being and being the two-fold role of language. How are we to understand language as the bridge between entities and the meaning of Being?

The answer to this question seems to be that any philosophical approach to the understanding of language must begin with the realization that language is essentially an aesthetic or artistic phenomenon. We can approach language *only* as poetry. This is not because poetry gives us delight, rather it is because poetry reveals the meaning of things as well as existence itself. It is in and through language that we manage to see beyond the mere factual existence of entities to their meanings and to see beyond, for example, what a jail is to what it means to be in jail. Perhaps it is even possible to extract our involvement from inauthentic everydayness to authentic self-understanding only through language—indeed only through language as poetry.

Heidegger and his oriental visitor discuss the Japanese word for language, *koto-ba*. Apparently *ba* means "leaves," especially as in a cherry blossom; *koto* is approximated by the English "gracious delight," with an emphasis on the sense of bestowal contained in the notion of "grace" (the Japanese *iki*). So, it would seem that language is a blossoming of bestowed grace in which the very taking of delight in the bestowal is the kind of understanding given only by language and which is missed entirely by mere direct experience.

The notion of "grace" deserves at least a brief comment. Heidegger claims that, ontologically, it is not *we* who speak but rather language itself does the speaking (*Die Sprache spricht*). Hence the gift of language is literally a bestowal—that is, something given as a gift. Gifts are given, not because of what we do but because of who we are, hence they are given because of our existence. Since this is not a metaphysical claim, we are relieved from having to imagine some pre-existing entity called "language" somehow speaking "through" us as if we were instruments. Rather, on the ontological level, this means that when we think about what it means for us to speak, our language as a source of meaning is not merely the sum total of the words we use or hear. Rather, in thinking about language we think of it as prior to our words. Since nothing can make sense to us unless it can be articulated in speech, the very ontological reality of this being-able-to-talk is one of the fundamental origins of being meaningful at all. To say that language speaks is to deny the intelligibility of a prelinguistic understanding that only *uses* language. Thus the communication theorists who argue that language is merely a vehicle for ideas are entirely mistaken in their backward view. Language is not communication. What would be communicated? Ideas? Thought? But both ideas and thoughts presuppose language; hence language must be prior to communication.

Heidegger distinguishes "telling" from "showing" and argues that language in the truest sense is the latter. Propositional language does indeed "tell," i.e., communicate, but to speak as showing is to let language reveal meanings; hence it is fairly easy to see that language as showing, which is ontologically prior to language as telling, would find its proper realm in poetic, rather than merely communicative, speech.

This may seem somewhat mystical, or at best metaphoric, and far from the precise analyses of *Being and Time*, but one would be mistaken if these essays were dismissed in this way. The same fundamental ideas are there: the ontological difference between entities and what it means to be, the insistence that language must somehow fit into Heidegger's critical understanding of truth as uncoveredness, and the insistence that language is itself not an entity but a mode of existence. The analysis of language in the later works may be more suggestive and enticing, but it is no less rigorous or precise. Indeed, for one willing to admit that perhaps there is a kind of philosophical truth that can only be gained by an appreciation of poetic thought, the essays are a serious contribution to our understanding of language.

TRUTH

Heidegger's famous analysis of truth as unconcealment is richly developed in his later writings, in many ways far surpassing the fundamental but elementary sketch outlined in *Being and Time*. In the earlier work Heidegger seems content to show that ordinary, everyday events and things could be true insofar as their meaning or that even their simple occurrence could be somehow revealed or disclosed. But in the later works he seems to want to reserve truth only for the loftiest of notions, content to allow ordinary things to be seen as true only in a derived or secondary sense. The reasons for this are obvious. If truth is the disclosure of Being itself, it hardly belongs in the ubiquitous and trivial clamor of daily distraction and prattle. In the essay "On the Essence of Truth" (*Vom Wesen der Wahrheit*) Heidegger presents a startling but profound claim: the essence of truth, he says, is the truth of essence (*Das Wesen der Wahrheit ist die Wahrheit des Wesens*). Reflection on this simple sentence contributes significantly to the understanding of this important account of the nature of truth.

In an age and tradition that has listened to the Wittgensteinians protest against the validity of seeking out essences, Heidegger's various titles (The Essence of Reasons, The Essence of Truth, The Essence of Language, etc.) seem curious and even quaint. We have grown dubious of the entire enterprise of seeking an essence. Wittgenstein's criticism goes something like this: Suppose one wonders about the essence of love, for example. But what is the problem? We know what love is. Romeo, by his behavior, is recognized as loving Juliet. You and I can identify it in others and in ourselves, we use the term correctly in sentences, and we know how to distinguish love from non-love. In short, since we use the term correctly and can identify it when it occurs and since we obviously know what it means, what else is there to look for? Aside from these obviously beneficial kinds of awareness, there simply is no other meaning, no hidden "essence" to love at all. Is not the vague, misguided and amorphous search for the hidden essence merely a conceptualist game that leads nowhere? If the point is to render a definition—and what else is an essence except a good definition—then hire a skilled lexicographer, not a philosopher. Most terms are not so precise as to have only one exact meaning or essence; rather the single term covers a family of overlapping but not identical usages, so that "essence" can be replaced by the notion of "family resemblances." The key to understanding a term, according to this argument, is usage and an analysis of the various usages of the term in kindred situations.

Of course, the Wittgensteinian protest is quite valid if our inquiry is into a single, covering definition. But Heidegger argues that by "essence" we mean precisely the opposite of that which can be culled or achieved by an analysis of daily usage. Rather, an essence is the fundamental way in which we think about the meaning of a term or idea, and this thinking about meaning is the realm of truth. It is possible, for example, correctly to define a mother as a female parent. But the essence of a mother—i.e., how we understand the meaning of what a true mother is—is to reflect and wonder on those qualities that make being a mother worthy of our thought and interest: her endless love, her willingness to forgive beyond what is deserved, her tireless self-sacrifice, her ferocious protection of her young. Of course, not all female parents are like this, and thus we say that they are not *true* mothers. This is not a mere ideal, however. One can be a *true* mother without being a *good* mother. A good mother may restrain her instinct to protect in order to instruct; but one who fails to do this, just because protection is of her essence, may not be a good mother but she is surely a true mother, i.e., her actions make sense *because* she is a mother.

In this way, the term "essence" comes to mean "how we think about what it means *to be* such-and-such." And if this is the case, the Wittgensteinian assault is made with unloaded weapons, for an essence could never be uncovered by an analysis of ordinary word-usage.

Essence, therefore, must be seen in an ontological, not a metaphysical, sense. As long as substance-metaphysics is the dominant way of thinking, the Wittgensteinian protest is probably valid. But as soon as the ontological difference is introduced, the notion of "essence" returns as a meaningful notion, because we are not talking about things but about meanings.

Truth is about essences, Heidegger says. Thus, only those whose business it is to step back from ordinary usage and reflect upon what we must think in order to understand the ontological meaning of something can reveal truth. Poets and thinkers, sacrificers and founders of states, in establishing or revealing the fundamental ways in which we think, are thus alone revealers of truth. In saying that truth is concerned only with essences, Heidegger is saying that the search for truth cannot be found in the mere analysis of true sentences. Why indeed is truth so honored if it can be elicited from simple but true sentences like "Paris is south of London"? Of course, this sentence or proposition is true, but only in a derived sense of correctness. This truth cannot be what Socrates labored and died for; this truth cannot make us free, as Christian letters tell us; this truth is not equal to beauty as Keats finds on the Grecian urn. So there is a loftier, even elitist, notion of truth that is rarer and "truer." For Heidegger, the truth that is the uncovering of what it means to be can only be found in the study of essences. Since "essence" for Heidegger is identified as that which makes something what it is, the rather lofty definition becomes almost analytically true.

By retaining the original insight of *Being and Time*—that truth is uncoveredness—and by reflecting deeply on the meaning of essence—that which makes the Being of a thing what it is, in the sense that essence shows us how to think about what it means *to be*— Heidegger has enormously enriched his original insight into the nature of truth. He has returned it to the central place it had in Greek philosophy. We must not confuse truth with knowledge. For the Greeks, *truth* was the center of philosophical inquiry; for the modern and contemporary thinkers, *knowledge* is the center. But truth is the ground of knowledge, and hence must be more fundamental. It is the jewel in the crown of thought. We now can *think* again, and not merely calculate. If Heidegger's placing of truth in the center of thought has altered our recent thinking, as it certainly has, then he deserves to be recognized as the prime and deepest thinker of our age, to whom we owe a debt of gratitude.